DEMENTED

ETHAN MORDDEN

DEMENTED

THE WORLD OF THE OPERA DIVA

Franklin Watts 1984 *New York / Toronto*

FRONTISPIECE:
EMMY DESTINN AS THE
EPONYMOUS HEROINE OF
THE BARTERED BRIDE

The material quoted in this volume from *The Prima
Donna's Handbook* is fully protected by copyright.
No further use whatsoever may be made without the
express written permission of Ethan Mordden, on
behalf of the estate of Lotte Heinotz.

Photographs courtesy of
Opera News: frontispiece; pp. 153 top, middle right, bottom;
154; 155 top left and right; 156; 158; 159 top; 160 bottom.
Michael Rosenthal/The Santa Fe Opera: p. 153 middle left;
Eleanor Morrison/*London Record; Opera News:* p. 155 bottom;
Foto Allotta Federico, Palermo: p. 157; Presseburo Salzburger
Festspiele: p. 159 bottom; Guy Gravett/Glyndebourne Festival
Opera: p. 160 top.

Library of Congress Cataloging in Publication Data

Mordden, Ethan.
Demented, the world of the opera diva.

Bibliography: p.
Includes index.
1. Opera. 2. Women singers. I. Title.
ML1700.M7 1984   782.1'092'2   84-11907
ISBN 0-531-09754-4

CONTENTS

The author wishes to acknowledge his strategic collaborators: art director Judie Mills, who troubled to design the book for deftness despite an overwhelming schedule; cover artists Vince Marchica and Honi Werner for their verve and wit—Honi, I should add, designed my first dust jacket twelve books ago, and I look about forty and Honi looks like a teenager; the invigorating Jennifer McFeely, who let me keep the red pen; editor Paul Hirschman, calmly superb, who not only caught me on the usual stylistic infelicities but checked facts like a team of researchers.

And, mainly, I thank my dear editor Liz Hock: for her enthusiasm, sympathy, and support, which included even letting an author run wild through the house to vet sample pages, second-guess the castoff, make a mess at the water cooler, and generally create panic and furore, his two favorite things. Here's to you, kid.

Again to Dorothy Pittman,
as she asks the musical question,
"Harbor Lights."

No one can love the theatre
without liking women.
Noël Coward

PREFACE

This is a look at opera's great woman singers, and at the elements of their professional lives, the wherefore and procedures of diva. I have let the international opera scene itself dictate format by topic, and thus have made no attempt to control a representative list of famous names. There are too many divas of historical, artistic, and personal importance for a book of this size to honor them all. To the reader who feels that his favorites have been slighted I say, one, it is not my work to reify your (or anyone else's) biases; and, two, go thou and write thine own book to thy specifications.

I have decided not to name those who granted me interviews, as more than half asked to remain anonymous, supporting my contention that opera is a more dangerous business than its buffs realize. In my youth I spent two years on the staff of *Opera News* magazine, and therefore heard a great deal more about opera's backstage than the general public does; some of what I heard was, to speak gently, shocking. Even when a scandal occasionally does reach the newspapers, its teeth are pulled, leaving the story to read as a solution without an equation

I would like to thank the grandchildren of Lotte Heinotz, who granted me permission to quote extensively from her groundbreaking study, *The Prima Donna's Handbook,* long out of print and never before translated into English. Unfortunately, Heinotz' heirs also wish to remain anonymous. I suspect they may be a bit embarrassed by their grandmother, a singer who, on the few nights she was allowed to play a lead (at that invariably in some emergency), left the opera house in fear for her life at the hands of outraged music lovers—yet who had the nerve to write a primer for opera stardom. I hope I may spark interest in Heinotz' fascinating work, which outlines the ruinous difference between the opera world of a golden age and our world, where the unique is attacked and attractive mediocrity sets the standards. As Lotte Heinotz meant her book, so do I mean mine: as a cautionary work.

INTRODUCTION

THE INTERIOR CONTRA- DICTIONS OF DIVA

*It can never be a quiet life
in music.*
Carlo Maria Giulini

We must dare constantly.
Janet Baker

*I think they like it when it
looks as if you're going
to kill yourself on stage.*
Carol Neblett

We're all finite.
Teresa Stratas

M

aria Callas paces her dressing room before a performance. Some little distance away, on the stage of a great opera house, awaits the ennobling challenge of Rossini, Bellini, Donizetti, Verdi: the urgency of narrative; the instruction of character; the intent phrasing of a line, colored, loved, hurled, bent, observing itself even as it comes to life; the ideology of historical style, the responsibility to the work; and the simple bottom-line hazard of stamina, of giving what is required, forcing muscles to obey. This is highest calling and hard labor.

And Callas says, "I'll teach those stinkers out there."

The public. Some have come to be shown, adventuristically, daring Callas to meet her reputation. Some, her admirers, have come not only to experience her art but to defend her from the attacks of those sworn to her rivals. Some have come for the excitement, opportunistically, and might fall into either camp, depending on how the evening levels out. If Callas is in poor voice, or even suffers a faulty high note, they'll boo and whistle with the anti-Callas faction. If she pulls it off, they'll cheer till the authorities have the house emptied.

It's amazing that one of the most acclaimed singers of the age is also one of the most vilified; but opera is at its most ecstatic when it is most dangerous, most reckless, and most ungrateful. Opera is as much an improvisation as it is re-hearsed, as perverse as gallant, the most collaborative possibility in the arts. In composition it may be rigorously controlled: a single author can conceive a project, write the text, set it, and score it. But once handed over to the theatre to stage, it is subject to the abilities of a conductor, a stage director, a designer, a chance mixture of who sings each part any given night—and, of course, to the mood of the public. Opera is made of battling parts: Verdi's *Rigoletto,* or Zeffirelli's Covent Garden *Rigoletto,* or von Karajan's or Kubelik's *Rigoletto,* or Gobbi's Rigoletto and Sutherland's Gilda and Pavarotti's Duke—not to mention librettist Francesco Maria Piave's *Rigoletto.*

These contradictions as to who is in charge grow when one expands from a performance to a season, a career, an epoch. What is opera? Production fights composition. Glamour wheedles dedication. Fame disturbs concentration. Talent is timbre here, musicianship there, then acting, then looks, then just being famous: and becoming more famous inevitably follows. Talent is at war—with other talents, with the state of the art, with critics, with voice-wrecking "modern" composers, with audiences. "Don't worry!" Callas assures us. "Don't worry! When I'm furious, I'm at my best!" She had to be—furious *and* best; that is the problem. Opera's standards are so high, its demands so extraordinary, and its people so highly strung, that the more a singer gives to opera, the more opera exhausts the singer: as artist, as athlete, as person. Opera devours. "A grand profession," mezzo Betty Allen has called it, "but a dirty business."

Opera is comprehensive. It can take in, all at once, singers who simply open wide to let loose pure velvet—and singers who must rise above an inferior instrument through force of personality; or musician-singers who can master a complex score in a week—as well as those who learn only simple roles, at that from phonograph records; or singers who play a very few roles in a certain inflexible way no matter where they are—along with singers who maintain a broad repertory and grow in each part from production to production; or singers who trouble to send every word of text clearly into the theatre—while holding dialogue with those who speak only notes and have never bothered to read through their librettos. There are imposing and garish singers, fresh and ruined, generous and solipsistic. Some consider themselves heir to the greatest traditions in Western art as cavaliers and colleagues; others take the money and run.

Consider now the other parts of opera, comparably contradictory. Some directors are little more than traffic cops, cuing the chorus and letting the principals take care of themselves, while some concentrate on characterological relationships and leave the merry villagers to an assistant. Some conductors work with their singers, some against. Some are obsessed with authenticity of style, while others make everything sound like Puccini (except Puccini—then they sound like your dentist). Impresarios can be fair or vicious, designers can make one look like anything from a suave goddess to a vicious pear, and the public changes from one cultural capital to another. In London they are loyal; in Parma they'd boo their mother off the stage as a warm-up. In Vienna they want it the way it used to be (and disagree among themselves as to how that was); in Paris they enjoy despising a novelty. New Yorkers will clap for almost anything, as if every performance were their first, or their last; the Milanese sometimes let their ancient reputation as The Place With the House do their clapping for them.

What is opera? At one level, it is the volatile public, a collection of ruthless factions. It is exposure at the highest level, with no quarter given because a singer's health is below par and, therefore, yields erratic voice—no matter how often the public has heard that voice in fine form. "I'll teach those stinkers out there." Yes, you have to, each time out, or else. Or else (as when an ailing Callas gave up partway through a pitiful Norma in Rome in 1958 before a fancy audience headed by Italy's president, Giovanni Gronchi) they will wait outside the stage door to assault you, defame you in the press, and hold obscene festival all night outside your hotel. Why must the stinkers be taught? Why are they ferocious? True, opera is largely about love and death, war and peace, duty and obsession, all provocatively delineated in the music. But, however much opera flaunts these verities, it usually does so in the form of solemn pageant, the posing supers, grandiose sets, and wayward acting draining the violence of its juice. Opera is about passion, but opera is not invariably passionate.

Then what ignites opera? Divas: for at their best they are passionate as a rule. What is opera? Divas, the great ones. Yes, the men have shared pride of place. Enrico Caruso, Titta Ruffo, and Boris Christoff, for example, inspired musicians and stimulated operagoers on a profound level. Or think of Rubini, Mario, the de Reszkes, Antonio Scotti, Beniamino Gigli, Richard Tauber, Tito Gobbi, Jon Vickers, and Luciano Pavarotti. Men swell the catalogues. But don't the men seem less colorful than the women? Do the men get into truly attractive trouble, or control such dashing parts, or engage aficionados in bitter controversies over technique, vocal state, and interpretive flair, as the women do?

On the other hand, we should not overestimate opera's element of diva-watching. Opera is *works,* four centuries' development of composition. The most significant names in opera are not those of singers, conductors, or directors, but those of Monteverdi, Mozart, Verdi, Wagner, Britten, and other authors. *This* is opera, surely. Still, as with any lively art, it is difficult to separate the theory of what is written from the fact of how it is performed. Few would deny that *Norma* comes off better with Pasta, Ponselle, or Callas than without, that *Der Rosenkavalier* is somewhat less than it should be when Lehmann or Schwarzkopf isn't the Marschallin, that *Les Troyens* is going to feel somewhat hollow now that Baker has left the theatre.

Joan Sutherland once called herself "a very ordinary human being that has been given a really rather wonderful voice," but there is nothing ordinary in diva. There are ordinary singers, journeymen of mediocre identity; but no one thinks much about them. They are placeholders, filling out casts when the more elaborate interpreters are unavailable. They are weak in voice, musicianship, temperament, and commitment, four basic qualities that comprise stardom in opera. At that, not all divas—not even the most impressive—have all four. Rosa Ponselle surely did, but Callas was weak in voice and had to make up for it with extraordinary musicianship and commit-

ment. Flagstad's voice alone excused her lack of temperament, while one of Flagstad's successors in the Wagner heroines, Birgit Nilsson, acquired temperament over the years and
another, Martha Mödl, seemed to lose voice early on and had
to depend on temperament and commitment (and her public's
recollection of earlier greatness) to carry her through. Some
singers have made their way entirely on voice and musicianship—Montserrat Caballé, for instance; and when one has such
beauty of voice and perceptive musicianship, this is easy to do.
Caballé is a crack musician who can sight-read her way through
anything—Robert Jacobson jokes that he can hear her paper
knife slitting the leaves of her brand-new scores on her recordings. But her lack of commitment leaves her sounding the
same in every part. Still, she is ahead of her colleagues who
try to get along on voice alone—and at least one diva, Olive
Middleton, lacked everything but commitment.

One thing that makes operagoing endlessly fascinating is
that these qualities vary from person to person. Temperament
in Janet Baker and Fiorenza Cossotto becomes two very different things. Voice in Leontyne Price and Leonie Rysanek
splits wide, nearly into opposition. Musicianship is one idea to
Régine Crespin, quite another to Renata Tebaldi, yet both had
it: both projected the voice into song rather than let song push
them from note to note. Sutherland is wrong. She is not an
ordinary person, for if she was one once, a life in opera has
rendered her extraordinary by function of art.

If there is an essential quality in diva, it is voice—what
Walter Legge called "an immediately recognizable personal
timbre." Lotte Heinotz, a curiously unpopular singer of minor
roles active in Vienna in the early 1900s, emphasizes this factor in her classic pamphlet, *Der Weltsopranführer (The Prima
Donna's Handbook),* written when Heinotz retired, at the ur-
gent request of the city of Vienna. "All the world of the diva,"
Heinotz writes, "may be divided into five parts: voice, profile,
costume, entrance, and death scene. But if you have the first
part, the rest will take care of itself." Heinotz then draws a
distinction between what she calls the "Stimmdiva" and the
"Kunstdiva"—roughly, the singer and the artist. The distinc-

tion is requisite to an understanding of one of the most inherent controversies in opera: the question of which is more useful, the stand-and-deliver sensuality of sound (Stimme means voice) or the intelligent, dynamic, versatile impersonation (Kunst means art). Most useful to art, of course, is the diva who has both natural voice and polished artistry—Elisabeth Schwarzkopf, say. But some who tend to one side or the other have aroused the most fervent factions, and do seem, in the fullness of what they do, essential to the age. A great Stimmdiva might be Fiorenza Cossotto or Martina Arroyo, famed for the sheer luxury of sound they bring to certain roles but less than the ultimate in bringing these roles to life. In the realm of the Kunstdiva, think of Lotte Lehmann, often vocally insecure but a subtle painter of text; or of Marie Collier, so consumed by the romance of being Minnie of the golden west or the 342-year-old Elina Makropulos that one scarcely noticed the rough singing; or of Anja Silja, who shattered her instrument singing everything every other day but remains surpassing as Lulu, *Wozzeck*'s Marie, and *Mahagonny*'s Jenny. Heinotz offers a useful difference between the two types: "The Stimmdiva's idea of preparing Gounod's Marguerite involves learning the music and ordering her outfits. The Kunstdiva reads Goethe."

It's a simplification, but informative nonetheless. The Kunstdiva does at times reveal an intellectual approach, a desire to learn from opera. She will take on new parts, even new kinds of part, plume herself on her linguistic ability, and might even support new work. The Stimmdiva prefers to tour her accustomed parts from house to house, sings in her native language, or in one adopted one, and despises what little she knows of contemporary composition. The twain will never meet; nor will their devotees. "Who cares," Stimmdiva fans ask, "how adventurous a soprano is if her high notes wobble?" Conversely, aficionados of the Kunstdiva complain, "So what if she can hit notes—but can't reach the character?"

Another distinction, developed at the Met in the 1960s, lies in the argot of "demented" and "filth." Demented is opera at its greatest, a night when the singers are in voice, in role, in glory. Everything fits. Filth is disaster. And note: not thrilling, admirable, or inspiring, but *demented:* insane. Not unfortunate, regrettable, or (God forbid) forgivable, but *filth:* corrupt. Stimmdivas are less likely to suffer a night of filth than their vocally less well endowed colleagues, but then it is the Kunstdivas who most frequently achieve the ecstasy of demented, because so much of it depends on fabulous interpretation.

Certain roles, too, feed the scheme. A first-rate Tosca is, by the nature of the role, demented: a psychopathically jealous prima donna who murders a brute, sees her lover murdered in turn, and leaps to her death. Anything less than demented isn't Tosca. This holds as well for such roles as Amneris, Carmen, Musetta, the Queen of the Night, Isolde, and Elektra. Obviously, demented suits characters who do a lot of raging and scheming. But less apparently excitable characters— Lucia, say, or Mimì or Octavian—can in the right hands attain demented. On the other hand: should they?

Opera is the richest of the arts, at its most fulfilled when it comprehends dance and design as well as the melding of music and theatre. This very comprehensiveness is demented, an artistic and organizational challenge of almost utopian impracticability. Add to this the hysteria of the public and the nerve-racking exposure the stars must submit to and one realizes why opera's people seem a little mad when they are most "operatic." "A singer can receive a $5,000 check," Evelyn Lear says, "then enjoy a grand dinner and a great night of love . . . and wake up the next morning with no voice. Not a single note. Or you can feel miserable, pick at your food, lose sleep . . . and wake up with *nothing but* voice." Fitness is elusive, defiant of control. And there is the "dirty business" angle. "We're all whores," says Lear, "waiting for the pimps to get us jobs."

No other art or business so tests its practitioners. Actors who learn their craft and play suitable roles usually do not fail. Pianists or violinists who master technique and secure good instruments have, at worst, slightly off nights, which their audiences readily forgive them. But opera is the marathon art— a physical exertion—in which all the singer's senses are working at once, to follow the conductor, act the scene, phrase the lines: to sing. Act too strongly, sing too well, and one will exhaust oneself halfway through an act, literally run out of voice.

Athletes have it easier than opera singers, though singers are a form of athlete—some of them say they lose three or four pounds a night when onstage. A baseball player who fails to hit a home run isn't booed out of the stadium. A runner trying and failing to break a record has our sympathy. But a diva who misses a famous high note is in Big Trouble. Even if one is playing to a public with a relatively high booing threshold, the polite applause at the spot where an ovation is appropriate can strike with a terribly hollow thud. One reason why *Aida* is performed less often than the other very popular Verdi works is a single note, a high C at the end of Aida's third-act aria, "O patria mia." There is no avoiding the note and, because of the scale-like passage that leads up to it, it stands out even to ears that have not heard *Aida* before. There are actually first-rank and very popular divas who avoid the role because that one note creates so much tension it ruins their lives. Every time they sign a contract to sing Aida, the months leading up to that note make them nervous wrecks and the months after are like getting over a bad marriage. Yet, like it or not, they *must* sing Aida, for it is a keen acting-singing part in a masterpiece, and opera's main energies bend toward such works. The public loves to hear it; conductors love to serve it; designers love its spectacle; and impresarios love the box-office receipts. Here is yet another contradiction: we demand that the singer take dares and turn on her if she slips. Why do it, then? Why not play safe? Because there is no safety in opera. It's too grand.

"The chemistry of the great role," Lotte Heinotz writes, "is the science of the diva. Ask yourself who you are and whom you might become. You must learn how to astonish them." We are going to learn how Callas, Sutherland, Farrar, Melba, Malibran Freni, Sills, Stratas phrased their answers to this question the diva must ask herself, and what hazards and assistance they met with on the way to demented. Will the director set them off beautifully, expose their weaknesses, hobble their strengths? Will the conductor coach them to eloquence or drown them out? Who is in charge of opera? We must learn, too, of the diva's rise and fall, how she trains, builds her reputation, maintains it, then knows when to leave. "Your last act," Lotte Heinotz warns, "must be your best!—whether it be Brünnhilde's Immolation, a Donizetti-Bellini mad scene, or Carmen's confrontation with Don José." And surely the final seasons of one's career are as crucial as the last forty minutes of a given performance. Your last act!—how quickly it may come. Speaking actors may go on forever, conductors don't become legends till their dotage, and accountants never retire. Singers have a limited prime.

We will see how differently certain divas take Heinotz' advice. Some dwindle into character parts, unable to make a final break with the stage; others make that break in good time, after their prime but before ruin sets in. Some linger too long but make up for it in an official last night of a great role with excellent supportive colleagues in a festival atmosphere of hail and farewell. And, by one of those miracles that keep one coming back to the opera house "just in case," the years melt away and the diva reclaims the zest of youth.

We must consider also a possible fifth basic quality in diva: audacity. This especially distinguishes the singers who fascinate. Great divas have more than stage presence—they have life presence. "You must learn how to astonish them": and be willing to. Grace Moore shows us how in a tale that finds her unpardonably late for a concert before a women's club in Westchester. Moore had done her best to make it, arriving to the sirens of a police escort, but, having sat in the middle of nothing for an hour, the audience greeted her with silent ire. Moore looks great, feels great, and is ready to sing, but the atmosphere needs warming up or the recital will never go over. So Moore puts on her nicest smile, hikes up her formal gown, and turns around, crying, "Ladies, you just must see these darling panties I have on!"

She has them. After a startled moment, they laugh, applaud, and relax, ready to listen. Divas know how to astonish and we must learn how to love them.

CHAPTER

1

THE
VOICE

*Madame Ponselle proves to us
that the finest singing—
given a good voice to begin
with—comes from the constant
play of a fine mind upon the
inner meaning of the music.*
Ernest Newman

*All I know is that from about age
fourteen I had a fully-rounded,
opera-like dramatic voice.*
Rosa Ponselle

*The voice is an instrument
of service.*
Evelyn Lear

In the opera world of the 1980s, there are few if any "sopranos" as such. There are, rather, *types* of soprano, classed by vocal and emotional range, by the agility in decoration we routinely term "coloratura," by lung power—even sometimes (informally and incorrectly) by physique. Yet, in the years when the woman singer became the essential opera star, there were only "sopranos," all singing more or less the same repertory and, ideally, having gotten the same training in some variation of the Italian school.

Obviously, there was quite some variation in the voices themselves. Maria Malibran, for instance, seems to have been a mezzo-soprano or possibly contralto who developed an extension of her upper register through expert guidance, hard work, and sheer nerve. Yet she sang Rossini's Rosina and Desdemona, Bellini's Norma and Amina, Zingarelli's Romeo— all roles also sung by her contemporary Giuditta Pasta, a high soprano who came by her upper register naturally. Other women of their era, roughly the early middle 1800s, similarly shared parts, for, with ancient opera dead and French opera stylistically isolated, theatres sustained a rather narrow Italian repertory, a compendium of relatively current works grounded by *Don Giovanni* and *Le Nozze di Figaro,* only a few decades old at the time.

How different the repertory is today, and how diverse the categories of diva. To speak of Katia Ricciarelli, of Marilyn Horne, of Helen Donath, of Yvonne Minton, of Hildegard Behrens, is to pull into one sentence a compound of mutually exclusive systems. There are loud, delicate, clumsy, and fleet voices; there are voices that can burn at white heat all night and voices that never seem to warm up; voices that inspire and voices that bore; sweet floated high voices like fairy bells and low dark ones like Vlad the Impaler coming to take you away. With an active repertory stretching from Monteverdi to Britten (some 350 years' worth) to take in varieties in language, performing style, and compositional idiom, the soprano has become faceted, ranged, sundry.

She was not absolute in the hierarchy at first. In the earliest operas, performed by enlightened amateurs for their friends, the closest thing to a star was the very experiment of opera itself, the so-called "new music," rapt declamatory paragraphs. Then, in operas given at princely courts, the star was the local lion himself, a duke or prince celebrating a wedding or the like. We know next to nothing of the backstage atmosphere of the first opera houses that were open to the public. But as the first substantial collection of posters, journalistic reports, and apocryphal tales comes into view, in the early 1700s, we find not sopranos but castrati in primary position. Star sopranos were competitively featured, and they had their followings. Still it was the "male soprano" who took the greater glory.

The castrato was, as the word tells, a man surgically ruined before puberty who grew up to sing with the icy brilliance of the child and the lung power of a man. The unique combination did not sit as well with audiences in all cultures as it did in Italy and Italian-oriented centers such as Vienna: the French were disgusted and the British, though eventually amused, never did quite know how to take it. Italianophile aficionados cried *"Evviva il coltello!"* (Long live the knife) at the castrato's verve, his startling coloratura, his trumpeting high notes. His peacock vanity, too, enchanted, especially in the royal and chevaleresque roles favored by his genre, *opera seria*. Reformers, however, wished to see opera make closer compact with artistic truth, rid itself of ceremonial excesses, and concentrate on musico-dramatic storytelling—and the castrato was the most spectacular excess of all. The turning point came in 1774, when Christoph Willibald Gluck rewrote *Orfeo ed Euridice* for Paris. Gluck's first Orfeo, in Vienna, was a castrato. In sensible Paris Orphée was a tenor. Down with the knife.

Tenors did not take over the castrato's perquisites. The tenor voice had yet to be broken in, established, expanded: but the diva was already an institution, and in due course supplanted the castrato in verve, coloratura, high notes, and, yes, vanity. It was the age of bel canto ("beautiful singing"), though the term is younger than the age, dating from a time when singing was ailing and its physicians needed a phrase to write on their prescriptions. In the 1700s beautiful singing was taken for granted; beautiful was what singing was, period. But by the 1800s singing wasn't always beautiful, or so we're told.

Actually, it was not that beauty had left singing, but that dramatic emphasis had come into it. Bel canto, to digest the vast amount of material in its file, consisted basically of, one, a faultless legato line and, two, the inspired decoration of that line. The one is ecstasy, the other festivity. Bel canto is a melding of soul and abandon, the whole designed to encourage the *instincts* of the vocal musician, the legato as intense as communication can be and the decoration suggesting improvisation, an explosion of virtuosity. But the composer's reform, from Gluck through Rossini on to Wagner and Verdi, emphasized different kinds of line and began to suppress the decoration. Composers now wrote the intensity into their scores and outlawed improvisation. Verdi, in mid-career, took to writing out the cadenzas that singers traditionally extemporized; Wagner, early on, dispensed with them altogether.

Already, in the late 1800s, opera has created a diversity among the types of diva, vocally and dramatically. Gluck's Armide, Alceste, and the second of his two Iphigénies call for a singer with a strong middle range and classical aplomb—in effect, a dramatic mezzo without the title. Gluck's Paris had not yet become the major opera center and his divergence from the norm did not harass sopranos of the international stages. Later, however, in Meyerbeer's day, opera was making major history in Paris, and some of *his* experiments registered heavily—Fidès, the mother in *Le Prophète,* for instance, a contralto with a solid top B, written for Pauline Viardot. Fidès was a new idea in lead roles, "the burgher woman," in critic Henry F. Chorley's words, "without youth or beauty." Before Fidès, divas tended to the princess mode in character. Verdi surely took note when he conceived Azucena, the mother in *Il Trovatore.** Moreover, while the woman leads in Verdi's earlier operas generally conform to types common to Bellini, Donizetti, and Mercadante, his later operas offer a new genre of heroine in Hélène, Amelia, or Aida, so unlike their predecessors that one speaks now of a "Verdian soprano," distinct from Mozart's Donna Elvira, Bellini's Amina, or Donizetti's Maria Stuarda. And Wagner's heroines are a breed entirely apart, their titanic commitment to love, vengeance, or a utopian dream delineated in music deliberately planned to reinvent opera, to sound the way utopia might feel.

Composers have wrested control from the singers, each great writer now developing an individual vocal repertory. Back in the 1700s, when the diva was queen, this would have posed no difficulty, for singers routinely altered scores to suit their voices, fame, and fancy. Every star had her trunk of specialties, to be forced willy-nilly into any piece no matter how irrelevant to the action. Whole scenes might be cut, replaced perhaps by new arias run up by whoever happened to be handy. Obliging and outraged composers alike retailored parts to suit the voice of the moment, for the success of the work depended on the success of the singer. Integrity of composition became important after 1800, though not till 1847 could Verdi stipulate to his publisher that theatres could contract for Verdi's

*Writers have been reconsidering this cliché of opera criticism. Fidès is indeed a burgher (she runs a tavern), apparently sane, knows and likes her son's lover, and sings elaborate vocal decoration, while Azucena is a gypsy, starts, continues, and ends psychotic, shares stage with but never meets Leonora, and sings a relatively undecorated line. However, *in performance* the two women show marked similarities, especially in their relationships with their respective sons. Perhaps the point is not that the roles resemble each other, but that in giving a woman lead to a mother rather than a sweetheart, Meyerbeer opened up new characterological possibilities for the mezzo-soprano.

operas only on an as-written basis; at that, this was, for the
time, arrogance. Verdi could tolerate a diva: he married one,
Giuseppina Strepponi. But he would not tolerate unsolicited
collaboration from one.

Another factor in the diversity of vocal casting may be the
most significant one in the history of the diva: the Romantic
era's escalating hunger for dramatic urgency in heroines. This
is a complex matter, for Romanticism is complex, made as much
of pathetic innocence as of turbulent self-hatred; or as much
of a carefree stroll through a sunlit glade as of ghastly conjur-
ings in occult places. Médée, who murders her children to torture an unfaithful husband, is a paragon of Romantic opera—
but then so is Beethoven's Leonore, who disguises herself as
a youth and takes work in a prison to save her husband at
gunpoint from a tyrant. Romanticism is Faustian, at once
needing and mistrusting the devil. One might expect such an
era to raise up a squad of male avatars—signing pacts,
breaching gulfs, shaking the world. But it was the diva who
became opera's Romantic icon. Even the era's essential *Faust*
opera—Gounod's, from Michel Carré's play *Faust et Marguerite,* drawn from Part One of Goethe's epic—gives the heroine
more telling variation than the hero. Yes, he signs his pact,
with Hell. But Marguerite gets the folkish Ballad of the King
of Thulé, the Jewel Song, a Spinning Song, a face-on confrontation with the devil in church, and a transcendent death.

Perhaps the most Faustian moment in the Romanticiza-
tion of the diva was Richard Wagner's infatuated response to
Wilhelmine Schröder-Devrient's Leonore in Dresden in 1824.
Schröder-Devrient was the first of the Kunstdivas, to whom
commitment outranked voice. To Wagner, this was not just a
performance, but a heroistic call to arms; he virtually dedicated the rest of his life's work to her that day. And what
Schröder-Devrient did for Wagner, others like her did for audiences all over Europe: they changed the perception of how
opera worked. The other divas whom the Romantic age adored,
like Pasta and Malibran, seemed, like Schröder-Devrient, to
foreshadow the twentieth-century diva of emotional projection—the tender voice pushed beyond safety because passion
overwhelms (as it did Lotte Lehmann), or the middle-weight

voice taking on heavy work out of artistic obligation (Maria Caniglia), or the beauty surer in theatrics than intonation (Maria Jeritza). As the dynamic heroine—Gioconda, Brünnhilde, Valentine—replaced the bel-canto heroine, so bel canto began to disappear. The legato line broke up, troubled by verismo's sobs and shudders. "It seemed to me that the music was so wedded to the story," Gemma Bellincioni tells us of *Cavalleria Rusticana*, "that together they became a single entity, enabling me to reveal to the public my own artistic ideals." Here is the cataclysm, the turning of the gyres, from opera as pure song into opera as acting song. "I broke away from every outmoded tradition of the lyric stage," she goes on, "abandoning myself to 'recitar cantando' [musical declamation]."

This is not an isolated event: Bellincioni created* Santuzza in the world premiere, so here speaks the influential heroine of a vastly influential work. Various reasons have been advanced for the dramatization (and, say some purists, the demusicalization) of the diva, but none carries as much weight as this intensification of her psychology: in vocal plan, in stage action, in the orchestration that she must sing against. A favorite alternate explanation, that theatres have been growing larger, forcing singers to push for volume, is nonsense. Only in America have opera theatres been growing; in Europe the architecture has been stable for well over a century. The present La Scala opened in 1778, La Fenice in 1837, Covent Garden in 1858, the Paris Opéra in 1875, and the state theatres in Munich and Vienna, destroyed in wartime bombing, were rebuilt virtually in replica of their originals, opened in, respectively, 1825 and 1869. It is true that orchestral pitch has risen since Beethoven's time: the A sounded by the concertmaster just before the conductor enters the pit is more like a B compared to what Schröder-Devrient sang to. Still, the difference of a whole tone, even in the upper reaches where it may mean the difference between striking a secure B flat (which

---

*Some question the use of this verb in the context: surely Mascagni and his librettists created *Cavalleria*. But years of usage have made *create* the official operatic idiom for "play the part in the first performance." It's also a lot less clumsy.

almost any diva can) and striking a C (which a surprising number can't), has not affected opera singing as much as composition and characterization have.

Because, in threading song into the web of story, opera made narrative more crucial than bel canto. Thus composers goaded singers; thus singers complied. As Bellincioni noted when she met the raw honesty of verismo and saw how it thrilled the public and satisfied her artistic ambitions, one could no longer, simply and beautifully and elegantly, sing. One must become one with the music, fade into it: as Malibran did when, as Desdemona, she believed Otello was going to strangle her and ran around the stage in terror; or as Garden who ignored the audience and said, "The part I was playing had become me"; or as Claudia Muzio did, for legend reports that she sang herself to death like *Hoffmann*'s Antonia, because she had a weak heart, or, better, because she was too tragic to live.

At length this ever-sharpening narrative thrust created diverse types of soprano, for as Wagner is different from Verdi and both of them are different from Mozart and all three are different from the differing Massenet, Strauss, Berg, and Britten, so are some stories different from other stories. The classic "soprano" of old, who could more or less handle all lead roles, gave way to the specialist. To keep it simple, let's accept four woman voices in opera today—the lyric, the leggiero, the spinto, and the dramatic—plus the mezzos, who also maintain lyric and dramatic wings. Fach, German for "category" and international opera argot for "vocal type," structures a chaotic world repertory, with quaint disinterments from the past on one hand and bizarre new wave on the other, with ancient houses one week and newfangled ones the next, with the provinces loving you and the cultural capitals yawning, with helpless hack directors who concentrate on grouping the chorus attractively and arrogant superdirectors who see *Roméo et Juliette* as a metaphor for Marxist revolution and set it inside the liver of an unborn panda. Fach is *your* roles, your traditions and potential, from your inspiring forerunners in the great roles to your amendments and improvisations when you hit your prime. "Fach," Lotte Heinotz warns us, in *The Prima Donna's Handbook,* "is Bible. Study it, know it, cherish it."

The lyric Fach might be the most basic, or the purest, in opera, dependent entirely on the natural beauty of the voice and the sweetness of its expression. It lacks the power to ride an orchestral climax or to cut through a big ensemble. To understand the lyric's appeal, consider Mary Garden's oft-quoted recollection of Melba's high C at the end of the first act of *La Bohème:* "The note came floating over the auditorium of Covent Garden: it left Melba's throat, it left Melba's body, and it left everything, and came over like a star and passed us in our box, and went out into the infinite. . . . My God, how beautiful it was!" *Beauty* again, always. But let us not condescend to the lyric—most of the heroines of the pre-verismo repertory are lyric, or open to lyrics with a little adjustment.

Gounod's Marguerite, perhaps, is the dead center of the lyric Fach. The role depends on a bit of coloratura (in the Jewel Song), a bit of muscle (in the Church Scene), and a bit of theatre-filling bravado (in the Final Trio), but is mainly a matter of a dear voice with the musicality and imagination to suggest the naïveté, wonder, and bewildered despair that Gounod so handsomely laid out. Bigger voices can sing Marguerite; in *Faust*'s Victorian heyday, when the public couldn't get enough of it, virtually any singer who could lay his or her hands on a costume slipped into it, and it must have been interesting to hear a sizable voice go all out in the Church Scene or the Final Trio. But Marguerite is a village girl. She has been nowhere, seen nothing, and has no interior resources to fall back on when a gentleman seduces her, kills her brother, and abandons her. She goes mad. A true lyric timbre, with its advantages in vulnerability and plangency, makes a better effect than the more confident darker instruments. This may be what diva-watchers who prefer lyrics are fascinated by: sheerest innocence.

A lyric with no ambitions to enlarge her repertory can run a nice career alternating her certain leads with quasi-secondary parts. Pamina, Despina, and Susanna; Massenet's Manon; Donizetti's Adina; Luisa Miller and Amelia Grimaldi; Mélisande; and Mimì and Liù are highlights of her itinerary, with stopovers amid the "little sister" parts—Micaëla, Gretel, Nannetta, Strauss' Zdenka and Sophie, Massenet's Sophie, Marzelline in *Fidelio*. However, it is the lyric's fate to see her big sisters take the flamboyant parts such as Fiordiligi and Arabella, and many lyrics attempt a breakout in what might be called "crossover roles." If her training was sound and her top is fit, there are the coloratura leads. Or there is Violetta Valery, a center of greatness in diva and a lyric role, yes: but one with a tricky first act* and a performing tradition that takes in big, sumptuous voices as well as expert coloratura-vendors.

Alternately, lyrics can graduate themselves to larger parts; after some years, many voices expand naturally. Still, one must prepare one's advancement carefully, pace oneself onstage, and not bounce in and out of Fach from night to night. At the New York City Opera, Carol Neblett recalls, "I'd sing Manon, then coloratura, then heavy stuff, mixing it all up. The voice got big and unwieldy." And she adds something of a personal nature to the science of singing: "You have to be happy to sing well. . . . A woman sings with her ovaries—you're only as good as your hormones."

Lucrezia Bori offers a case of the success, and the hazards, of a breakout career. Bori's fame depended less on her voice then on how she used it: with an intent pathos, the phrasing captivating and the characterization sensualistic. Though anything larger than Micaëla or Nannetta taxed her instrument, Bori constantly balanced light roles with some quite heavy ones—Butterfly, Manon Lescaut, and even Octavian in *Der Rosenkavalier*'s Italian premiere at La Scala as *Il Cavaliere della Rosa*. Too, Bori sang at the Metropolitan, then the opera world's largest auditorium.

In 1915 Mascagni's *Iris* nearly finished her. Toscanini talked her into it—it was for only four performances—and after all Iris is a barely pubescent girl who is kidnapped and taken to Tokyo's pleasure quarter, just the part for Bori, with her exquisite, fluttery charm. Shortly after *Iris* was over, Bori's vocal cords developed nodes, that mysterious terror of the

---

*The repeated "gioir" in "Sempre libera" alone has undone many a light voice, as it lies very high and must be musically varied at a dramatically tense moment. Take the trouble to sing it right and your scene may lose its gumption; act it, to hell with the notes, and that's just where the notes will go.

profession, often climactic. Nothing mattered to Bori more than opera, and to ensure the success of the removal operation, she took four years off, spending one literally mute and cut off from the world. Her comeback was cautious—Zerlina at Monte Carlo, a light role in a small house—and it went well. Two years later she returned to the Met for a suspenseful and ultimately triumphant evening in *La Bohème*. Bori then reigned as one of the Met's elect personalities, so "Metropolitan" in name that after her retirement in 1936 she stayed on as the company's most glamorous fund-raiser, advisor, and diplomat.

The career of Bidú Sayão is instructive in another way: How to Become Famous and Beloved While Singing Only Lyric Roles in the World's Biggest House With the World's Smallest Voice. Brazilian and a pupil of Jean de Reszke, Sayão started as Lakmé, Lucia, Rosina in the soprano transposition, and other coloratura heroines. She came to the Met's attention in the mid-1930s, when they needed someone to take over for the retiring Bori. Though, like other light sopranos, Sayão had her eye on the fascinating possibilities in Butterfly and Desdemona, her coach (later husband), baritone Giuseppe Danise, steered her back to Fach; the opportunity to step in for Bori gave Sayão a ready-made repertory appropriate to her fragile instrument.

In the event, Sayão's Manon, Mélisande, and Juliette were remarkable. Her voice was so tiny that in *Le Nozze di Figaro* Sayão as Susanna would emit little chirps and giggles in ensembles just to make herself heard. But in an intimate moment, like "N'est-ce plus ma main?" in *Manon*'s St. Sulpice Scene, she was compelling, filling the house with personality and an acute feeling for language. (This of course is what made her Mélisande so telling—some call it her great achievement.) Sayão's fourteen Met years, glowing against the flame of the seductive Bori, prove that a gifted lyric is more than just another pretty voice.

Today's lyrics are under pressure to cross over that Bori and Sayão never knew. The shortage of big voices, the money and PR hunger of impresarios and agents, the reckless manipulation of youngsters by conductors in need of protégées, the collapse of tradition, and the lyrics' own impatience are all problems; and, too, there is the Tosca Syndrome: big, loud roles make you famous and little silly ones don't. Today's public doesn't pack a house to hear a Zerlina or Adina; they want Divakunst, the art of being demented. Can anyone become famous singing Mimì?

Mirella Freni did, in 1963, in a Scala *Bohème* with Gianni Raimondi, staged by Franco Zeffirelli and conducted by Herbert von Karajan, that enchanted Europe. It went to Moscow and Munich, sets and all; it was filmed; Freni and Raimondi were opera's couple of the year; and Zinka Milanov gave her the ultimate accolade: "She sounds like a young me!" A Great Alliance was forged: not with Raimondi, but with von Karajan, who made Freni his protégée. In the old days this was one way to know you had arrived. The public may like you for any number of reasons, but a musician admires you for one reason only: you're good. A musician's admiration meant first dibs at new roles, important new productions, and sharing in the wisdom of the ages. Nowadays a musician's admiration means you're going to sing roles too big for your voice.

Just a year after the triumph in *La Bohème,* Freni tried Violetta at La Scala, also with von Karajan, and did so poorly that the management rushed Anna Moffo in as a replacement and the public outdid itself with nasty letters and atrocious phone calls. But, rather than resign herself to a lifetime of Marguerite and Manon, Freni regrouped, restudied, and persevered. Her Mimì improved to champion status, and she erased the bad memory of the Scala Violetta with Elisabeth in von Karajan's *Don Carlos* in 1975 at Salzburg, and then, four years later at the same station, with Aida. The Salzburg monster production, radiant with stars, copping headlines and a recording tie-in, is the biggest single event in opera today. To succeed in one is to ascend to the profession's heights. And of course these times Freni and the Meister were on von Karajan territory, where anyone unhip enough even to consider booing would be shown the instruments of torture, as they put it in the days of the Inquisition.

Anyway, no one considered booing, for Freni had somehow managed to encompass the Verdian soprano's Fach. To put it bluntly, she's terrific in it. She may have had to sacrifice some of her former warmth, and she knows she cannot utterly give herself to the Verdian ring without damaging her voice. "Who makes her do it?" Renata Tebaldi once asked. Who else? Still,

Freni has demonstrated the fluency of the lyric, the adaptability. She knew you can't say no to von Karajan; but knew
also that you must husband your resources. Freni is bold, not
foolhardy. She pulled it off. Besides, why attack the woman
for attempting to widen her experience? Evelyn Lear will sock
you if you make a Freni joke. "Because this woman has the
most perfect vocal technique," says Lear, "she is unappre-
ciated! Because she shows no agony!' But then a lyric who did
show agony wouldn't be a lyric anymore: she'd be a scared
spinto.

The leggiero voice, the one that handles the coloratura
heroines, is less adaptable. Mimìs with ability in fioritura can
dabble in *I Puritani*—as Freni has done—but Elviras often lack
the sensual body for *La Bohème.* For that matter, Bellini and
Donizetti need more than a brisk attack and a thousand tiny
notes machine-gunned into the ozone. Elvira is an avatar of
Romantic pathos, the spinner of dreamy mad arabesques; and
Norma and Anna Bolena are genuinely formidable women.
Unfortunately, generations of birds have reduced the leggiero
repertory to patty-cake embellishments. "But I don't *want* to
be a coloratura!" Mary Garden cried when Mathilde Marchesi,
teacher of Emma Calvé, Emma Eames, Nellie Melba, and Sig-
rid Arnoldson, outlined a course of study. Garden wanted to
turn into magical women, not babble roulades. Coloratura,
Marchesi coldly told Garden, "is the only beautiful singing there
is." But all Garden could hear in it was a fairy piping in an
enchanted glade. It might be beautiful; but it isn't real.

Not all coloraturas are of fairy proportions. "My dear boy,
we can't let her be seen," Thomas Beecham told Walter Legge
when the sizable Lina Pagliughi arrived to play Gilda in one
of Beecham's international seasons at Covent Garden. "She
looks like a tea cosy!" And the most notable leggiero of the
golden age (and Pagliughi's teacher), Luisa Tetrazzini, loved
her *table d'hôte.* By the time she came to stardom in this century's first decade, she had swelled to hefty hourglass proportions. "Some are born to be thin," she supposedly told a Philadelphia newspaper, "others to be fat. I belong to the latter
class." And she wasn't complaining: she was exulting.

Surely Tetrazzini's figure hampered her portrayal of the
consumptive Violetta, the dainty Lakmé, the pranking teen-

ager Rosina? On the contrary, Tetrazzini's appetitive swank added to her singing in any role, for hers was a buoyant art, daredevil and life-loving. She would come into *La Traviata*'s first Party Scene throwing kisses and waving to friends—not those onstage, but those in the audience—then find some chance to extricate the hemline of her gown from some planned hindrance during a showy scale, and polish off "Sempre libera" with a high E flat as she picked up her train, threw it over her arm, and gaily made an exit, still holding the note. Other Violettas filled their gowns more discreetly, but few had more fun in a costume than Tetrazzini.

All this came through in her singing. We have books on *The Joy of Cooking* and *The Joy of Sex;* if there were a *Joy of Coloratura,* Tetrazzini would have been the one to write it. Though she first absorbed repertory by listening to her older sister's practice and made her stage debut by leaping up from her seat in a second-rate theatre in Florence to offer to substitute for an indisposed soprano, she spent her seasoning years touring through South and Central America and thus knew her business thoroughly by the time she reached the international scene. Critics worried about her inadequately equalized registers, but it may be that a leggiero with distinct lower, middle, and upper voices is saucier, more ebullient, than one with a seamless composition. There's something wonderfully perverse in a passage that jumps from the heights to sudden depths, and Tetrazzini's glorious top was matched by a secure bottom. (Opera folklore recalls a weak lower register, but her records disprove this.)

In the golden age Adelina Patti remained the standard by which lyrics and leggieros* were judged, and Patti's were perfectly married registers. But I wonder if Patti could have made Philine's "Je suis Titania" or Rosina's "Una voce poco fa" so

---

*The two Fächer were relatively interchangeable then, for coloratura was a fact of life in training and performance, a duty and pleasure. Not till about 1890 and the rise of "realism" did composers come to regard coloratura as "unrealistic" and generally cease writing it. In Patti's epoch, roughly 1861–1919 (from first fame to death), lyrics couldn't avoid the decorated line and leggieros sang any role not of Wagnerian weight. Patti even sang Aida—as did Tetrazzini, who instituted the unforgivable but delightful interpolated high E flat at the close of the Triumphal Scene that Callas revived in her Mexico City Aidas.

devilish: the *joy* of coloratura. Tetrazzini respected opera's nobility more than its honesty, as when Patti herself erupted out of her retirement castle in Wales to hear Tetrazzini at Covent Garden and Tetrazzini, upon entering, bowed homage to Patti, diva to diva. This seems, even for the day, inartistic. But Tetrazzini was a woman of loyalties, to her repertory, to her public, to her friends. How many other divas can one name whose best friend was a tenor?*

Tetrazzini's roles, emphasizing coloratura, announced the arrival of a specialist, and her successor Amelita Galli-Curci completed the revolution by singing almost nothing but coloratura. Hers is a strange career, centering on New York and Chicago only, bedeviled by intonation problems (especially a tendency to sing flat), and cut short by a goiter operation. Yet hers is an extensive reputation, for she made it, largely, on her phenomenally lucrative Victor records. Later on we'll consider the crucial part that records play nowadays in building a career; in the early 1900s the primitive reproduction and prohibitive cost of the discs and equipment made them somewhat subsidiary. Caruso recorded well, to say the least; he virtually placed the phonograph, and the phonograph placed him as the tenor of the age. So recordings could be made a weapon. Galli-Curci made them hers.

It's not entirely clear why. She had none of Tetrazzini's glitter or sense of humor, her voice itself was ordinary, and she had nothing new to say in music that was, in her time, already two generations old. Melba sang Puccini, Caruso created roles by Cilea and Giordano, and Mary Garden seems at times to have sung nothing but premieres. But Galli-Curci prepared a kind of leggiero rolodex in her Rosina, Elvira, Amina, Lucia, Gilda, Violetta, Lakmé, Dinorah, and the Queen of Shemakha in *The Golden Cock*. True, she sang Mimì and Butterfly, but emphasized these larger roles mainly in Chicago, where she was so popular she might have sung Boris Godunof with success. She had stage presence enough to bring off Violetta, and by luck her first records came out in the late 1910s, just when the phonograph was becoming acculturated

---

*Enrico Caruso. Tetrazzini was also close to John McCormack.

in living rooms from San Francisco to Prague. Chances were, the first record you bought was a Caruso; the second, a Galli-Curci. Hers are not great records, for she was not a great singer. Still, as the historian and aficionado Michael Scott notes, "Is there any other famous soprano on record who so often and so obviously sings out of tune and yet does it so endearingly?"

The Patti standards have utterly collapsed by now, yet the leggiero (as the technically most exposed singer) is still held to account for false intonation, wayward decoration, aspirated runs, and underwhelming charisma. The repertory has partly vanished—what house performs *Dinorah* or *Lakmé* today?—but the revitalization of Mozart and his contemporaries and the increased popularity of Richard Strauss have yielded new sets of roles. *Die Zauberflöte* was not often performed outside of German lands till rather late in this century, yet the Queen of the Night, a role comprised entirely of two arias, some lines of dialogue, and a few notes in the finale, has become the leggiero's *ne plus ultra*. One can build a career on it, for singers who can encircle its star-flaming coloratura smack up to the high Fs (which no voice can guarantee—some nights you hit them and some nights you don't) and who can also flame star-like (as the character must) are rare. "How to make a sensation *[Sternstunde]*," Lotte Heinotz muses, "is the obsession of the neophyte." And the obsession of the arrived diva?* "How to make a *second* sensation." If few of the lyric's parts are sensation-makers, the leggiero can become news as the Queen of the Night; whereupon, every company will try to sign her Queen and thus ensure another series of *Zauberflöten*. Lucia Popp's Queen looked so good that she was recruited to perform it with the Bratislava Opera when still a student, and the gargling Cristina Deutekom and ferocious Edda Moser similarly became famous in the part.

Edita Gruberova is the latest in the line, and perhaps she best demonstrates the modern leggiero's versatility. I doubt that either Tetrazzini or Galli-Curci could have grown so impressively as Zerbinetta, the coquettish dancer in Strauss' *Ariadne auf Naxos*. The German alone would have defeated them;

---

*Heinotz' term is the tautological neologism *Divagöttin*.

and could either have negotiated the shifts in thematic narration that Strauss and his librettist, Hugo von Hofmannsthal, put Zerbinetta through in her big aria? First, in
recitative, a disquisition on how truly women love; then, in terse
arioso, a curse on how falsely men love; then, lyrically, a personal report on constancy and inconstancy, with a florid cele-
bration of the latter, the high notes tripping to and fro as Zerbinetta does at the court of love among her swain—Pagliazzo!
Mezzetin! Pasquariello!; and at last the vivacious rondo, relevant to the myth at hand: like Ariadne, she surrenders to man
as to a god . . . but, always, a new god replaces the old one.
Once a competent Zerbinetta, at ease in the coloratura and on
call at every major house to authenticate their Ariadnes,
Gruberova became at length a human Zerbinetta, tracing the
complexities of a woman who can appreciate the ideal but ac-
cepts the way of the world.

Leggiero contains a subgroup of sopranos who make
themselves famous for a freak high range rather than for any
certain role. They may from time to time appear as Zerbinetta, Gilda, or the Queen of the Night, but they feel more
comfortable singing concert pieces on the borderline of trash—
an Air and Variations, "The Carnival of Venice," or a Ländler
with a yodel refrain and oompah cowbells. Opinion-makers don't
approve of this; they hear meretricious, even unwholesome art.
But the public enjoys them: not necessarily an operagoing
public. Ellen Beach Yaw, Maria Galvany, Erna Sack, and Mil-
iza Korjus among others varied in the extent to which they
considered an elitist theatre career part of or a mere adjunct
to their appeal as whackadoodle *artistes.* Yaw was utterly out
of her element in opera (fainting at the close of Lucia's mad
scene, she looked, one critic wrote, "like a pan of spilt milk"),
while Erna Sack sang the standing leggiero parts, even created a new one, in Strauss' *Die Schweigsame Frau.* Korjus, too,
sang opera, but did not find herself till she came to Hollywood
to play a diva in MGM's *Wienertorte* d'après Johann Strauss,
The Great Waltz. It's interesting, at last, to hear what one of
these crazy voices sounds like when it isn't singing—Korjus
talking is like a baby imitating Mae West.

It is when we gain the bigger and darker voices that we reach true Divakunst. If the lyric's salient quality is innocence and the leggiero's is agility, the spinto's is distress—showing that agony that Evelyn Lear mentioned. The word spinto ("pushed") was first used to describe the nineteenth-century evolution of the lead tenor from light dexterity (Nemorino, say) into dramatic weight (Radames). Sopranos turned spinto in the verismo years, when composers habitually wrote on the edge of the registers, especially at dire moments when the most committed singers are so rapt in their parts that they cannot hold back and protect their instruments. But who can resist the spinto repertory—Tosca, Butterfly, Francesca da Rimini, Iris, Fiora, Maddalena, Isabeau, Parisina, Wally, not to mention comparable roles in non-Italian catalogues? These are women who live on the fault line, love too well, and die with *panache*. Some of their antecedents had mad scenes. These women have whole mad operas. It's possible that Galli-Curci made her career in America rather than in her native Italy because verismo had fed a taste for defiant love and death that Galli-Curci's voice and temperament could not satisfy.

It is demonstrably true that a generation of Italian sopranos broke their art upon the wheel of verismo. Bianca Scacciati, a favorite at La Scala, found when she presented her Turandot at Covent Garden that what was sincere to Italian ears was shrill to English. The management sent her home and called in Florence Easton, a singer who controlled her resources so securely that she sang everything from the teeny-tiny Lauretta to Brünnhilde and Isolde. Agreed, Easton was an outstanding musician, with nearly a hundred roles, any one of which she could sing on a day's notice. The point is not how good a Turandot Easton was, but how dangerous the spinto Fach is to the singer who isn't strong enough for it. Too many weren't: because spinto isn't really a Fach at all. It's a graveyard for lyrics.

Spinto is a euphemism. There are really only two kinds of voice, the light and the heavy, and there is no way to induce the heavy: you either have it or you don't. Spinto is the name by which light voices have dubbed themselves heavy, and so

Scacciati's coevals ruined themselves. They were dedicated and
extraordinarily musical performers, but they were also unsteady, with squally top notes and bludgeoned chest tones. "I
belong to the group of singers," Maria Caniglia very eventually observed, "who gave too much of themselves."

Yes, one might say that. For Caniglia, famous as an example of letting the voice broaden through experience from lyric
through spinto to dramatic, made her debut, aged twenty-four,
as Strauss' Chrysothemis, a short but big role, of Rysanek cal-
iber. Having reigned as a Scala favorite for twenty years,
Caniglia woke up one day in 1950 to find her "group of singers" retired or dead, leaving a shortage of dramatics that impresarios thought Caniglia might fill singlehanded. Well, if
you're going to sing with an on-and-off top, poor breath control, and a sluggish attack, you might as well sing Norma,
Abigaille, Gioconda, and Minnie as sing Mimì.

Thus the lyric who declared herself spinto allowed herself
to be declared dramatic. Leontyne Price makes a notable point
in assessing her capability as "lyric with a dramatic thrust."
Price has the weight of color, of brightness—but that won't get
you through Minnie (as Price learned at the Met in 1961). Price
dubs herself "a juicy lyric," describing an area between lyric
and spinto that only a strong-willed singer can maintain, and
quotes the advice of her teacher, Florence Page Kimball: "Sing
on your interest; don't use the principal."

Nevertheless, there is something vastly admirable in Caniglia's dedication, particularly to performing new works. It is
typical of changing times that the outstanding Italian spinto
of the postwar generation, Renata Tebaldi, sang classic rather
than contemporary repertory, though, given the drab, remain-
dered quality of composition in her day, one cannot blame her.
Tebaldi was cagey in judging scores. She had true spinto possibilities, a gorgeous sound flaked with steel for the vicious bits.
Her "Ecco un artista!" in *Tosca,* at the tenor's execution, stays
vital in recollection: sung, not screamed, but really sung, the
words scraped out in desperation, yet the notes full and intense. But no Abigaille for her. And when Tullio Serafin offered to coach her in Norma slowly and carefully—Serafin, the

wizard of Fach—Tebaldi said no. She must have heard one of Caniglia's attempts.

Tebaldi's most memorable roles have to an extent defined the spinto repertory—Desdemona, Tosca, Butterfly, Manon Lescaut, Adriana Lecouvreur, Maddalena di Coigny, a Violetta somewhat overtaxed in Act One, an opulent Mimì, a very careful Minnie, and finally, when the voice is ready, Santuzza, Gioconda, Amelia in *Un Ballo in Maschera,* Elisabeth de Valois. At that, some of the last roles she gave only to recording tape, unwilling to risk them in the theatre. Because the voice was beautiful enough to be called, seriously and often, *the* voice of the day, it was easy to forget the Tebaldi was as well a highly expressive artist, not an important actress but a finely musical interpreter. Early in her career, in *Giovanna d'Arco* in Venice in 1951, she showed how an extraordinary singer can distill the excitement of character entirely from within line, phrasing, and accent. But thereafter she grew careful, as if she had studied the example of the spinto generation before her and understood the corrosive effects of passion in performance. Because she was careful, she was able to conquer vocal problems that set in suddenly and horribly in the early 1960s, to return glowing and true and ride out her last years with dignity. But because she was careful, she never broke through, in any part, to that summit of demented whereat singer and actress come together explosively, definitively. With Tebaldi it was the song; she was the Stimmdiva with artless Kunst.

Today spintos are three for a penny, as much of the repertory needs high-pressure voices and popular taste runs to high-pressure performances even of lighter parts. Verismo spoiled not only vocal technique—it spoiled the public, led it to demand a diva singing on her principal every night. However, like Tebaldi, some wise sopranos are alert to tradition and their personal physiology of voice. They resist crazes. Margaret Price is one such: the Welsh soprano's career has been well founded on Fach. Her first roles included Cherubino, Nannetta, and Amelia Boccanegra, and by the 1970s she had become an outstanding Mozartean. It's a grand instrument, evenly registered and brilliant at the top. Price is so certain of what she can do that, strictly for purposes of recording and with a sympathetic conductor, she taped a spectacular Isolde, a treacherous part even for dramatic sopranos. But then a medium-sized voice in sharp focus is at times more intrepid than a big, loose one. At the climaxes, with strings surging and the brass wild, Price stays afloat. Here is a spinto who can defeat the modern demand for vocal miscasting.

The temptation to sing a role beyond one's powers is not new. There are famous cases throughout history, such as Nellie Melba's one attempt at the *Siegfried* Brünnhilde at the Met in 1896, on the advice of her mentor Jean de Reszke. One of the few tenors Melba could take standing up, de Reszke later claimed it was the *Siegfried* Woodbird he had recommended. But Lillian Nordica's coach E. Romayne Simmons claims that de Reszke talked Melba into Brünnhilde to oust Nordica, an Elsa and Venus who had just taken up big-lady Wagner (as Isolde to de Reszke's Tristan) and scored, in the opinion of de Reszke's ego, an uncomfortably spirited success. One can imagine how de Reszke exploited Melba's vanity to protect his own: "Just think, Nellie—Nordica came to the Met in *your* parts. Marguerite, Ophélie. If she can move up to Brünnhilde, why can't Melba?"

However, Nordica's was a strong voice in transition, Melba's less strong and already set. The question is not why did Melba attempt it, but why did no one talk her out of it? Melba's teacher Mathilde Marchesi tried to. When Melba came to Paris to coach Brünnhilde with her, Marchesi refused to have anything to do with it, and let fly with a few choice observations on Wagner's vocal writing in general. And from the moment Melba opened her mouth on The Night she realized the difference between getting through Brünnhilde at the piano and getting through it on the stage of the Met. "I have been a fool," she said. She didn't say it often.

The Melba Brünnhilde and similar calamities are isolated disasters. Today, miscasting has become a Fach in itself. It is as if sopranos feel they can be classified by the roles they sing, no matter how indifferently they sing them. A Norma is a dramatic soprano. You sing Norma, you are dramatic. But are you competent, what the Italians call "correct"? No. The role doesn't define the voice. The *voice* defines the voice.

The dramatic soprano, the true one, may occupy the most defined Fach of all. Certainly there is nothing more noticeable in a dramatic part than an underdeveloped instrument. The high notes shriek or gently slip flat, the upper middle register implodes, the low notes hide. The fatigue can be awesome—underpowered Turandots and Elektras have provided some of the most notorious evenings of filth, so terrible even the gallery is afraid to boo. The dramatic's essence is power, physical and emotional, from Isolde to Salome, from Norma to Turandot. Yet notice what a variety of styles the four roles present, especially as compared with the more homogeneous lyric or leggiero repertories. Isolde is a woman struggling for a sense of self in a heavily male-ordered age; Salome is a child of semi-barbarians. Isolde treats universals of honor and passion; Salome watches, pouts, dances, and kisses a bodiless head. Isolde dominates the first act, shares half the second, and closes the third of a very long evening; *Salome* is over in eighty minutes. Isoldes are drawn from the biggest veteran sopranos; an ideal Salome is more lithe than loud. (Strauss hoped to hear a sweet lyric in the role and offered to rescore and transpose it for Elisabeth Schumann, who had possibly the smallest voice in the history of the German mouth.) Norma and Turandot are even farther apart: the one a woman burning with jealousy, her line embellished to the utmost; the other a tense virgin who must learn to love, working the unencumbered lines of the verismo period.

The four roles do require much in common: endurance, smashing high notes, low notes that speak strongly, and the unique touch of Divakunst. Has any one singer brought off all four? Callas could have done it, but never sang Salome. Nilsson was famous for three of the quartet, but she couldn't have sung Norma. Eva Turner, one of the two or three greatest Turandots, was an admired Isolde, but canceled her first Norma to be with her ailing father and never got another chance at it. Montserrat Caballé sang Salome early in her career, grew up to Norma and even Turandot. But Isolde?

Perhaps it is best to think of the dramatic Fach as comprising two crossover subcategories: the lyric-dramatic, who commands legato as well as power; and the heroic-dramatic, who relies on strength. Isolde, really, demands both types; Norma primarily the former; Salome (because of the orchestra) and Turandot (because of the remorselessly high tessitura) the latter. One might regard the Fach ethnically, the Italians on one hand and the Germans on the other. Let us take Gina Cigna and Kirsten Flagstad as our models thus.

Cigna, though French and a student of Emma Calvé at the Paris Conservatoire, became an exemplar of the verismo dramatic, coaching with retired exemplars of the preceding generation and falling wholeheartedly into the contemporary Italian repertory. She branched out into Monteverdi, Gluck, and Strauss, but made her name as Norma, Turandot, Aida, Gioconda, the *Ballo* Amelia, and in Respighi, Zandonai, and Mascagni. At Covent Garden and the Met, her huge voice delighted the public; but her erratic technique and fluttery intonation irritated critics and connoisseurs. Poetic phrases alternated with platitudinous phrases. The complexities of Turandot—balancing the ice and fire—were beyond her. Her Norma was ramshackle. Her Aida and Gioconda were interesting in terms of sheer force, and her devotion to living composers apparently made her special as Isabeau and Francesca. But it would seem that Cigna had, too often, no basis but force on which to build. She was a dramatic one takes for granted, a willing worker and—except in bel canto—somewhat touching. But never altogether inspired.

Flagstad's concentration on big Wagner, and her assumption of this repertory only after twenty years of lyric and spinto heroines, places her apart—as does the breathtakingly warm quality of the voice itself, its middle register developing an almost unearthly richness over the years. It came straight out, clear, full, and pure. Cigna, beloved in Italy, never won over a following elsewhere: Cigna came out strained. Flagstad became a sensation at the Met and Covent Garden and stands in memory as the essential Wagnerian despite superior competition. Frida Leider's voice was more ravishing, Florence Austral's majesty incomparable, Helen Traubel's emotional involvement more generous. Later, Birgit Nilsson's strength of character (because of the size of voice) outdid everyone's. Flagstad lacked temperament and sensuality. She was the hausfrau as diva; when she wasn't onstage, she was knitting.* Her notable quality was her singing itself, her resolute projection in a day when other sopranos—Cigna, for one—had trouble just hitting notes. Coming offstage after a Met *Fidelio* in 1951, Flagstad said, straight out, "There is not another singer living or dead who could have done what I did out there tonight."

It would seem, then, that dramatics have it harder than their colleagues. But the one soprano whom everyone is agreed on as the great singer of the century—incomparable instrument and flawless art—was a dramatic soprano. She had no training to speak of, made her stage debut at a major house with an illustrious cast with no prior operatic experience, and quickly became a marvel universally acknowledged. Her Norma, undertaken when she was thirty, proved that a dramatic needn't sacrifice agility for power. Tullio Serafin rated her one of the century's three "miracles," along with Caruso and Titta Ruffo. And the recordings bear all this out: it was a luscious voice, dark, even in scale, and able to do nearly anything. Arturo Toscanini fell on his knees before her when she came back to congratulate him after a concert, and the if possible even more austere Victor de Sabata told her that her rehearsals for *La Vestale* in 1933 were "the greatest musical experience" he had had in the theatre. Here was the voice that defines and transcends Fach. It was a fluke, ideal in an age of shattered ideals.

It was Rosa Ponselle, who thoughtfully retired at what appeared to be the height of her fame and never explained why, thereby passing into one of opera's most inveigling legends. How does a diva become extraordinary? "As far back as I can remember," Ponselle wrote in her autobiography, "I never had what I would call a 'girl's voice.' . . . My singing voice was al-

---

*"It is not true that I knit in my dressing room!" she told an interviewer; scotch a favorite Flagstad legend. In her dressing room she studied the score of the evening. Nevertheless, in almost every Flagstad story that doesn't take place in her dressing room, she *is* knitting. Nor is this an isolated case—Joan Sutherland does needlepoint.

ways big and round, and even as a teenager I could sing almost three octaves. I never recall the slightest trouble swelling or diminishing a tone."

Serafin was right: she was a miracle, neat. Ponselle had one weakness, a limited top range; she picturesquely spoke of "the high C" as if it were a once-in-a-season horror, something you aim for when you go for broke. She always had a dependable B flat; after some years everything above it became risky. Yet, given what Ponselle could do with her instrument, its few disappointments are of small account. Her legato was literally *legato*—"bound" in artistically rational connection, wonderful and surprising, yet so right that one realized as she sang that she might have written the music herself. Her staccato was perfect, "like rows of equally matched pearls," Walter Legge thought, "with a glimpse of light separating each one." She could toss off coloratura divisions with the kick of a whip or the sigh of romance, and the great velvet of sound never seemed to give out or fall out of tune. Ponselle was an Eve of sopranos, the first of kind who unaccountably delayed her entrance till her kind was almost over. She was an authentic lyric-dramatic, one in whom power was simply the producing medium for golden-age singing.

Can one name a lyric-dramatic today? Joan Sutherland might qualify, for, though she mainly sings leggiero parts, the voice is surprisingly large. Montserrat Caballé, too, suggests the dramatic's verve while keeping her trademark pianissimo high notes in trim. Still, they are exceptional. The postwar dramatic is almost inevitably a heroic—Amy Shuard, say, who rose through the ranks from Sadler's Wells to Covent Garden, from Musetta, Marguerite, and the *Boccanegra* Amelia on to Elektra and Brünnhilde. As Scacciati's sincere but uncouth Turandot displeased the British, so did Shuard's tense, formidable Turandot disappoint the Italians. Shuard, Eva Turner's pupil, sang the part in the Turner style, alas without the blazing Turner high notes. The Italians want a warm squandering of voice, in the verismo manner, or a cold magnificence of voice, as with Turner or Nilsson, an Italian favorite in the part. Shuard had authority and depth but neither warmth nor magnificence. Her Elektra was one of the best I've seen, but

Italian audiences wouldn't have liked it, either: in these parts they don't want appropriate; they want *wild.*

Wild, perhaps, would be Gwyneth Jones, a heroic-dramatic with voice to spare. The Welsh soprano started as a mezzo, underlining the solid foundation that supports the dramatic's top. This was wise of Jones, or perhaps fortuitously salubrious: for too many singers sail into dramatic parts before their lower and middle registers are composed and end up, or, rather, continue with wholly unsupported voices that fall to pieces as one listens. Yet Jones may have leaped the course once she hit stride, for she took on a heavy schedule and suffered sloppy patches. However, when Pierre Boulez and Patrice Chéreau cast her as Brünnhilde in the Bayreuth centennial *Ring,* recorded and televised, they were virtually declaring her the Brünnhilde of the age.

And Jones distinguished herself. Earlier in her career she was an acceptable Sieglinde, generalizing the character's warmth and desperation. She worked harder as Brünnhilde, smoothly blending the woman and the archetype without scanting the role's epic resonance. Brünnhilde is goddess and mortal, a hero's wife and a hero herself, obedient and mutinous, a world-saver and world-ender. How many voices suit such combinations? Is the role singable at all? Just getting the notes out is hard enough; then comes portrayal! In the second act of *Götterdämmerung,* when she is dragged before the Gibichungs to become Gunther's unwilling bride, Jones' Brünnhilde felt so wretched that she bent nearly in two, her head inches off the floor. She made strong contrast with Jeannine Altmeyer's Gutrune, the two women both in white dresses but Altmeyer pert as a beauty queen, frolicking and even smooching with Siegfried. How different Jones' Brünnhilde was from the customary seething arrogator. And at the mention of Siegfried's name, she looked up, saw him, tottered, and fell, a woman in utmost ruin. As Siegfried's apparent treachery was brought out, Jones gathered Brünnhilde's self-possession and charged back upward, now an immortal in utmost fury. After Siegfried took his oath of innocence on the spear, Jones rushed forward and pushed him away to take her own oath, her voice in full cry and the high notes bitten out and flung off. Later her Immolation Scene was equal to the task of closing the apocalyptic epic. If she lacked Flagstad's security and Austral's white-hot top, still she undoubtedly fulfills the role's requirements, and has become somewhat symbolic in opera—of the Welsh vocal tradition, of the postwar British dominance in the realm of the acting singer, and of the lure, for heroic-dramatics, of the Wagnerian heroine, as strong now as ever.

With the mezzo-soprano we begin again with the table of sizes and skills: Frederica von Stade is lyric, Marilyn Horne florid, Tatiana Troyanos dramatic. As with sopranos, the distinctions are not rigid. All three of these women sing Adalgisa; von Stade is known for her Octavian, a strenuous role generally thought to be beyond the lyric's reach; Horne, in her apprentice days in Gelsenkirchen, Germany, sang big soprano roles, including Minnie; and Troyanos' extended range has given her rights over parts in soprano territory such as Kundry, *Ariadne*'s Composer, and Handel's Cleopatra.

Each of the three, Americans of international stature, instructively represents an aspect of the contemporary opera scene. Troyanos was born in New York, studied at Juilliard, and made her debut with the City Opera at its old home on Fifty-fifth Street. But, like many of her compatriots of the postwar era, she made her name abroad, resident in Hamburg. The average German house being far more adventurous in repertory than most theatres, Hamburg exposed Troyanos to modern composition in steady doses, taking in the world premiere of Krzysztof Penderecki's *Die Teufel von Loudun,* in which Troyanos created the vicious, sexually obsessed Sister Jeanne. Modern vocal writing is fiendish almost as a matter of course; and when it treats vicious sexual obsession it really goes wild. Troyanos came through unscathed; still, she doesn't sing much modern opera anymore.

Von Stade, too, created reputation in Europe, where she unveiled and developed her celebrated Cherubino, Mélisande, Rosina, and Penelope. However, after study at Mannes, she had joined not a foreign company, but the Met, where her sumptuous voice and melting stage presence netted her such gala parts as the Third Boy in *Die Zauberflöte* (a debut role she shares with Lotte Lehmann), one of the Unborn (and unseen) Children in *Die Frau Ohne Schatten,* and Wowkle, the laconic Indian servant in *La Fanciulla del West.* "Ugh!" says Wowkle. Once free of the Met's heedless maw, von Stade found herself in lead roles wherein she helped infix her generation's outstanding ability to deal with opera as singing and acting text. It is not likely that the postwar exhumation of Monteverdi-era opera could survive without von Stade, Richard Stilwell, and the others in this group of young Americans more intrigued by their music than their billing.

If Troyanos is the American star illuminated in Europe and von Stade the singer energized by text, Horne is the deputy of the revival of golden-age ideals launched by Callas and Visconti and taken up by Sutherland and Bonynge, who made Horne their cohort. In her grand range and superb technique, Horne recalls the days when there were only "sopranos"; so, indeed, she bills herself, letting the distinction of Fach shine forth in what she does rather than in what she is called. To Callas the revival was exalted mission, to Sutherland an experiment in Fach, to Horne the indicated course of action given her vocal endowment and the openings in the repertory that she alone could fill. Besides, how can anyone resist singing Arsace (in *Semiramide*) when you can dress and make up to look like The Little King?

Horne's tradition takes her back to Pauline Viardot. It is an outmoded tradition in all but vocalism. Everything else in opera has changed—composition, staging practice, fidelity to the authors' conception, and the relation of the stage to the public. But the standard of great singing has not changed. It was high; it is high. Horne's attention to the composer's markings, her elated bursts of coloratura, her *acuti,* her fluent, feeling line build a one-woman theme park entitled Music-land. Her chest tones are a treat—yea, she passes them out like candy, and once, jokingly, she threatened to record a disc of old favorites to be called *Chestnuts for Chest Nuts.* It is true that, in singing Adalgisa, Horne overturned golden-age tradition, for both *Norma*'s woman leads are sopranos, the younger Adalgisa presumably going to a younger and lighter voice. Modern taste prefers a dramatic mezzo in the part, and the sight of Horne and Sutherland, arms clasped for "Mira, o

Norma," became one of the sights of our time—most piquantly so on television on the old "Ed Sullivan Show," where opera always added that touch of class to the vaudeville. But it is notable that one of Horne's greatest parts, Fidès in *Le Prophète,* is the Viardot role that redirected mezzo-soprano history.

The vocal scene is further textured by subcategories—the German soubrette, say, basically a leggiero who sings sidekick parts, or the French Dugazon and Falcon, named for unique singers who uncovered new genres. Because the French love categorizing, the Dugazon is available in sizes: *jeune* and *mère* (roughly, "ingenue" and "veteran") or simply *première* and *deuxième* ("first" and "second").

Yet, however much we study the categories, it is not Fach that fills our ears, not the projection of a (we hope) lovely voice. It is expression that impels us: how the singer uses voice to narrate characterologically. I speak not of acting *per se* but of musicality wedded to acting: of the dynamics of singing, of the person the composer and librettist imagined, of the insight of phrasing.

There can be no doubt that singing has become less imaginative since the early 1900s. Modern taste prefers a rigid tempo and no variety of color, with perhaps a touch of zing on a high note. All lyrics sound alike; all dramatics sound alike; all Mimìs and Carmens and Sophies and Turandots sound alike. This is why there is no one today "like" Melba, Farrar, Muzio. Our sopranos are discouraged from trying (if they can at all) what Melba's age regarded as what one might call standard individuality. Each singer *inflected* his music; this was the vitality of the golden age: why it was golden in the first place.

It is gone. Today's singers largely perform like an army, under bans of "fidelity to the score" and other nonsense that would have astounded the composers of those scores. Wholesale revision and rude improvisation they banned the first chance they got, certainly. But they were not composing for robots. On the contrary, distinctions of voice and approach were not only taken for granted but written into the scores. And so, within the limitations of this counterfeit "fidelity," or especially because there is so little difference from mouth to mouth, we look for the arresting talent, the unlike diva with personality and insight: with dynamics. Voice itself, in such an age, becomes less important than individuality.

Thus Jarmila Novotna, whose voice was undistinguished, even dull, could hold a theatre on edge by the way she used it. (Her knockout looks didn't hurt.) Thus Callas, even in her tattered later years, could hearten her adherents and humiliate her detractors with the utter rightness of a phrase. Thus Zinka Milanov, despite an industrial-strength physique, would grip the imagination with a soaring line, as if the composer had written this line in the only possible way it should sound and with just this Milanov in mind to sing it—that tone, that love, that freedom.

"I want to be judged," Mary Garden said, "not alone by my singing or my acting or my stage appearance, but by these combined into one art that is entirely different from the rest." It is far more than what you were born with; it's what you make of it, going for it not because show biz says so but because the work and you, the singer, are at one great strength together and all the terrorism of artistic challenge and the public's show-me defiance is out of mind. You have left The Business behind. You are well cast, in good voice, and inspired. You have temperament, you have been seasoned in the provinces and tested in the cities, and your politics is art. Nothing, now, can hold you back—that is more than voice, more even than solid training. That is a talent exclusive to opera, where stupendous singers deal with the absolutes of life—love, honor, and death—as if their lives depended on it. And you take it, the great blinding size of it, and contain it.

There is nothing as big as a gifted diva in her prime.

CHAPTER

2

MUSICIANSHIP

She had no voice, but she knew so well how to direct her breathing and thereby to create, with so wondrous a musicianship, the true soul of a woman, that one thought no longer of singing nor of voice.
Richard Wagner on
Wilhelmine Schröder-Devrient's
Leonore

There are not many born performers.
Jennie Tourel

In September of 1969, a party of aficionados headed from New York to Philadelphia by automobile to catch a performance of *Nabucco* at the Academy of Music. The cast promised Peter Glossop as the Babylonian king, Salvador Novoa as Ismaele, and Ezio Flagello as the Jewish High Priest, but the sole reason for the trip was Elena Souliotis' Abigaille. Souliotis had made her debut in Naples as Santuzza in 1964 and in the ensuing five years had become a sensation in the lyric-dramatic Fach. She was Greek and clearly headed for Norma, so there were comparisons with Callas. Moreover, she sang like Callas—not with that technique or coloration or patience, but with the same accents, as if she had learned her parts from Callas' records, the way one might master Swedish. There was no question that when she was in voice, she was dynamite: had already been so in this very part, on a complete recording made just as the world had turned its ear upon her swelling fame.

In the car the aficionados cheerfully traded wild stories and sweeping opinions. Philadelphia trips made them expansive and giddy, for Philadelphia opera (by either of the city's two companies, the Lyric and the Grand, long since merged) was of the last-minute, inadvertently daredevil kind at which anything may happen. One might hear an unheralded new star in the making or see aged choristers keel over during a finale. Scotto and Caballé sang arcane bel canto; forgotten tenors made intemperate returns. At Joan Sutherland's *Lakmé* a dresser put an oversized helmet on Anastasios Vrenios and he played Gerald, until the second act, with no face above the lower lip; and as Mary Curtis-Verna's Manon Lescaut died on the deserted plains of New Orleans, a bag lady entered the Academy's Spruce Street stage door, trudged grumbling behind Curtis-Verna in full view of the audience (who sat deathly silent, in the Philadelphia manner), and went out the Pine Street door. There were demented nights, nights of filth, and wonderful nights when nothing happened for about twenty minutes and then suddenly all the scenery fell down.

Yet after a while our aficionados of the *Nabucco* trip grew serious. How many foolish performances can opera afford to give before it caves in on foolishness, on hack producers and no rehearsals and ignorant singers and political appeasements? True, the aficionados' home base, the Met, was no Philadelphia. If nothing else, it had the money, the rehearsal time, the major singers, and something like a hundred thousand in help backstage. And there were the aficionados' visits to Bayreuth, London, Milan, Santa Fe, San Francisco. Still, there was a queasy feeling about the future possibilities in their operagoing, a feeling that the art had been on the decline since before they were born.

The talk turned to superlatives on the best, the worst, the most. Matthew Epstein said, "There are five great voices in opera today. *Five.*" Epstein was just then embarking on a career as an artists' representative that would eventually make him the most influential man in American opera who was neither a conductor nor a director. He bore an encyclopedic knowledge of the field, never forgot a performance, and could instinctively, immediately, and ideally cast any existing opera, including some he had never heard, including even a few he had never heard *of.* He had the gift. And his five great voices were: Arroyo, Caballé, Crespin, Price, and Rysanek.

The company struggled to understand him. The five greatest—

"Not greatest," Epstein replied, "as if there were more. These five. *Netto.*"

"You think they're the greatest singers today?" someone asked "What about Sutherland?"

"I didn't say 'great singers.' I said 'great voices.' There's a difference."

"Then who are the great singers?"

Epstein reflected, then shook his head. "There are so few it's not worth making the list."

The group considered this. Was the gold eroded, the age inconvertibly corrupt? Was the best they could hope for an evening in which, twenty minutes along, the scenery falls down? One of them sadly asked, "Is there life after Callas?" and another, inspired by the popular notion that Souliotis was destined to carry on where her compatriot had left off, asked, "What about Souliotis?"

"That voice," Epstein decreed, "is a house of cards. And it's just about to blow."

It blew that night in *Nabucco* in the Academy of Music. Where once Souliotis rode this bronco of a part like a cowboy king, now—and from then on—she was flying all over the corral. The stormy scales that had glittered like sculpted ice now were pebbles, each of a different shape and texture. The high notes had stung; now they itched. Worst of all, there seemed to be no plan to the performance other than to get through it. There was no artistic endowment, not even of a cursory nature. Debates as to whether Souliotis was Stimmdiva or Kunstdiva were stilled. She was neither. Still, she became famous by example as the first of several notable house-of-cards stars, scaling upward out of nowhere overnight, in demand everywhere, compared to Callas as a rule, and suddenly suffering disasters and largely disappearing from the international scene.

Once, such disappearances could be laid to retirement for family reasons, as with Lisa della Casa, or because of a medical emergency, as with Galli-Curci. Now we have reached an age of opera singers who have no musical centering. They know nothing of the art, they do not endure training, and they cannot hear the phrases in a secret ideal vision which they then fulfill for the public. Once, anything less than this in opera was lewd. Now it's conventional. Regardless of the quality of voice, singers are not to a fine extent *singers* anymore. They are becoming an army of mouth-workers.

This would appear to be the last days of the Kunstdiva, the beginning of the end of great musicians of the voice. Let us get our bearings deep in the golden age, to compare the divas of Kunst and Stimm' at some remove from our own ears, tastes, and controversies. Let us take the word of Henry F. Chorley, one of the most frequently cited critics of the nineteenth century. An undistinguished writer of novels, plays, and poetry and in music no more than an amateur, Chorley is far from choice as an opinion-maker. Yet he is certainly preferable to his successors. Chorley, in the style of the day, exercised a passionate involvement in the quality of contemporary music. Today's journalists—in America especially—are reporters who hope to recount the particulars of a performance, to build a reputation on the measured, virtually opinionless nature of their writing. They can make a glory sound like a disaster—partly because they wouldn't know one from the other, but mainly because they cannot summon up the exuberance that the rest of us feel for the musical theatre.

In Chorley's age a critic earned his reputation for fanatic inclinations and hostilities. One knew where one stood with him. Where one stands with Chorley's vehement distaste for Wagner is something for each reader to assess for himself. "But," says Ernest Newman, himself oft-quoted and a Wagnerian, "even if we admit that his point of view was possibly only one out of many . . . it is always the point of view of a man who knows every in and out of his profession." Chorley's taste in composition and performance ran to the Italian style, giving him (Newman again) "a remarkably acute sense of the musical and more especially the vocal values of the operatic world of his time."

In other words, Chorley is a better judge of singers than of composers. Let us hear him distinguish the capabilities of two stars of the mid-1800s, Giulia Grisi and Pauline Viardot. Grisi was a Stimmdiva:

What a soprano voice was hers!—rich, sweet, equal
throughout its compass of two octaves (from C to C)
without a break, or a note which had to be managed.
. . . Her shake was clear and rapid; her scales were
certain; every interval was taken without hesitation.
. . . In the singing of certain slow movements pianissimo . . . the clear penetrating beauty . . . was so
unique as to reconcile the ear to a certain shallowness
of expression in her rendering of the words and the
situation.

In brief, "the beauty of sound was more remarkable . . . than
the depth of feeling." Chorley excepts Grisi's vigorous or angry scenes, wherein he feels she excelled. Still, he thought her
best parts were the result of adopting what she liked of her
colleagues' conceptions rather than of any original views. "Her
Norma," he adds, "doubtless her grandest performance, was
modelled on that of Madame Pasta." In Grisi, then, we have a
great voice and an expert technique, but something less than
great in acting heart and individuality of temperament.

In Pauline Viardot Chorley cites a singer more sensitive
than sensational, one of inferior natural equipment but surpassing imagination and intelligence. As the younger sister of
the beautifully ill-fated Maria Malibran, Viardot had "the dis-
advantageous shelter of a family name," the two women's father being Manuel Garcia, tenor, composer, and the most famous teacher of singing then and now. But this is beside the
point. Her disadvantages were mainly physical and vocal. She
was not beautiful; nor was her voice. Onstage, however, she
was electricity—not for acting *per se* but for what character
she could put into her singing. Her London debut as Rossini's
Desdemona "seized the musicians," Chorley noticed, "more
powerfully than it fascinated the public." Unlike Grisi's voice,
Viardot's was no natural glory:

Here and there were tones of an engaging tenderness,
but, here and there, tones of a less winning quality. In
spite of an art which has never . . . been exceeded in
amount, it was to be felt that nature had given her a

rebel to subdue, not a vassal to command, in her voice. From the first she chose to possess certain upper notes which must needs be fabricated and which never could be produced without the appearance of effort.

A problem voice, however, could not penalize such conviction of character as Viardot could bring to her singing. Clearly, it was not a question of how great the voice was, but with what greatness Viardot used it, Kunstdiva. Her Orphée awed Chorley:

> The slight, yet not childish, youth, with the yearning that maketh the heart sick, questioning the white groups of shadows that moved slowly through the Elysian Fields . . . The wondrous thrill of ecstasy which spoke in every fibre of the frame . . . at the moment of recognition and of granted prayer; these things may have been dreamed of, but assuredly were never expressed before.

As I've noted, fans of the two kinds of singer dispute their preferences. But opera needs both kinds as surely as it wants a Sutherland Norma to balance a Scotto Norma, one more beautiful and one more truthful; or Mödl's Isolde to amend Flagstad's. There is no one way in which to hear a given part, and there is too little of greatness now to elect any approach as the sole approach. Musicianship created the Kunstdiva: it was the thing she had in place of a superb voice. If she could not sound marvelous just by opening her mouth and pouring, then she would create a marvelous sound by cooking a more careful recipe. "See the whole country of trees and oranges and the sky!" Jennie Tourel would urge a student singing Mignon's "Connais-tu le pays?" The voice is a painting. " 'And there I want to die'—feel you are there already!" The voice is experience. "You are not Mignon," Tourel warns. "You are *thinking* of Mignon." The voice is a notion, inventive, protean. "Remember that her life is terrible, it's nothing." The voice reflects the subject of the music, counts the words as much as the notes. "Then you *are* Mignon."

Tourel was another Kunstdiva, her coaching a verbalization of the art of singing character. As one character differs from another, so one's performances differ—if only in the way one's phrasing sights a certain emotional goal, from Mignon to Octavian to Carmen. But students today prepare for a world increasingly concerned with polish, evenness, and sheer voice. In the provinces the old method of putting oneself into a role to the utmost hangs on, as heathen ritual did in the early Christian era. And as we all hang the holly at Christmas, we still appreciate, every so often, the old verismo singer with color and guts. Indeed, one of them—perhaps the last of the true divas—actually penetrated one of the world's grandest companies and has reigned as house soprano despite a militant faction oathed to destroy or at least despise her. (More about her later.) Still, we are losing the twentieth century's great innovation in opera production, the portrayal that thinks about the words, as Tourel urges, and feels them. Nor are we going back to the Patti style of handsome singing for its own sake, because the technique that Patti's coevals took for granted is in ruin.

The pervasive influence of recordings, moreover, with their antiseptic poise, their retakes and notes spotted in and remixing, their drab excellence, has taught a false ideal of voice without personality. This is hardly what Mozart, Bellini, Verdi, or Massenet had in mind; on the contrary, they wrote for specific voices and personalities. Too, Herbert von Karajan's momentous Salzburg style, wherein singers are gentled into the instrumental texture, or, rather, muzzled like dogs with a tendency to bite, has carried us further, into an idea of voices with one personality: that of Der Meister. This would have seemed even more bizarre to opera's composers.

Granted, von Karajan's High Suave Equalizing has brought forth some exquisite performances, even a *Don Carlos* with a lot of genuine Italian blood in it. But von Karajan blends his style under laboratory conditions at Salzburg with hand-picked teams of world-class stars who suit the style and also with plenty of time in which to distill the meticulous personality of his Salzburg alchemy. Elsewhere, with singers of a grainier individuality and conductors with a less compelling vision, this attempt to homogenize the diverse sounds of opera cannot work. Yet there are those who make the attempt. Coaches caution singers against "enacting," critics want every piece dished out with Salzburg cream, and the public expects live performances to sound as if von Karajan had doctored the tapes. Singers are trapped.

Ironically, in the years when von Karajan was just coming into his fashion, when he headed the Vienna State Opera and finally resigned because he couldn't get the sound he wanted and had to found his own Vienna in Salzburg, he himself gave some of his most successful performances with the singer who stands as the antithesis of the icily pretty but uncharacterized sound that von Karajan has helped foster. This was the singer who redeemed the expressivity of bel canto from the leggiero's superficial technique; who reclaimed opera's history from the density of the verismo effect, teaching the austerity of Classicism, the injured beauty of Romanticism, and post-Verdian realism as *separate* styles; who stimulated two generations of conductors and directors; who made each phrase in a role as crucial as any other, rather than spare herself and spoil the art between the high points. This is an outstanding historical figure, ranking with Malibran, Viardot, Toscanini, and Mahler: Maria Callas.

Callas inevitably touches upon every chapter of this book, for her exploits were wide of reach. She is somewhat like Viardot, Chorley's "tones of an engaging tenderness" mingled with those "of a less winning quality." It was a flawed voice. But then Callas sought to capture in her singing not just beauty but a whole humanity, and within her system the flaws feed the feeling, the sour plangency and the strident defiance becoming aspects of the canto. They were literally defects of her voice; she bent them into advantages of her singing. She was pure Kunstdiva, making more than having. The instrument was not that large, given her Fach, but its incisive metal told throughout the largest auditoriums, and her range took her from A below middle C to a high E. This is what she had. What she made was a musical information of what was happening in her characters, a searching virtuosity. Suffering, delight, humility, hubris, despair, rhapsody—all this was musically appointed, through her use of the voice flying the text upon the notes. This is musicianship.

Callas' Lucia was a revelation after the Galli-Curcis and Pagliughis, her Norma a dread glory after Cigna, her Tosca in effect a revival of a neglected and misunderstood classic. Who are the great singers? The Stimmdivas can endow a stirring performance, but in the end they pass, leaving their mark on nothing. It is not great voices that best serve opera, but those voices that understand the great music, the understanding of Kunstdivas. Through the defensive misrepresentation of Callas' detractors, the simplistic synopses of journalists, and the public's inability to come to terms with something as complex as an acting singer (and because the voice was truly unsteady, some notes "managed," others wobbling or running with acid), Callas has grown into a legend of an actress who could barely sing, who forced her way into opera and somehow got away with it.

No one who knows opera could say this honestly, for those who cannot sing will not survive there no matter how hard they act. This claptrap critique sometimes affronts other unique talents—Chaliapin and Mary Garden, for instance. He bellowed and she bleated; they got through on charisma. Rubbish! The records tell otherwise. It is in fact primarily as a singer that Callas made her history, in the way Lucia's skittery anguish, Norma's struggle between reason and hatred, Lady Macbeth's ambition, Tosca's tactless warmth, and Violetta's opulence and despair *sounded* on her voice, line for line, in notes colored as no other singer in living memory could color: for strength, darkness, breadth, pallor, radiance. The voice is a painting.

Yes, the woman could act. At the very moment she entered, you saw in full Aida, Anna Bolena, Gioconda, felt their eyes on you even before they uttered a sound. Her Lady Macbeth seemed to pounce, her Norma to advance, her Amina to glide. As Iphigénie she instilled an aura of condign doom, as Médée cast the bitter shadow of the unconquerable woman, as Violetta sought protection under the cover of independence. The gestures—so authentically antique, yet, strangely, devised entirely on her own—were completely equalized into her stylistics, with one set for the Greeks and Romans, another for post-Renaissance royalty, a third for more contemporary characters. Yet all this was subsidiary to the heavy Kunst of developing the psychology of the roles under the supervision of the music, of *singing* the acting. The voice is experience.

It was Callas who inflamed the feud between the fans of Stimm' and Kunst. Before her, Stimm' was sensuality of sound and Kunst was intelligence of character: the natural talent versus the resourceful performer. No one, no matter how partial, ever tried to argue that mezzo Ebe Stignani illuminated her characters. Stignani was an unsophisticated woman without a shred of glamour or theatricality, no more vivacious as Eboli than as Azucena, no more regal as Amneris than as Ulrica. "I am not an interesting woman in any way," she said. All she had was a magnificent voice, good instincts, and the experience of working with teaching musicians like Toscanini and Serafin. She was Stimmdiva in its essence. Conversely, the soprano Gilda dalla Rizza was an exemplary Kunstdiva, finessing an unappetizing timbre with a host of character insights and vocal details.

The choice—need one make one, instead of enjoying both—was clear. Any ear could take pleasure in Stignani, for if she was dull onstage, her singing had pulse and sweep and ultimately, if generally, served character. But many took exception to dalla Rizza. Puccini, oddly, adored her, his "cara dolce Gildina"—oddly, because he was a voice man from first to last. Mascagni and Zandonai, too, sought her out for their operas, and she was thought to be unrivaled as Francesca da Rimini and—so Puccini said—Minnie. Yet there were incredulous reviewers and puzzled shakings of the head whenever she sang. Tenor Giacomo Lauri-Volpi said she used her voice "rather to express the emotions than for purely musical effects," and after two acts of her Covent Garden Butterfly, the *Times* "began to long for a phrase of clean, true, and unemotional singing."

There are artists whose reputation stands between the schools, such as Claudia Muzio, who in her youth displayed loveliness of sound but no particularization of sound from role to role. Though her technique didn't "speak" all that easily, as a Stimmdiva's would, still the effect was of a natural singer, ravishing and unfussy. As the years went on, however, her sense of interpretation developed to an amazing degree, and at length she Romanticized herself into a Kunstdiva, generating a profound air of tragedy here, a whispering pathos there, deftly maneuvering a failing instrument, and reading Germont's letter incomparably in a famous recording of "Addio del passato." As a youngster, then, she was delightful; as a veteran she was unique. If she couldn't make the A list through Stimm', she made it at last through Kunst; and of course dying relatively young and heartbroken gets one's legend off to a fine start, as those who neglected her when she was available suddenly collected her memory for their catalogue of greats. Turning back to consider her tale, they noted her theatrical background (her father, Carlo, was a stage director at major opera houses, including Covent Garden and the Met), her classic dark beauty, her concentration on verismo heroines. And lo, she was entered on the lists as the Duse of Song. The term had caught on earlier, but mainly among her smallish following; now it was general history. And this somewhat spurious history recalled a woman of grandest tragedy, her delicate, winning charm forgotten in favor of heavy Divakunst. Tosca, Giorgetta, Angelica, Refice's Cecilia, written for her to play the Saint of Song. And, naturally, Violetta: "Teneste la promessa . . ." Though her youth was unquestionably that of the warm and lovely singer, Muzio was reevaluated to reinforce the cult of Kunstdiva—as if one couldn't be both artlessly gifted and a superb artist at once. As if one embodied *either* the music or the character, made lovely noise or arresting interpretation.

Callas shattered the choice, for her interpretation was based on lovely noise: if not on how the voice wanted to sound, then on how she could force it to sound. She sang as if she had the most beautiful voice in opera—and sang so beautifully that she might as well have had such a voice. Thus she moved opera back a century to the age of Viardot, to the acting singer, Stimmkunstdiva. It was inevitable that Callas turn to golden-age bel-canto repertory, then, and inevitable that she lead its revival, for much of it had fallen into abuse and neglect. No wonder she had so much trouble, then, in establishing herself, garnering bad reviews for her triumphs and resistance from some of the major houses. Her Fach was so outdated it was novel, so those who comprehended what she was determined to do were vociferous in their support and those who didn't comprehend shocked into retaliation. But she taught those stinkers out there, purposefully, in the very repertory Kunst-divas most feared, the voice roles: Lucia, Amina, Elvira, the unspeakable Norma. That, early on, her sizable instrument and very forward timbre gave her a working relationship with Brünnhilde, Isolde, Turandot, and Gioconda did not confuse the issue, for she dropped these cards of entry as soon as she had the chance to proclaim herself in bel canto and made a point of not gorging on verismo roles, the refuge of voiceless Kunst. She sang a few such, and recorded a few more, but at the core of her work was a strident assertion about the obligations of the voice.

Thus the feud with Tebaldi: Callas rightly saw her as her closest rival, despite Tebaldi's avoidance of florid parts. In public, Callas emphasized Tebaldi's inability to compete, her lack of versatility. "How can she challenge me?" she asked a radio interviewer in Chicago. "Can she sing the operas I sing? No . . . I have no rivals now." The words print coldly, but as she spoke, Callas would sound a touch modest, if firm, always thanking those who liked her, always hoping they would. "It's a matter of opinion," she would say; no, in her unspoken opinion, it was a matter of fact. Callas sang everything, and who could compete with that? "When my dear friend Renata Tebaldi sings Norma or Lucia on one night, then Violetta, la Gioconda, or Medea the next—then and only then shall we be rivals." This was the quoted Callas. But in private, not for attribution, Callas knew that she and Tebaldi were matched on one level: as sopranos who would force the roles out through singing. And the singing would be good or the singing would be poor.

At the time, Callas and Tebaldi did seem beyond comparison, so opposed were they in sound and temperament; and at length Callas was not to be rivaled. Occasionally there was a flurry of challenge in the air. Anita Cerquetti sang Callas' dramatic roles and was the one who replaced Callas as Norma after the notorious walkout in Rome. But Cerquetti's physique remained heavy after Callas had gone lithe, locking Cerquetti out of the Lucia–Amina–Anna Bolena circle so inherent in the bel-canto revival. Nor could Cerquetti tackle Puccini as Callas did, always thinking she was slumming but singing in thrilling style. Later the Turk Leyla Gencer was at times mentioned in a Callas connection. But Gencer's hooty sound and abuse of the glottal attack disqualified her from comparison, and her plastique was strangely pedestrian. There was Souliotis, too, for her five years. To the end, Callas' singing was beyond equal, her repertory past counterpart, her acting antique yet immediate. From chapter to chapter we will see how unmatchable her reform was.

Yet at length a diva did come along who could vie with Callas on major counts. The newcomer, Joan Sutherland, had a big, flexible instrument, endless technique, a cultural belief in bel canto, and one thing Callas never had: a great natural-born voice. Sutherland does not extend herself much as an actress and has not made alliance with a director of Visconti's imagination. She does not contrive or get trapped in stage intrigues. And she has lasted quite some time—over three decades at the present writing. (Compare this to Callas' twelve or so good years followed by decay.) So the differences are telling, yes. But it's worth remarking that Sutherland has been mistyped and in a certain way underrated, just as Callas had been. For where Callas was the expert singer dismissed as an actress, Sutherland is the expert singer dismissed as . . . an expert singer.

She never complains or breaks down, so people think it's easy, or isn't important. And a few just criticisms have followed her since that first life-changing Covent Garden Lucia in 1959, especially that her droopy arabesque is more a cartoon rendition of bel canto than a mark of the style, and that her mouthy diction fails to meet even international opera's lowish standard. Then, too, it's usually the Stimmdivas who inspire the huge followings, get their choice of the new productions, grab the top salaries, sell the most records—all of which Sutherland does—and for some reason this kind of success offends some people.

So Sutherland has her disbelievers just as Callas did. They fumed as the Italians dubbed her La Stupenda (to complement Callas as La Divina) and can be seen in the opera house on Sutherland nights obviously resenting the anticipatory tension in the auditorium as curtain time nears. (Then why did they come?) Those of them who write get rather exercised when Sutherland shows no signs of taking their expert advice on what roles she should sing, what language to sing in, and how she might improve her taste in conducting. Most of all, they deplore the way in which Sutherland uses her power as a heavyweight star—or fails to use it, perhaps. Never was a star less the prima donna, never more agreeable. Given only that managements agree to let her work with her husband, Richard Bonynge, and occasionally indulge their participation in the Massenet revival, Sutherland will put up with a great deal. Here's another reason to think of Sutherland as Callas' opposite: the woman who changed the course of opera history, from the singing through the staging to the contract with the public, always had to have her way. Who has made parlous headlines more than Callas, and who less than Sutherland?

Yet it may be that Sutherland is a historical figure comparable to Callas in several ways—and that it is in Sutherland's at times intently expressive singing, not in her virtuosity, that the Australian best revives bel canto. Callas is supposed to have said that Sutherland set Callas' rediscovery work a century back in time. Thus Callas herself alleged the essential difference between the two sopranos: the Greek put the bite back into these operas and the Australian took it right out again. And so many people think. Yet to regard Callas as the Kunst and Sutherland as the Stimm' of modern bel canto is to celebrate apparent differences while ignoring subtler, shared values in communication.

The differences, again, are notable. Photographs of Callas in action have virtually become the icons of opera-as-religion, and what concentration of character they show. Here is no serene saint: her Médée, a flashing mask, all eyes and mouth;

or her raptly pining Violetta; or her Amina, a bashful china figurine. Sutherland, on the other hand, always looks the same no matter the role, a bit like a Christmas tree just before the little lights are plugged in. On stage, Sutherland registers no visible tension. One sees nothing. What one hears, however, is urgently communicated, singing as character. What has obscured this is, first of all, that mushmouth pronunciation, which defeats belief that Sutherland is aware of the meaning of her lines. (In her defense Sutherland points out that few of those on the yonder side of the footlights know the words any better than she verbalizes them, including the critics.) Secondly, there is Sutherland's odd habit of changing views on a role from year to year in such tiny ways that it's hard to notice the differences and easy to catch her in between her seasons of more potent involvement with character. Unless one follows her from booking to booking, one keeps missing her when she's on.

How differently Callas and Sutherland began. Each had to leave home to launch her career, but Callas then fought as a lone wolf on a freelance basis from house to house while Sutherland, after three auditions, settled in at Covent Garden and stayed put for a decade. Callas passed a stormy time of implanting her unique ideals while Sutherland quietly inaugurated her studies in bel canto. Callas also knew from the beginning what she could use and what not, where Sutherland needed advice. Here the two stories diverge sharply, for where Callas ran through a series of conductors and directors, teaching as much as she learned and fighting sooner or later with almost all of them, Sutherland committed herself to Bonynge's personal school of bel canto as protégée and wife.

It's a cute story. They had known each other in Sydney, and in a musical context, but were not collaborators till they met again in London. Bonynge immediately recognized Sutherland's potential. It was even then a surprisingly big voice, with a leggiero's possibilities in delicacy but a dramatic's thrust. "Quite cold," Bonynge recalls. "Steely, strong and even. And not much more. Not terribly expressive, either." It wanted developing—and Sutherland's repertory wanted focus. At her Covent Garden auditions she had sung Mozart, Weber, Bellini, Wagner, and Verdi. Not unnaturally, she was taken in as a kind of "principal in general utility." "They doled me out anything that didn't fit anybody about," she says. "I sort of got the leftovers. . . . It was 'Well, maybe Sutherland can manage to sing that' or 'Give her that as well.' " Early on, Sutherland's path crossed that of Callas, when the youngster sang Clotilde in the sensational Callas-Stignani-Gui Covent Garden *Norma* of 1952, and one may be sure that Sutherland and Bonynge listened carefully. Here, in Callas' Druid, was bel canto at the apex, for Callas had been over into the past and it worked. Callas, in her turn, listened to Sutherland's Lucia and was impressed enough to drop the role as soon as outstanding bookings were fulfilled.

Surely the two Lucias were extremely different? Surely. Yet it was as much Sutherland's energy as her technique that made that first entree into Donizetti so fetching—remember that London was by then a Callas town, rife with the memory of her dramatically vital exhumations. A flatly vocal Lucia, however dazzling in cascade of notes, would not have gone over as Sutherland's did. And, yes, those who were there recall an *incisive* Sutherland, confidential in recitative, elated in cadenza. But almost immediately thereafter Sutherland and Bonynge reworked the part. They smoothed it out, evened it, drooped it. It lost color. It grew dowdy. At the same time Sutherland was learning other roles, and some of these at first seized her imagination. Then these, too, would languish and lose their grip. Where Callas would sharpen, Sutherland would dull.

Thus, while Sutherland's virtuosity is consistent, her communicative greatness is only elusively remarkable. In some roles it lies dormant; in others it projects enchantingly. Some music, it seems, tells her something; some other music she scarcely hears. Recording Sieglinde's "Du bist der Lenz," she stands in working clothes in the studio, posed in concert-hall stance before the score, pouring out voice and more voice, each line like another. This is no Sieglinde. It's Wagner only by a technicality of authorship. And when the chore ends, she closes the score with a gesture of "Thank heaven that's done." Yet her recording of Gounod's Marguerite—not imaginably a "Sutherland part"—finds her with the wrong voice and style (and language, though she sings it in French), yet with an alert feeling for the story, on a line-by-line basis. This is Marguerite.

Why was there no Callas-Sutherland feud? This, if nothing else, would have defined their respective positions *vis-à-vis* bel canto, for it is as expressive singers above all that they were able to enrich the world repertory with their archeology. No doubt Sutherland isn't the feuding type; though, for all that, neither was Tebaldi and that didn't protect her. Perhaps Callas didn't feel up to it. As Sutherland's first Lucias were bursting into renown, Callas had just made the fatal connection with Aristotle Onassis that was to destroy her, and she would soon begin her withdrawal from opera. Whatever she said publicly—and the public Callas was heavily edited, *all' improvviso*—surely she knew that in Sutherland Stimm' and Kunst were as inseparable, however differently, as they were in Callas.

Voice and art are indeed inseparable in bel canto: in all opera. Beautiful singing is, in fine, beautiful expression of what one sings of, and to that extent the very notion of a Stimmdiva as opposed to a Kunstdiva is wayward and modern, relating to the collapse of vocal purity in the verismo era (when weeping and screaming edged Stimm' to the side) and the growth of expressionistic composition (wherein Stimm' fears to tread). In the 1800s, when the bulk of our standard repertory was written, voice and art were partners—not always equally so, as Chorley's two divas suggest. Still, the idea that a diva can sing without "acting"—without expression—is as foolish as the idea that a diva can act without singing. The major difference between Callas and Sutherland lies not in some imagined monopoly on portrayal or voice but in how far and how consistently one or the other was equipped to take voice into art.

The difference is temperament.

CHAPTER

3

TEMPERAMENT

To defy personal despair is the artist's most blessed gift.
Lotte Lehmann

We pay to the last farthing for everything we take from the world.
Janet Baker

She behaved as a woman should do only with her husband.
Kirsten Flagstad
on Lotte Lehmann's
Sieglinde

Don't be picturesque. Be stunning.
Lotte Heinotz

Temperament, in diva, is made of like parts of confidence, imagination, and guts. In her handbook Lotte Heinotz proposes five rules of temperament *[Einzelwesenregeln]* for prima donnas, whether aspiring, arriving, or exalted:

Temperament is caprice. Travel like an army; object to costumes, sets, and tenors as a rule; cancel periodically. Otherwise you will be taken for granted.

Temperament thrives on danger. You cannot become important without taking risks. If you want to be cute and beloved, sing Micaëla. If you want to be famous, sing Carmen.

Temperament must be controlled. Pace yourself: in an act, for an evening, through your career. Leave something to grow on, or there will be nothing left in you *but* Micaëla.

Temperament allows no competition. Charity is pious and loyalty admirable. But a feud to the death is a box-office sell-out.

Temperament is ruthless. Each day, do something vicious to somebody. This will provide anecdotes for your autobiography.

The capriciousness of diva is as old as the diva herself; most of opera's classic diva stories tell of silly capers as opposed to, say, pledges of philanthropic intent or feats of gourmet cooking. A tale that thrilled America in the late 1870s was the Great Dressing-Room Disturbance, one of the headaches that impresario Henry Mapleson suffered on an almost daily basis. Mapleson had taken a company to Chicago, where the house held two important dressing rooms, exactly alike, in the stage-left and stage-right wings. Mapleson's primary draw was Etelka Gerster, so imposing an artist that the great Patti called her rival (and other things). Gerster held first option on the rooms, and chose the one at stage right. This act virtually declared the stage-left one as the second-diva room—but what happens to one's logistics in a three-diva opera like *Le Nozze di Figaro?* Minnie Hauk, the Cherubino to Gerster's Countess, took possession of the second room at three o'clock on the afternoon of *Figaro* with her dresses and trunk. Marie Roze, the Susanna, retook the room at four, having Hauk's property moved out. At five-thirty Hauk's agent not only took the room back but had it padlocked, yet Roze—who, by the way, was at the time Mapleson's daughter-in-law—called in a locksmith, broke in, and occupied the room. When Hauk returned and found herself displaced, she marched back to her hotel and canceled.

Unable to get Hauk to budge, Mapleson began *Figaro* without a Cherubino. Not till midway through the second act— "after considerable persuasion by my lawyers," Mapleson recalled, and having missed her two arias—did Hauk consent to appear. The episode inspired a revel in the press, unto diagrams of the dressing rooms and the wonderful motions of the trunks. The Great Dressing-Room Disturbance.

Ah, that was a golden age. But formulae in caprice were most thoroughly set down later, at the turn of century, when press reports fed legends of spendthrift styles of living and rampageous acts of vanity. Take Nellie Melba, a favorite source of journalistic report and one of the makers of the pattern of diva, superb in rivalry, incorrigible in trivial onstage oneupmanship, and terrible in her rage. Melba, too, had a passion for dressing-room honors—hers, in Covent Garden, could be used by no one but Melba, whether or not she was on that night, or even in England. "MELBA," one read upon the door, and "SILENCE! SILENCE!" There was her voyage on the Twentieth Century Limited from New York to Chicago, a tour so lavishly appointed with retinue and appurtenances that it caught the approving eye of the haughty society reporter Lucius Beebe. Exploit caprice and, if you're of sufficient standing, the world will respond: plover's eggs *en croûte* with caviar were unavailable in New York, Beebe tells us, but this was one of Melba's favorite dishes, and the Twentieth Century "lived up to her standards." She got her eggs. "They always lay early for [Mummy]," Sebastian says of his fabulous mother, Lady Marchmain, in *Brideshead Revisited;* Melba seems to have cut a comparable swath. She insisted on fetching the highest salary going. No matter how excellent her colleagues, Melba had to get at least a pound higher, even than Caruso.

It may be that Melba's public would not have enjoyed her as much if she had been amiable about her fees, ate ham and eggs, and traveled as you and I do in a seat for one. In Melba's day, opera stars held the patent on world-stage glamour, as film stars do today; even actors of that era were not as colorful. What actress maintained, as Melba did, her own muster of knights, rewarded for various services to Queen Nellie with a jeweled tiepin in her initial and graded from gold to platinum? And whom did it hurt if Melba chose to act colorfully, other than those singers who came within striking distance of the diva without the requisite humility? It hurt young John McCormack when he sang with Melba at Covent Garden and attempted to share a curtain call with her. With a wave of her hand she dismissed him from the scene. "In this house," she announced, "nobody takes bows with Melba." There were times when one couldn't take a bow *without* Melba, as Giovanni Martinelli discovered when he heard the public calling him by name. Him, too, Melba waved back, for she took a different reading of the ovation. "How they love their Auntie Nellie," she fondly mused, sailing out to take another call.

Tenors can take care of themselves. A diva's caprices go

too far, however, when they cancel a performance, for some of them seem to regard canceling as a sacred duty, whether or not they are truly ill. Some divas despise canceling as cowardly. Joan Sutherland would rather go on in questionable voice, with a discreet announcement, than disappoint those who bought tickets to hear her. But Tatiana Troyanos suffers from a stage fright so fierce that she has at times to be firmly escorted from her dressing room to the stage, and even Rosa Ponselle, who might reasonably have believed herself the most secure singer of her day, with the most positive public, trembled horribly in the wings throughout her career. Ponselle radiated nervousness; she made her colleagues nervous, the stagehands nervous, the bats in the eaves nervous. Why? Melba tells us: "When you are climbing up, you just do your best. When you are the diva, you have to be the best always." It's the pressure to be as good as you have established you can be, to be permanently top. Mary Garden, for one, had no patience with this sort of thing. "If you know what you're going to do," she lectures, "you have no reason to be nervous." But what if you don't know what your voice is going to do?

The most consistent canceler of the modern age is Teresa Stratas—unfortunately, for she is one of the distinctive artists, always different, always opulent, and, among other things, the unrivaled Lulu of her time. Considering that this is the essential diva role in *the* post-Romantic masterpiece, and that Stratas was chosen, virtually inevitably, to create the world premiere when Berg's third act finally slipped out of his widow's mad eyrie, this is quite a credential. Stratas' friends would warn her that her self-willed and spontaneous behavior would get her into trouble, for the backstage of opera is calculated and Stratas is alive, self-propelled. Yet she must hold the record not only for quantity but quality of cancellations, as when she canceled Lulu in a "Live From Lincoln Center" telecast. (Julia Migenes deputized.) Even Montserrat Caballé, Stratas' most potent contender in the sweepstakes, has not pulled off anything as magnificent. Caballé has instigated near-riots for no-shows at La Scala, but this means disappointing thousands. A Met telecast involves millions. Having scaled this Everest of indispositions, Stratas had nothing left to cancel but her career; and did. How can such an exciting singer live without singing?

The pressure Melba spoke of, to be the greatest time upon time, tells us why temperament is as tense as it is capricious. As one gains character in this business, one loses, perhaps, one's gentility. Beverly Sills' famous tale of Learning How to Survive at La Scala is telling. She was the diva ingenue, not a melting maid exactly but a local girl who had suddenly made good, tried Lausanne and Vienna, and was now testing her talent on the major international stages. Her manners were typically American, forthright, pleasant, understanding. But that is not how one gets what one needs from La Scala. The production was *L'Assedio di Corinto,* the role originally Renata Scotto's, and there was the matter of a dress made for Scotto in gold. Sills wanted it remade in silver, and asked very nicely, as who wouldn't? Time passed. The dress was not remade. Sills asked again, nicely. Again she was yessed, not honored. So she took the costume, folded it into a square, borrowed the wardrobe mistress' scissors, and cut it in half. And that's how Beverly Sills got the costume she wanted.

This is learning the trade. Callas, who inculcated Italian house style in her first years, was a champion at confrontation and demand. To Callas, the enemy was not just impedient staff, but anyone who stood between her and her objective of a perfect performance. Rehearsing *La Sonnambula* at Edinburgh, she was distracted by whisperers in the orchestra stalls. Suddenly she stopped singing, took off her glasses, walked downstage to the footlights, and said quietly and rigidly, "Either you talk . . . or we sing." A very stillness ensued.

No one doubts that Callas had total temperament—the terror of Médée, the vanity of Violetta, the self-belief of Norma. There were nights when temperament got her through more than voice and art did. In Callas, temperament was danger, love of it and fear of it, a contract between artist and public based on what she would do and what she would convince them not to do to her. "You are cowards!" Régine Crespin cried, rising from her seat to denounce booers hectoring Marion Lippert's Turandot at the Paris Opéra in 1972. *"Vous êtes des lâches!"* So they are; does a one of them undergo the challenge of singing Turandot? On the other hand, at the premiere of the Met's disastrous Peter Hall *Macbeth* in 1982, there was Eva Marton, lustily booing with the rest. And she knows what challenge is; she sings the challenge roles, not Mimì or Adina. "You cannot become important without taking risks." True. But should not temperament lead one as surely away from the hopeless challenges as toward the likely ones?

"Temperament must be controlled." Don't confuse your emotional content with your vocal capacity. Don't mistake commitment for temperament. Commitment is a dedication that enables the diva to execute a role to the very elation of her ability, to her nth. Commitment is not, itself, ability. Without the requested voice and stamina, avoid hopeless challenges, no matter what glory awaits you if you get through them: because if you can't, you won't.

All her life Lotte Lehmann had her eye on Isolde, the summit of her idea of selfhood as a German soprano, a highest possible service of her art. Yet, though she took on Turandot for its Vienna premiere, she hovered forever on the edge of Isolde. Her Sieglinde tasted of it; oh, how she wanted it, and what she could do with it—the wounded stillness of the opening; the explosive Narrative; the ambiguous potion, for love or death? (for both); the celestial return at the end; the Love-death. At one point the conductor Franz Schalk, at Lehmann's urging, tried to work out a game plan by which Lehmann could get through it. "So be it my end!" she cried. "Could there be a better way of losing one's voice?" Isolde herself says much the same thing when signaling the start of the love duet with the torch: "Die Leuchte, und wär's meines Lebens Licht, lachend sie zu löschen zag' ich nicht!" (Were it my life's light, I'd not quail at extinguishing the torch!) The price is high, the art higher. Schalk thought a more restrained conductor than himself might be trusted, but Isolde would have ruined Lehmann, and Lehmann knew it. That Turandot didn't go smoothly as it was, and Isolde is three times as long and ten times as fiery. In the end, she let Lauritz Melchior and Leo Slezak talk her out of it. Temperament is a boon; there is no demented without it. But it is a trap as well, luring singers to tackle roles that are (the singer thinks) *temperamentally* suitable. They as well attempt roles that are vocally congenial but temperamentally beyond them, like the cool beauty Emma Eames, of whose Aida James Huneker wrote, "Last night there was skating on the Nile."

Lehmann is the classic example of a singer in whom temperament and voice are not equalized. The tone itself had extraordinary personality, with a womanly intimacy that made her Sieglinde and Marschallin indisputable treasures; she could "whisper" a line into the largest house as if sharing a confidence. But technically it was not an apt instrument. Her breathiness was so pronounced it virtually became a component of her singing style, and her habit of "swimming" through her music, as the Viennese put it (*schwimmen,* meaning imprecision in rhythm and pitch), raised an important eyebrow every so often. Temperament can sabotage a performance, not least one by such an artist as Lehmann. In opera, one cannot walk onstage psychotically turning into one's character, as Eleonora Duse did. Duse was the real thing—when playing Camille she coughed blood. But Duse did not have to listen to the orchestra for her cue, or follow the baton in an ensemble when other voices crowd the senses and one cannot hear the instrumentalists. Mary Garden claims that she took Duse's approach, that her roles "became" her. But had she not kept an eye on the conductor, she could hardly have gotten through the first five minutes of her career,* much less the rest of it. An actor can lose himself in his theatre; a singer, never.

The temperament we normally associate with the diva is not that of the ogre nightingale who reveals Norma to us, but that of the megalomaniac who takes Norma out of the score into life, savaging tenors, exasperating impresarios, agonizing conductors, and generally depressing everyone who knows her. She may be most querulous with fellow sopranos. "Tempera-

---

*It was an intense five minutes—Louise's "Depuis le jour." Garden made a fluke debut, taking over for Marthe Rioton in mid-performance at the height of *Louise*'s sensational first run at the Opéra-Comique. Coming onstage at the start of Act Three, Garden had to launch herself in the big aria without a note of preliminary, a rare instance of a career's beginning right on top of the tiger.

ment allows no competition," Heinotz warns us, and was she not herself the offended party in a brief and in the event rather tepid feud organized by a benchwarming comprimaria from Zagreb? Diva wars have excited the opera world since the days of Handel, when Francesca Cuzzoni and Faustina Bordoni climaxed their London rivalry, onstage in Bononcini's *Astianatte* is 1727, in spontaneous physical combat. The one sure way to avoid a rivalry—given that a diva wants to; many do not—is to be the only one around who sings your particular roles, for even the most incomparable and unchallengeable singers have been compared and challenged. There were Malibran and Sontag, Grisi and Viardot, Melba and Tetrazzini, Lehmann and Jeritza, Callas and Tebaldi. Each rivalry is different from the others. Some are started by one diva, or both, or by critics or fans. Some are local, like that of Handel's two prima donnas, and some international, the latest ones including recordings, books, telecasts, and gossip columns among their ingredients.

Some are sneaky. In her prime as the Met diva with the most Personality, Geraldine Farrar was vulnerable to unflattering comparisons, for her technique lacked agility, her voice could not live up to her adopted Fach, and her inability to hold back in performance—which is what made her so compelling an artist—ate away at the instrument. Especially galling to her was the Met arrival of Emmy Destinn, an enemy from Farrar's Berlin days with possibly the most ravishing voice of the time; the two would pass each other in Met hallways in absolute silence. But Farrar cleverly disarmed comparison by contracting her repertory as the years went on, centering on a few roles in which she knew she was supreme. Potentially every soprano's rival, Farrar ended as no one's. She left the theatre in triumph, still glorious, and could thus be generous with her colleagues in her autobiography, *Such Sweet Compulsion*. Marian Anderson she calls "superbly gifted," Melba's "dazzling coloratura effects" she freely admits were beyond her, and Florence Easton she likens to Lilli Lehmann in their versatility. Suddenly we come to a reference to a "prima donna of secondary importance" who sang Desdemona to Leo Slezak. But this was Frances Alda, a first-rater if there ever was one and the wife of Giulio Gatti-Casazza while Farrar was at the Met and Gatti running it. Alda was outspoken, litigious, and—significantly—a singer who, like Farrar, specialized in contemporary roles. One imagines that when these two women crossed paths the fallout was notable. Destinn you could freeze out, but Alda liked a ruckus. No wonder Gatti's photographs always show a sorrowful man holding his head in his hands. Still, how deft of Farrar to wait so long to dispatch Alda; and so gently, too. This is rivalry *après la lettre*.

Some rivalries exist only in the minds of the public. That between Maria Malibran and Henriette Sontag was a natural one, for after Sontag had taken Paris with her ineffably sweet song came Malibran to offer her more intent one, Kunst contra Stimm'. Though Malibran's letters reveal a forgivably human resentment of Sontag, in public the two were handsome colleagues. They gave concerts together, and even rose above factionalist provocation. In a famous story the two shared the stage in London to great acclaim—but when Malibran stooped to collect a bouquet, someone in the stalls roared out, "Leave it there, it's not for you!" Malibran calmly replied, "I wouldn't deprive Mademoiselle Sontag of the flowers. I would rather give them to her myself." Sontag reaffirmed this noble act a few weeks later at a solo concert when she offered a bouquet to Malibran from the stage.

At times natural competition turns into energetic disputation, with even the most gracious divas leading the dispute. Driven beyond patience by the machinations of Giulia Grisi, Pauline Viardot finally made her stand. Grisi had been singing Viardot's roles, not well, and disrupting Viardot's performances by withholding from them the tenor Mario, married to Grisi and considered crucial in the success of the operas Viardot sang. Finally Grisi suggested a sing-off: *Norma,* with Grisi standing to Viardot's Adalgisa. Fine, says Viardot—only Viardot sings the Norma and Grisi can play *seconda donna*. It never came off, for some reason.

The Melba-Tetrazzini battle was inevitable, given Tetrazzini's popularity and Melba's vanity. Her hold on Covent Garden was solid enough to defend it from many an incursion, but Tetrazzini slipped in during the autumn off season while Melba was in Australia—in one of Melba's roles, Violetta. The house was not filled, so Tetrazzini filled it herself: with her talent. Sensation ensued. Most offensive of all, for Melba, was Tetrazzini's youth, for it enabled people to hail her as "the new Melba."

Actually, Melba was a lyric and Tetrazzini the new type of leggiero specialist, and they only crossed boundaries in *La Traviata* and *Rigoletto*. Still, two camps sprang up, for one or the other, as they did later in New York, where the critics seemed to regard it as indispensable to point out how much fleeter was Tetrazzini's embellishment, how much more invigorating her sense of rhythm. Surely Melba still had the more ravishing voice, and unquestionably held herself together better as an actress; but Melba was infuriated nonetheless. How *dare* the woman try to sing better than Melba?

The Melba-Tetrazzini rivalry, involving two Stimmdivas, really boils down to personal taste: one prefers this voice and personality or the other. More potent rivalries are those involving singing actresses, for these address a veritable ontology of the diva: what is their origin, their purpose, their duty? Devotees can argue the merits of Sutherland as opposed to Freni, and vice versa, without coming to hard words or blows. But try them on Sutherland and Callas, and the passions burn. Perhaps this is because the Kunstdiva herself is passionate.

A great feud, then, was that of Lotte Lehmann and Maria Jeritza when they were both resident at the Vienna State Opera. Their doings were hot copy in a city that virtually lives on scheming and gossip, and the pair improved upon the Viardot-Grisi *Norma* project by appearing together onstage—unfortunately for the Viennese, never as antagonists. Lehmann sang Sieglinde to Jeritza's Brünnhilde, the Dyer's Wife to Jeritza's Empress (in *Die Frau Ohne Schatten*), the Composer to Jeritza's Ariadne, keeping their claques busy swelling or boycotting the applause at decisive moments.

Jeritza, a diva of the Heinotz school of aggressive competition, enjoyed the row, and Lehmann played her part, too. Her modesty and generosity as an artist, or let's say as a person alone in a room with a Schubert song, are famous. She is dedicated to music. She is enthralled by it. She must be too nice to be demented; but she was demented. Opera poured out of her. "If she had been born in Texas," Walter Legge wrote, "they would have called her a gusher." What other soprano, getting her big chance by substituting for a colleague (in Vienna, as the Composer), would go out there a youngster, come back a star, and still suffer inwardly in sympathy for the singer who lost her part? What other soprano would have said of her Turandot, "I liked Maria Nemeth's better"?

Yet put Lehmann in a room with a soprano who could share her roles and she feuded with gusto—with Jeritza for the title of *Wienerdiva,* later with Viorica Ursuleac for first legitimacy in Strauss heroines, a contention embittered for Lehmann by Ursuleac's pull with Strauss' favorite conductor, Clemens Krauss, Ursuleac's husband. It's worth remarking that, an era later, when Lehmann turned teacher in Santa Barbara, the pupil she seemed to get along with most easily was Grace Bumbry, who in voice and temperament is as unlike Lehmann as a singer can be. Lotte Heinotz, who was in Vienna throughout the Lehmann-Jeritza rivalry, recalls an electricity in the house when either one was announced. She seems to shudder even as she writes: "It was a time of superb frenzy, of glamour without equal and tension beyond measure. What a tigress that Jeritza was!" Lehmann could be gentle, Heinotz recalls. "But I wouldn't want to fall asleep with my finger in her mouth."

The most vicious diva feud in memory is the one that never occurred between Maria Callas and Renata Tebaldi. Sparked by the press and fed by fans, the rage rose in Callas, not in Tebaldi. Callas, the unloved daughter, the two-ton canary who, as a novice, saw agents and impresarios suppress grins when she entered a room, could never forgive herself for having started as a loser. She had to finish, always, in every part, on every last note, the absolute winner. "If an ordinary artist has a Cadillac," she once asked, "how can I have a Cadillac, too?" She must have the best and be the best: temperament is fame as well as art.

Tebaldi, who felt no rivalry and who had thought opera had room for everybody, was bewildered and kept her dignity. It wasn't easy, for at the time when both women were on the rise, Callas' husband, Battista Meneghini, kept the Greek diva living in a state of siege bounded on all sides by cabal, dissent, and terrorism, protected only by Meneghini, the loyal manager and lover. Rare was the night of a Callas performance on which Meneghini did not flutter into her dressing room to reveal yet another conspiracy to unseat Callas. A demonstration is planned, the impresario looks wily, the stagehands are restless, the brown paint on the forest backdrop has a threatening smell. That half these alarums were imagined and the other half exaggerated did not matter: Callas, too, thrived on this sort of thing. Too many people had opposed her without good reason for her to have to wonder about any of her enemies' reasons now. Believing that she was humiliating enemies as well as inspiriting her following heartened Callas. Winners do not just win: they *smash* the villains. "It's him or me!" she cried, countless times. It's her or me! It's them or me! Of course it was. From her mother on, everyone had ignored or despised her. A few even managed to do both.

The Callas enemies list took in various officials, critics, musicians, singers, hangers-on, and so forth, and these were in many cases scornful characters. But so sensitive was Callas to attack of any kind that she fought even with trusted advisors. Her partnership with Giuseppe di Stefano is recalled as one of the great postwar duets, yet half the time, when they weren't making music, she was swearing he would never sing with her again. Then out would come another Callas–di Stefano record, and it looked a little silly. Even Tullio Serafin, the man from whom she learned the most, got the ax temporarily when he made a *Traviata* recording with Antonietta Stella that Callas thought belonged to her.

Then Tebaldi. Callas didn't need an incident to pin a feud to: they were doomed to be rivals because the very sound of Tebaldi was a threat to everything Callas intended to do and to become. Anyway, Callas found an incident in Rio de Janeiro when both women were down for an Italian season. In one version, Tebaldi sang an encore at a gala after suggesting that none of the company give an encore. In another version she organized a faction to hiss Callas' Tosca. The facts hardly matter. Callas wanted *assoluta* position—It's her or me! Tebaldi sadly agreed, abandoning La Scala to Callas rather than figure in a scandal.

Yet Callas herself asked Carol Fox and Lawrence Kelly to bring them both to Chicago on Callas' American debut, arguing that a multitude of stars provides security against emergencies of health or caprice, and shoots the season with excitement. It's good for business. Thus Callas could be lucid, could even admire Tebaldi. Though she once said, "She does not need either my admiration or my recommendation." Fox and Kelly had wanted Tebaldi but were afraid to ask her in fear of angering Callas. Didn't she play by La Scala rules everywhere? It's her or me? And did not Tebaldi say mean things about Callas to reporters? Did she? Callas thought so— "because," she told a radio interviewer, "things do not come out by themselves. If someone doesn't tell the press, the press doesn't imagine. . . . Sometimes [the press] can invent, but this is a bit too much of a . . . It's a bit too *evident*." True, after a while Tebaldi did begin to respond when reporters egged her on. But from the first she had been unwilling to play. "I have my public," is how she put it, "and she has hers." It sounds so simple; could they not coexist? Never: Callas must have it all, because deep in the secret heart that remembers back before the infant could speak and defend itself, Callas did not believe herself worthy of any of it.

Nor did the two women's partisans smooth the trouble over. Tebaldiani stirred noisily through Callas' performances, hoping for a sour note to punish; the Callas gang menaced Tebaldi. Enter then Elsa Maxwell, the most revolting of the vultures who batten on the vanity of the rich and famous and feed the avid idiocy of gossip-eaters. First a Tebaldiana, Maxwell switched to Callas after realizing that Callas had the chic. Meneghini thought Maxwell the ugliest woman he had ever seen, but Callas said, "Leave it to me," approached Maxwell at some celebrity do, charmed her, and put her in her pocket.

Do not underestimate the power of the Elsa Maxwells. Till that point, Callas had been as often attacked as praised. From that point on, Callas was VIP. Simply by befriending a hideous goon, Callas now traveled with the elite, won raves from the critics, and saw the press print her better rather than worse photos. But by then it was almost over, Meneghini, feud, and career. The feud had been unavoidable, though Callas handled it gracelessly, hurt Tebaldi, and even when they Made It Up, came ungenuinely into Tebaldi's Met dressing room complete with photographers and Rudolf Bing. It was unavoidable: because it defined Callas for the benefit of an obtuse world. It worked, too; but it gave her no joy. "I remember so well her words," Tebaldi later said. " 'I am so happy to have been present at your great success.' " But, Tebaldi went on, "It was a tragic moment in her life, for she had been abandoned by Onassis, for whom she gave up her career." Yet more telling is Tebaldi's comment of some years earlier, when *Time* magazine capitalized on the feud by printing Callas' alleged statement that Tebaldi "is an artist without a backbone." Replied Tebaldi, "I have one great thing that [Callas] has not—a heart."

Strange to say, Callas could be a quite decent colleague. She drove the lazybones mad with endless nitpicking rehearsals, but basically was the kind of singer who can talk only to other singers. She was gracious to Sutherland when the Australian looked certain to take Lucia from her, and was actually rather close with Giulietta Simionato. True, as a mezzo Simionato and Callas shared few roles. But Simionato was the essence of Stimmdiva, with a faultlessly attractive sound. If Callas could get along with Simionato—onstage in the same operas, too—she can't have been that hard a nut. She was virtually pals with Elisabeth Schwarzkopf, dangerously comparable to Callas in several ways. At the time they shared no stage roles and Schwarzkopf was furthermore the wife of Callas' excellent record producer, Walter Legge. Still, they were shockingly *bonne camarade* together, trading high notes in full voice at an improbable practice session over supper at Biffi Scala restaurant. Was Callas a mad collector of feuds, wallowing in war, or a purist who chose her targets sagely? She singled out Tebaldi with the care with which she singled out her bel-canto repertory, and for the same reason: to define herself as the world's greatest Stimmdiva. And when she drew the line, she did so firmly, even rhapsodically.

If Callas felt that the public was inclining to a rival diva in one of her parts, she would pray for a disaster to impugn the intrusive talent and vindicate Callas. When Delia Rigal cracked on that perilous high C in "O patria mia" in Buenos Aires just before Callas was to take over Aida, she regarded this as a gift from heaven; and she chopped those famous high E flats into her Mexico City Aidas to exacerbate a pushy tenor. Anyone, anywhere, could set Callas off, simply by holding a note in duet longer than she held it—as Enzo Sordello did at a Met *Lucia*.

"You will never sing with me again!" cries Callas.

"And I will kill you," replies Sordello. Note that while he makes an absurd threat, her promise she could keep. (He was promptly fired from the Met.) Callas had had her fill of the Enzo Sordellos; what singer hasn't? Too bad there are so few Tito Gobbis (and, we shall shortly see, Callas had her moments with him). The Tebaldi "feud" was gentled by Tebaldi's lack of taste for it; the Sordello episode ended with PR photos of him tearing up her picture and confronting her at the airport. They got him some attention, but they aren't flattering.

Temperament is ruthless. Some divas have been able to take control of a house to the extent of banning not just coarse baritones but promising rivals—Melba, for instance, at Covent Garden, not only on artistic strength but with the backing of formidable socialites. It seems amazing that Callas could rule so thoroughly at La Scala; how can a world-class house limit itself to one major talent? When a radio interviewer called her "the undisputed queen of La Scala," however, she did not bask in the fame but worried it, questioned it. In the event, she was deposed suddenly and completely. Still, despite the tensions excited by this or that scandal, Callas felt comfortable there, or at any rate appropriate, for its tradition and grandeur were unequaled anywhere. There is a famous photograph of Callas, artistic director Victor de Sabata, interesting consultant Arturo Toscanini, and conductor Antonino Votto discussing some matter during rehearsals for *La Vestale* that says it all. This is the house that resounds with the glory, and, given her repertory and standards, it was the place where she would make her history.

Still, she kept nobody out, not even Tebaldi—Callas would

surely have preferred to let the public compare them *in stagione*. What a stranger she must have felt at the Met, in those dark, shabby old productions thrown together by some moron of a stage manager with book in hand. But then La Scala ran on temperament of production, going for triumph or scandal with each title, while the Met ran on temperament of performer, keeping the sets and costumes ready to back up the latest visiting voice. One thing must be said in the Met's favor: unlike La Scala, it had a long-standing tradition as an almost open shop. Not even Frances Alda, who was sleeping with the boss, could hope to close it to her competition.

The Met was always hoping to be the biggest of the international houses: in repertory (until the 1930s, anyway), in roster, and in length of season. It is really the small theatres with their limited rosters that can fall most fatally prey to temperament, especially when a more or less indispensable diva suddenly hits international renown and comes home to renegotiate some perquisites of international proportions. The Netherlands Opera, which had launched Cristina Deutekom, found her virtually hiring the cast and staff for her *Norma*, and the results, dull when they weren't grotesque, actually roused the usually forgiving Dutch to register a distinct negative during the curtain calls. Worst of all, Deutekom is an atrocious Norma.

Closer to home, the New York City Opera found itself in the mid-1970s with perhaps one name in each Fach that could be called a box-office draw: Beverly Sills, of course, in leggiero roles, Catherine Malfitano for the lyrics, Carol Neblett for spintos, Johanna Meier for the lyric-dramatics, and nobody for the heroic-dramatics. Maralin Niska was filling in. There was no backing-and-filling room for emergencies. When Frank Corsaro staged *La Fanciulla del West* with Niska as Minnie, he had an impossibly tight rehearsal schedule and no support from the house. The backstage tension was acute and the piece turned out perfunctory, Niska at one point changing into a button-front dress in a trice, not even bothering to pretend that there wasn't Velcro under all those buttons. This *Fanciulla* was of the worst sort of American performance, a reckless garbage. Considering that Corsaro is the man who more than anyone else developed the City Opera staging style in his judiciously naturalistic *Madama Butterfly, Rigoletto, Faust,* and *Traviata*—and developed another possibility in the mixed-media *Makropulos Business,* also with Niska—it is shocking that he could not marshal house forces and do justice to Puccini.

All great divas have temperament; but are they all capricious, recalcitrant, ruthless? Some of them put all their temperament into their singing, which doesn't get them into classic anecdotes but does lighten the atmosphere backstage. Of course, as Sills learned at La Scala, in certain circumstances the house personnel don't respect anything less than the sumptuously rigid. And the public, too, wants a sensory overload. This may explain why Victoria de los Angeles has never quite made the list of the fabulous despite having one of the century's distinctive voices, exercising great versatility while emphasizing a few identifying specialties, and doing everything with great honor. Her colleagues never doubted her; her Mimì put Elisabeth Schwarzkopf into tears of elegy and envy. But de los Angeles left an air of sweetness and vulnerability even in roles calling for tension, and this, no matter how polished, isn't demented.

Perhaps demented needs the ferocious temperament. Could Renata Scotto love Gioconda so much lov'd she not Pavarotti less? But Janet Baker says, "I have to keep a sense of balance and preservation." She says this in regard to her decision to sing opera only in Britain, taking nothing grander than a recital or concert to foreign lands. Nevertheless, the statement might be expanded instructively, for Baker has kept her balance backstage while focusing her temperament onto her portrayals. She has sung Donizetti's Maria Stuarda, a role favored by divas of pyrotechnical emotions; Maria Malibran, one of the first of the new-style acting singers of the early-middle 1800s, was a favorite in the part. Baker was a great Mary Stuart, reining in her fury of injured merit till the great confrontation with the arrogant Elizabeth I, when the Scottish queen tells off her rival and Baker erupted with stinging *grandezza.* But when the music stops, Baker relaxes. It would be interesting to see how she would have handled the episode of the *Siege of Corinth* costume had she been at La Scala in Sills' place.

Actually, Baker encountered something similar while taping the English National Opera's *Maria Stuarda* for television. During the big confrontation, and just at its climax, Baker was distracted by a shift in attack from one camera to another. Apparently the director thought this would be a fine time to get a reaction shot from Elizabeth. This is risible, we know; opera's narrative travels line by line through the singing, and it hurts the dramatic flow to cut from Mary in mid-paragraph.

Baker stopped the proceedings. She was not angry. She just wants to learn why the technicians are doing this foolish thing. They hesitantly offer jargon about red lights, pushmi-pullyous, and who knows what else, but they take it again.

And again they cut away at the same wrong moment.

Baker slaps her hands against her waist, yet remains cool, perhaps mildly exasperated. *What* are they doing? The television director explains: he wants to capture, through camera motion, what Baker is doing in music. Now it's clear. It isn't smart opera, but it's acceptable television. In the finished tape as shown to the public, the camera looks on from an angle to capture both queens, Mary offending and Elizabeth offended. It works well. But had this been some other diva in another place, one can imagine the snafu boiling into battle. In Italy a dozen voices would instantly have begun to scream. In France there would have been a skirmish of reputations with résumés fixed; and the chorus would have walked out on strike, mainly because this is what French choruses do best. In Germany everyone's a civil servant and they would have ranged their arguments by rank, the present highest authority prevailing. Temperament, however, can be channeled, even—as with Baker here—gracious.

It can be silly, too. In an arcane corner of opera history there lives the memory of a diva too loony to be true, a woman long beyond her time of vocal ease who sang Tosca, Aida, Gioconda, and Sieglinde in a dingy New York ballroom to the accompaniment of whatever instrumentalists had wandered in off the street and for the wonder of a small band of faithfuls fetched as much by her audacity as by amusement at her inadvertent spoof. This was Olive Middleton, "Madame" to her fans and, in her heyday in New York in the 1960s, a symbol of how far temperament can take a diva.

Madame Middleton sang with the La Puma Opera Work-shop. This was not opera on the grandest scale. The chorus numbered six or seven. The scenery comprised—invariably, but ever in different positions—a tree, a huge cross, a sofa, a folding table, and pieces of wall. The orchestra ran to odd combinations—two clarinets, a trombone, and three violins, say, along with the piano—and the players would eat brown-bag dinners during the performance. La Puma was opera made for those—performers and spectators alike—who can't get enough of it on any level. This is opera bizarre: but it *was* opera, and it says something about how deeply runs the union between the artist and her public.

Why did she sing? Why did they go? Middleton had been a professional singer, as Olive Townend with Beecham at Covent Garden in the early 1920s, and she had a pro's standards. Sternly maintaining that youngsters must not tackle Norma, she waited till she was in her eighties before singing it, and wore a stuffed owl strapped to her wrist. Her sense of decor was uncanny. John Ardoin recalls her making her entrance in the last act of *Tosca* with matching luggage. (Well, of course. She's going on a trip, isn't she?)

Whatever else she lacked, Madame had temperament. That could be a joke, but it isn't meant as one. Ardoin calls her an "authentic original." Is *this* temperament, the result of the tension caused by being unique? Opera depends on the unique talent, but opera fears it as well, as Callas knew when she set out to force her way in. In some, temperament feeds on art alone; in others, it feeds on art and fame. For Olive Middleton, art alone would do, for she had missed out on the fame. For Callas, at the center of the arena, art must yield fame, position, clout. "Every year," she said, "I must have an even greater career." To have one, one must start with voice, musicianship, and temperament. But these alone are not enough. One must build on them, apply oneself, develop. One must have commitment.

CHAPTER

4

COMMITMENT

*The strange thing about a singer's
destiny is that you have to renounce
everything for its sake, and then
it's all over in a flash.*

Lisa della Casa

*Always a fight—that's been the
trouble with my career.*

Maria Callas

*Opera must draw tears, terrify people,
make them die through singing.*

Vincenzo Bellini

Opera is a mixture; when one part changes, every other part changes as well. The world of the diva has been affected by evolutions in instrumentation, in the ethnic balance of the repertory, in design technology, in realism of subject matter: she had in consequence to sing more powerfully, master languages other than Italian or French, hold the eye against a cyclorama, and portray a proletarian worker, a streetwalker, a lesbian, a scientist. One has only to attend a performance of Monteverdi's *L'Incoronazione di Poppea* or Lully's *Alceste* or Handel's *Ariodante* to see how completely the elements of opera have been reordered, blended, transformed. The older works have their words and music in linear narrative, singers in costume, players in the pit, recitative, arioso, and aria, yes. But to hear Sutherland sing Violetta and then Handel's Alcina, the one so embedded in liquid ensembles of sharing and confrontation and the other made of static *da capo* solos with a beginning, middle, and beginning; or to hear Frederica von Stade's gala Rosina, with all the vocal pranks Rossini delights in, then in Penelope's severely distilled "speaking song" in Monteverdi's *Il Ritorno d'Ulisse in Patria*—to hear how constantly riddles of procedure have been resolved over the years, in short—is to understand what pressures have encircled the diva's liberty.

Singers themselves have made a crucial change in opera's value system, made it relatively recently, and have held to it despite general belief that the results have already damaged opera beyond repair. They have revised their contract with the art, above all renegotiated their responsibilities, and those who have thus attained stardom set a dangerous example of "I'm all right, Jack," take-the-money-and-run artistic compromise. And "compromise" is a euphemism.

"The spirit is gone," says Jarmila Novotna. "It's all routine, catch-as-you-can, always in the dark." "The unity is gone"—this from Elena Nicolai—"and with it the entire structure." Maria Carbone says, "These young people don't feel anymore, so how can they express pathos, joy, or humor? They are all miserable; they hate their parents, their families, the world." They are arrogant and clumsy. "The theatre is a temple," Sara Scuderi observes, "not a football field." What is lacking? "Discipline," says Gilda dalla Rizza. "No dedication." Denise Duval calls it a "rat race." Gina Cigna arranged for her pupil Elena Mauti Nunziata to sing *I Puritani* in Palermo and sat back proudly at her protégée's success. The ideal part for the voice. Then the divetta announces that she is considering taking on Aida. "She will not study it with me!" cries Cigna. "I have given my very blood to these students, and it is most discouraging to realize that it has all been in vain."

The Prima Donna's Handbook is filled with advice on having feuds and grabbing *Sternstunden,* but Lotte Heinotz also counsels the presumptive *Divagöttin* in commitment. Like Giulia, the heroine of *La Vestale,* "the diva is a custodian of the sacred flame." Heinotz cites commitment to role, to composers, to tradition, to one's company, to art, even to colleagues. Opera's retired grandees, each time they are interviewed, all say the same thing about commitment: they had it, young singers don't, and the sacred flame is going out.

Some of them even say that opera is finished, but opera will survive. What it will be like is another matter. Certainly its stars today are much less dedicated than their predecessors. They don't think about what they're doing, don't become absorbed in a project, don't ask for guidance from the old singers who are the last links with Verdi, Puccini, Strauss, Wagner. These composers coached singers who passed on this inside knowledge, artist to artist, and oldsters live yet who might pass these traditions on in turn. But today's headliners are too busy to consult them—busy leaping off one stage to gain another a few hours later, busy sight-reading their way through scores in the recording studio (or doing a little overdubbing in case spontaneity somehow got out of hand and the tape sounds too vital), busy crashing television and the movies. Roles are not challenges to be met, but jobs secured and dispatched. They doze off on a plane, wake up somewhere, and race off to the opera house; if it's Tuesday, this must be *Norma*. If the stars do it, why shouldn't the kids imitate them?

The stars are not enjoying great careers, however. They may have voice and temperament, and no doubt they're making a vault of money. But they are not the Tetrazzini or Melba or Flagstad of the day: they are not doing their best, and every opinion-maker knows it. They are making little connection with style, with character, with intelligibility. A record-producer, trapped for a Pinkerton, is thrilled that Placido Domingo could be snapped in on little notice. "There isn't another tenor in the world," says the producer, "who could perform *Tosca* in the opera house one night, spend most of the following day in planes and airports, then drive to a recording studio to sing as Placido has this evening." On the other hand, his Pinkerton sounds somewhat like his Cavaradossi, and his Cavaradossi sounds somewhat like everything else he sings. These are the forgeries of art, assembly-line opera. It is prevalent, successful, and putrid.

A diva who practices commitment today runs against the rhythm of the business. Would there be a place now for Wilhelmine Schröder-Devrient, history's diva of divas, the inspirer and reformer, with her messy instrument? Would such lack of polish be admitted, such dedication encouraged? None had more commitment than she. Her astonishing gifts allowed her to choose among ballet, drama, and opera, and after trying all three she made her career as an acting singer— largely, it appears, because there weren't many then and there had to be if opera was to grow. It is possible that *Fidelio* might have waited much longer to enter the world repertory had

Schröder-Devrient not drafted herself to be its deputy. She was dashing, tender, superb; everyone who saw her says so. But could she sing? Chorley says no:

> Such training as had been given [her voice] belonged to that false school . . . of "nature-singing." Why not as well speak of natural playing on the violin or other instrument which is to be brought under control? A more absurd phrase was never coined by ignorance conceiving itself sagacity. Why not as well have nature-civilization?—nature-painting?—nature-cleanliness?

It must have been difficult to go on for twenty-six years with universally bad notices for one's singing, but Schröder-Devrient was a woman beyond the reach of received opinion. She lived as she sang, making her own rules—three times married, many times *amoureuse,* once divorced for adultery, the sensation of Dresden as much on the gossiping streets as at the Opernhaus. Her public utterances, however, insist on her position as upholder of the rights of German art. Her commitment to *Fidelio* above all cannot be denied; even Chorley thought her Leonore unequaled. It is not merely that she found it personally sympathetic, but that she performed it as if it made sense, as if it weren't an opera, as if—accepting the convention of the woman disguised in man's clothes and fooling everyone—*Fidelio* could have happened. (It is in fact based on a work derived from an incident that occurred during the French Revolution, disguise and all.) Even such an obvious touch of realism as her anxious checking of the prisoners' faces as she releases them for their moment of sunlight—checking to see if her husband is among them—was considered unusual at the time, as if no other Leonore had stopped to consider how she would react at such a crucial moment. Other such touches, together with Schröder-Devrient's self-willing intensity, provided a reformist rightness, a sense of destiny in the part, in Beethoven, in opera. No wonder she had such resonance to those who could hear with more than ears: with soul. Doubters might call her commitment the vanity of a woman who simply decided to sing opera whether or not she could. But one part of commitment is just this sort of rightness, comprehending the honesty of the art and heedless of the consequences. Any singer can learn a role; the committed one reveals it.

Schröder-Devrient's commitment to Beethoven has had many a counterpart in later days. Some singers will take what they get, some only want great roles. Some others feel an obligation to a composer, and will promote his less popular works, perhaps because they fancy themselves his stylists or because he needs ambassadors. Christel Goltz and Leonie Rysanek found themselves so comfortable with Richard Strauss' tessitura that they took on the onerous work of popularizing his later titles, though most of these are proved bombs even in Germany. Rysanek actually thinks the roles quite singable, but if you have her fluke voice, unsteady in the middle but securely brilliant at the top, they do wear well. Both Goltz and Rysanek turned up in *Die Ägyptische Helena* in a famous revival in Munich under Josef Keilberth in 1956, Rysanek in the role that neither Rethberg nor Jeritza could win with and Goltz in the higher line as Aithra, the seeress who attempts to reconcile Helena and Menelaus through magical intervention. Rysanek's high notes were the talk of a town that talks incessantly of Strauss. She deserves a medal. It may not be hard work to her—she says it isn't—but it is devotion. Who wants to spend an evening singing one's lungs out and then have everyone say, "My, it's dull"?

The Italian divas who sang when Puccini, Mascagni, Zandonai, Montemezzi, Respighi, and Pizzetti were active showed even greater commitment to their composers, for in this epoch sopranos and tenors were constantly forced to the upper range, emphatic outbursts marked *squillante* on high G sharps, B flats and Bs almost outnumbering the reasonable notes, and sudden lunges down to the lower register when all breath has been blasted away—all this in marathon parts. However, to Rosetta Pampanini, Gilda dalla Rizza, Augusta Oltrabella, and the rest of their sorority, it was honor and piety to sing such roles. Flawed though their instruments were (partly because of the workout they got in these parts), they put all they had into them and made them glorious. Now, waiting to die in apartments in Milan and Rome, they wonder why Mascagni's *Isabeau* and Zandonai's *Conchita* are virtually defunct. It's because the noted Italian sopranos of today don't extend themselves.

These operas are too special to disappear entirely, for the so-called verismo* era brought forth a sublime poetry of libretto and opulence of melody that cannot be matched by anything since. These were the last great days of new composition, when expressive vocal style, symphonic orchestration, and romantic tunefulness worked in dazzling collaboration. It was a festival of pageants. But it is largely novices who sing them today, only because they can't afford to turn down any legitimate job. "This man is going to kill me," Beniamino Gigli said of Mascagni, who wrote excruciating high tenor parts and then conducted them, appropriately, at the pace of a funeral march. Yet Gigli sang Mascagni, as a form of noblesse oblige. These special works demand special talents, so the great voices made the effort. Moreover, when the divas Gigli had sung with were scheduling retirements, after the war, Gigli habitually begged them not to. *Someone* must carry on the tradition.

What diva did? Renata Tebaldi, the bright hope of the postwar dawn, avoided this repertory, though her drawing power might have capitalized a production of anything; Tebaldi had the fastest no in verismo. She did make a specialty of Catalani's *La Wally,* probably at Toscanini's instigation, for he singled out Tebaldi for honors from the start and regarded Catalani as a sort of rich man's Puccini. Callas, too, might have helped out, but Callas despised verismo. Like Tebaldi, she tried *Fedora* and *Andrea Chenier* on a lark but never went near the more definitive verismo heroines like Isabeau or Fiora.

Magda Olivero of course made her name in verismo, for she sang everything in verista style, including Verdi and Janáček. Joining Olivero were the younger Clara Petrella and

---

*Verismo denotes a style of opera on realistic, contemporary, and usually proletarian or peasant-class subjects. However, because most post-Verdian composers used verismo's vocal writing in *any* kind of opera, the whole era is termed, loosely and confusingly, "verismo."

Virginia Zeani, all three forming a Kunstdiva tryptich, of more impersonational flair than vocal cream. Perhaps the last committed Italian diva was Marcella Pobbé, who quietly went about the boot from Trieste to Palermo keeping Isabeau alive. She was lovely in the part, however much a lyric out of her Fach, and it is worth remarking on the sighs the public would make throughout the piece. This is gorgeous music. But who wants to tackle such difficult work when one can get discovered singing Mimì and end up in a Salzburg *Grosserkarajanspiel?* Who cares for tradition today?

One diva does: Renata Scotto. Born to sing, with a sweet timbre and fluent musicianship, Scotto played by the rules as a leggiero apt in lyric parts, Stimmdiva. She got a terrific break five years into her career, taking over at the 1957 Edinburgh Festival in *La Sonnambula* given by the Scala company when the posters announced Callas. Consider what a slant the press took on the episode—arrogant diva offends a major international festival, blithely walks out on her last performance, pleads illness, then turns up—*immediately* after—in photographs of Elsa Maxwell's chichi Venetian ball looking anything but ill. And who turned a fiasco into a *Sternstunde?* Little Renata, cute as frangipane and, in the event, a very excellent Amina, perhaps the only soprano then working who could have pulled it off. The Italian press was particularly vivid in hailing the *coraggio* of the younger diva at the expense of the older's malign licentiousness.

In fact, Callas sang all of the *Sonnambula*s she had agreed to sing; the fifth, the one she missed, was announced without her permission. Typically, Callas said nothing publicly, expressed no concern one way or the other. She does what she agrees to do, no more: what she does, what she has, no one else does or has. And off she goes to the ball, letting—virtually inviting—the press to misrepresent the facts and savage her. As we shall see, it was the first act in the dissolution of the career—and, therefore, the life—of Maria Callas.

Oddly, the Edinburgh episode did not affect Scotto's career as importantly as it did Callas'. She became a favorite Amina in Italy, but remained trapped in the inherent acceptability of the lyric: no matter how good you are, the parts themselves forbid demented. Mimì is gentle, Marguerite innocent, Gretel (with Fiorenza Cossotto at La Scala) cute. This is not the material of fame. Scotto recorded, but only roles that everyone else had already done, like Gilda and Lucia, and when she turned up in EMI's Nilsson-Corelli *Turandot* as Liù, it was as a replacement (for Gabriella Tucci, who was hardly Scotto's equal in the part in the first place).

Scotto was growing. Her Butterfly was one of the best, the text pointed and the characterization interestingly taut, more tragic than pathetic. Most important in the light of what followed, Scotto was learning to apply *accenti* to carry her through the part, and learning how to save the voice in recitatives by aiming the interpretation rather than the sound. It was a great Butterfly. But she was giving it in places like Modena and Philadelphia. Alternatively, she should have become known as a Bellini specialist, for she was singing all his heroines (except Norma), even the uncelebrated ones like Adelaide (in *La Straniera*) and Zaira. Even when she made the Met, nothing seemed to take.

So she said the hell with it and became a Kunstdiva, tackling the great Italian roles, spinto and dramatic; taking it all as she pleased; measuring her sound, knowing she was trading warmth for power and irritating the natural wobble on her top notes, but seeing it through directly and shamelessly; taking up the slack left by her defaulting colleagues; slimming in the Callas manner, glamourdiva; making her prideful *fracassi* here and there, immensodiva; becoming first lady of the Met because no one else living knows what she knows about how Italian opera works; facing down the first actively hostile claque in Met history, because opera is at such a low ebb that the spark offends; and somehow seeing it through though the voice cannot live up to the musicianship.

In the authority with which she can invest her roles, Scotto tells us what they were like when they were new and the singers who created them were alive and influential. Her bel canto has the elated textual insight and the lavish musical flourishes. Her Verdi has the soaring line and structural consistency, laying out scenes in arches and blocks. Her early, modern-dress, verismo is shocking; her late, costume, verismo poetic. Better voices sing these parts with more body and security, but they are dull; they could easily feed their voices onto computer tape and let technology sing for them, parceling out the notes as each score reads, for only Scotto takes the trouble to distinguish Adriana from Hélène, Norma from Lady Macbeth. These women are not a chorus; each is different. Why not sing them differently? Scotto is the last of the mad-genius sopranos, dementodiva. When she goes, opera is in a lot of trouble.

Above all, she is mistress of the traditions, with a grasp on authenticity. Her studies, though, are not notable for historical advice, and she abjures listening to the teaching past on the phonograph. Preparing for a concert of Licinio Refice's *Cecilia,* she did not seek out Claudia Muzio's famous discs of two scenes from the opera, though the composer wrote the role for Muzio and conducted the 78s. What could be more authentic? "I make it a practice," Scotto told the *New York Times,* "never to listen to recordings of roles which I am singing. The role must be completely my own." Andrew Porter caught exactly the flaw in such independence: "That is rather like, say, proudly refusing the chance of a coaching session from Jenny Lind and Verdi while learning the role of Amalia in *I Masnadieri.*" Yet somehow Scotto has absorbed the lessons of the past, has separated bel canto from verismo, Bellini from Verdi. She has dared Norma, to general dismay; but it is the most correct Norma of the day. It needs Sutherland's voice, no doubt: but then Sutherland could use Scotto's delivery.

Scotto seems to have taken Callas' lesson that high Kunst always reverts to Stimm', that greatness in diva means taking on the Voice Roles, not slinking by on verismo. The two divas crossed paths here and there, most instructively in a *Médée* wherein Callas suggested that Scotto's one aria be cut. "Why she do that?" Scotto later asked in a television interview. She is smiling and amused; it happened long ago, and anyway Callas is now postwar opera's official saint. One dares not blame. One keeps it light. Yet Scotto has learned from Callas' toughness and can, when necessary, switch to heavy, because she has discovered how hard it is to move from lyric-leggiero to superdiva.

Consider her as Amina in Venice in 1961, still riding the fame of her Edinburgh success, with Alfredo Kraus. The two are in stupendous voice, he tossing off a high D with magnetic force and she plying the lyric's injured innocence along with the leggiero's spendthrift brilliance, suggesting a vital personality within the framework of village naïveté. She has the long Bellinian line, the éclat in fioritura, the verbal-musical sensitivity for the Sleepwalking Scene in the last act. She is intelligent and moving. She can go on doing this and similar roles forever and no one will care. Scotto is too sweet in a Callas Fach. She needs tension.

Scotto acquired it. Tension illuminated her Butterfly, strengthened her Violetta. She became less poised, more searching; less melting, more inquisitive. She took on the grand gestures, developed stature, saw now through the obstinate eyes of the veteran who wants what she wants. She had always been a lovely singer, but now she was as well an arresting actress. It was clear that the bigger parts—all her parts were big now—were overextending her. But she filled them with temperament, by now her outstanding feature. More and more, she became the Met's house soprano, by Fach a combination of Zinka Milanov and Magda Olivero, by voice a Stimmkunstdiva, by inclination something wild and new in Scotto.

By the mid-1970s this exploded into a creature of incalculable theatricality, in total command. Who else leaves so strong an impression as Berthe in *Le Prophète?* The role is a ghost in an opera for mezzo and tenor. Scotto recalculates the geometry to a triangle. Who else can inhabit the core of *Les Vêpres Siciliennes* with such vigorous disgust for the French villains that any production derives a historical foundation on her basis alone? It cannot be easy to play history in the Met staging, which appears to take place, all four acts, on Jacob's Ladder. But Scotto focuses the eye as she moves down it, leading the Sicilians in her first aria in still, coiled fury. At such moments, one begins to see why all great roles tend to Norma.

One sees also how much of stage presence consists not of fury given out, but of inner tension—who besides Scotto can cast such a spell in an aria that a Met audience is actually too entranced to applaud?

And who was scheduled for a punitive demonstration at the premiere of the Peter Hall *Macbeth* in 1982 and was saved only by the unexpected incompetence of the production as a whole? Who was delighted to receive the anonymous present of a Miss Piggy doll until some oaf told Scotto that "Miss Piggy" is her title* among her detractors (who, like Callas' enemies can forgive Scotto for being great but can't forgive her for *knowing* that she is)? Scotto proves the difficulty of being better than everyone else on flawed equipment in an era disdainful of any excellence but that of voice and fame. Freni is excellent: voice. Von Karajan is excellent: fame. But Scotto? Her following fear to admit that they admire her unfashionable, arrogant individuality. They'd rather give her their secret vote. Scotto herself has erred, feuding with one of the few tenors worthy of her collaboration, Luciano Pavarotti, during a *Gioconda* in San Francisco—and did so, unwisely, on that strange little camera that has begun to follow us around everywhere, saying nothing, then suddenly flashing us, in our worst moments, onto the world television screen. Someone made a documentary out of the *Gioconda* production—and there was Scotto, memorably fuming.

So Scotto's commitment is not that of Lotte Lehmann, pathetically going on just after her mother's death because there was no substitute acceptable to Vienna's standards; or of Teresa Stratas, who will not collaborate with the uncouth indif-

---

*The fans don't usually give singers code names. The first will do, yielding a delicious secret intimacy: Sutherland is "Joan," Freni is "Mirella," Marilyn Horne is "Jackie" (her childhood nickname), and so on. Scotto can't be "Renata," however, for this officially refers to Tebaldi, retired but ever present in many a heart. Satirical or vicious tags are on the whole not only rare but frowned upon as a shabby informality. Although—as with "Miss Piggy"—frantic buffs will rush in. Caballé, normally "Montserrat," is sometimes referred to as "Monsterfat," and even Callas was known to a few at La Scala as "La Greca Atroce" (the Atrocious Greek). Some fans are creeps.

ference of a skimpy rehearsal schedule for a Met *Lulu,* and walks out*; or of the Sutherland-Bonynge "house" like Huguette Tourangeau and Margreta Elkins, who have found an artistic niche as comradely as a provincial "concert party" troupe of the 1920s, good companions in a very decent sense; or of Kirsten Flagstad, who stayed in America long after she had decided she would be happier with her husband in Norway, simply because her charisma made Met visits socially and aesthetically desirable at a time when the Met badly needed a surge at the box office. This is commitment to company, to art, to one's colleagues. Scotto's commitment is of a different nature, balancing what opera needs with what Scotto needs, the commitment of personal fulfillment. Callas, too, had such commitment, and Scotto does at times seem like the modern Callas in slight ways. Both came into first fame as an eleventh-hour replacement, Callas as Elvira in Venice and Scotto as Amina in Edinburgh. Both glamorized themselves in mid-career. Both represent the tough, self-willed, and entirely operatic personality at home only at work. And both are controversial figures.

The differences, however, are more illustrative than the similarities. Callas was lyric-dramatic; Scotto more the leggiero. Callas adopted her artistic ethnicity; Scotto sings a natural Italian. Callas was known especially for Norma, Tosca, Violetta, and Lucia; Scotto has sung all four but made her greatest impressions in other parts. Callas had about ten years of prime and left the theatre forever less than two decades after her first important engagements; Scotto is nearing the end of three decades of constant stage work. Callas always had to be *assoluta,* preferably in operas that had one woman lead. She could tolerate a mezzo in the vicinity, as in *Norma* or *Il Trovatore,* but bridled at two-soprano operas and turned down *Les Huguenots* at La Scala twice—first as the Queen to Tebaldi's proposed Valentine, later as Valentine to Sutherland's Queen

---

*and stands up to the Met lawyers, and wins out of court, and takes her full salary for the contracted performances, and donates it back to the Met, and says, "What's a career, anyhow?" A few years later, satisfied with the accommodations, Stratas did sing Lulu at the Met.

(Simionato played the part). Scotto, on the other hand, is sport enough to play Musetta in *La Bohème,* secure enough with her standing not to worry about diva-rolemanship.

Callas had off nights so terrible it is a mystery why she didn't cancel more often; Scotto's proportion of on to off nights meets the professional average. Callas' family life was a musical comedy by Eugene O'Neill, from mother through husband to lover; Scotto's is domestic and serene. Lastly and mainly, Callas helped wreck her career in a series of dazzlingly wrong choices, especially the way she handled the Edinburgh walkout, especially in going on in the notorious Rome *Norma* when her voice was giving such poor response she could scarcely have gotten through "Every Day a Little Death," and especially in playing cat-and-mouse with Rudolf Bing while she was in Dallas singing Médée, knowing as sure as rain falls on open-air theatres that Bing hated being toyed with and loved making examples of arrogant stars.

Scotto's approach is entirely different. It is not entirely free of scandals,* but, unlike Callas, she isn't trying to collect them. On public occasions Scotto appears amiable, charming, and quaintly Italian where Callas was often severe, rational to a fault, and in that carefully unclipped English that made her sound like some alien intruder who had learned the language via tape on Mars.

Callas was a woman helplessly impelled by contradictory longings. Scotto is astute and in control. Callas' commitment could only be analyzed by a psychiatrist, for its drives—even speaking strictly of her career—were bound up in her agonies of family neglect and personal unworthiness. Her commitment to the golden-age Stimmfach was, on one level, just a way of trying to be the best. Scotto's commitment, on the other hand, is more easily read. With the passing of Callas, the collapse of verista traditions, and the rise of the academic performance of

---

* A note on this word, which means different things in English and in opera lingo. English-speakers tend to use it in a moral context, as anent the corruption of an officeholder, a sensual outrage in a religious situation, or adultery. Continentally, it refers to an artistic uproar in the theatre, whether through poor performance, mixed reception, or impetuous ad lib. Half of Callas' career, successes and failures alike, was scandals.

fidelity and polish and no guts, a gap opened and Scotto—who had been getting nowhere in particular anyway—moved in to fill it.

She had the musicianship and the temperament, she knew; as for voice, this she stretched. In the end she brought vitality to the scene and created her unique stardom. This contradictory give-and-take is Scotto's commitment, her way of retrieving the liberty lost when composers surrounded the eighteenth-century star with the unshakable integrity of composition. She has chosen. As Callas did, she demanded to reign, and has backed up the demand with her resourceful talent. She has chosen, above all, her roles. This is essential: for if roles don't define the voice, they can define the reputation, the profile. Let us examine Divakunst in action, then, in the Great Role: wherein a diva proves how resourceful she can be.

CHAPTER

5

GREAT ROLES

*She never acted the same scene
twice precisely alike, just as
in real life no one does the same
thing twice in the same way.*
> Rose Weigall
> on Jenny Lind

Please forgive me.
> Kirsten Flagstad
> after singing
> her last Isolde,
> Covent Garden,
> 1951

The Great Role was not basic
to early opera. The savants and musicians who created opera
in Florence at the end of the sixteenth century declared a clear
and expressive delivery of the text opera's absolute. Within
these parameters the notion of a favorite voice in a favorite
part was inconceivable, for the *dramma in musica* held the libretto to be more strategic than the music, and the two together an absolute beyond considerations of performer charisma. A singer was, in Adriana Lecouvreur's pungent phrase,
"l'umile ancella del genio creator"—the humble servant of creative genius.

Anyway, no part could be made favorite then: each was
written to be performed under the composer's direction on a
single occasion. So unlikely was the possibility of a repetition
that manuscript consisted of the melodic lines and some no-
tations—the musicians would improvise the scoring in rehearsals. Thus there would be no repertory of roles, no comparing the interpretations of a given role. This changed after
opera went public for a paying audience, and by the early
middle 1700s the structure of the opera world suggested the
enterprise as we know it today, with stars, impresarios, feuds,
critical persuasions, composers utopian and retrogressive, and
a general sense of a nightly, ongoing occasion with a past and

future as well as a present. In France, Lully's operas were regularly performed not only during his lifetime but after, allowing each promising new soprano to test herself against tradition. Eventually, Lully's works fell out of style, but when Gluck reset, in a new version in 1777, the same libretto that had served Lully for *Armide et Renaud* ninety-one years earlier, Gluck's new *Armide* reestablished the pagan sorceress as a familiar character open to personal embellishment. Armide became one of opera's early great roles—a part with a history.

Still, not till the Romantics conceived of opera as imperishable art were great roles counted in profusion. As the nineteenth century drove ever more deeply into its conflicted ideals of profound spiritual emptiness, useless but beautiful heroism, and wonderful doom, Mozart became a religion, *Fidelio* a humanistic credo, Cherubini's *Médée* a lesson in radical psychology. The great heroines were regarded as the major soprano's major challenge; she must try her authority against that of the singers before her, and must register in her turn as a point of comparison with those after. It is no accident that Wilhelmine Schröder-Devrient inspired Wagner to implement his impossible dream of a titanic ritual-theatre when she was playing Beethoven's Leonore. What other role of the time so stimulates all that is noble, fair, even titanic in an actress who sings? The picture of Schröder-Devrient heartening Wagner, the most impenitent revolutionary in opera history, while playing Semiramide or Euryanthe* is unseeable. Great Divakunst is provisioned by great parts, by—in the era at hand—the rich women of the Mozart–da Ponte collaborations and moving thence climactically on to Norma, most demanding of all and richest, if not in sheer narrative character, then in the nuanced majesty of vocal character. The death of Maria Malibran from a horseback-riding accident at the age of twenty-eight clinched the Romantic notion of a role almost too great to bear. Too bad Malibran didn't die singing Norma; that would have been perfect. At least Margarethe Schick went mad singing Médée. We have come to an age of superb prima donnas—

---

*Schröder-Devrient did, however, astonish Weber as Agathe in his *Der Freischütz*—not a heroic part but a key figure in a key piece in the German ethnic puzzle. Weber thought this soprano found more in the role than he had.

not just famous, vain sopranos and not just front-rank singers but acting singers of desperate commitment. Life was not big enough for them; they must live in legend. But their roles were big, and thus vindicated the legends. Historically, this is the beginning of demented.

Not every leading role is a great one, and of course divas of one kind of brilliance appear to poor advantage in parts calling for another kind. But there is an inventory of characters in which reputations are made and developed, an inventory that all sopranos support and admire. Operas about actresses or singers yield diva roles as a matter of course—Tosca, Zazà, and Elina Makropulos are studies in flamboyance because so are performers. Femmes fatales similarly give the diva a main chance, whether the lyric Lulu and Manon, the heroic-dramatic Kundry, Porgy's spinto Bess, or, for mezzos (and the odd soprano), Carmen. Another set of characters ripe for diva treatment are the "crazy lady" roles—Ortrud, Cassandre, Médée, Azucena, Lady Macbeth, Eboli, and Amneris, for example. Invocations to evil gods, dismaying prophecies, psychotic recollections, and the like make these parts endlessly fascinating, for while any competent Ortrud can curl a lip or look pridefully dour, Bayreuth's Astrid Varnay could open *Lohengrin*'s second act standing against a castle wall, arms straight out and features glowing in the darkness with a dream of vengeance, magnificently lurid. At such an image the entire opera becomes fresh, even startling. And it's the villainy that does it: how different can one Elsa be from another?

Vocal marathons like Turandot and Elektra stand among the great roles for the sheer sensation of sound they produce and the exciting aura of danger surrounding them. Something like the opposite of these are the Kunst roles, subtle and usually relatively safe, like the Marschallin. These have a sturdy bias of tradition (Lehmann did it this way, Schwarzkopf that way) and possibilities for innovation, and here the only danger is lack of imagination. There are whole subsections of roles that have become great simply because outstanding interpreters originated or rediscovered them. The school of verismo, with its Fedora, Francesca, Fiora, and others who crest to doom in ecstasy, sings with the memory of legendary practitioners, and the entire Rossini-Bellini-Donizetti catalogue, with its big act-finales and so-called mad scenes, leaped into splendor through the evocations of Callas, Sutherland, Scotto, and Caballé. Here we encounter roles already established as great along with those that promise to be—for if Anna Bolena and Tancredi have already been revealed by distinguished interpreters, who knows what beauties may not lie in Zelmira, Zaira, Pia de' Tolomei? Eve Queler's Opera Orchestra of New York had but to announce Caballé in Donizetti's *Gemma di Vergy* to add another great role to the list, though, for all anyone knew, Caballé might not have shown up and *Gemma di Vergy* may be another of Fritz Kreisler's forgeries.

A role does not peel great right off the score—a gifted singer must apply herself to it. But certain parts demonstrate her gifts better than others. Consider Carmen: the role is not only vocally exploitable but characterologically challenging in her Gallic matter-of-factness, textured, in the Card Scene, by a moment of tragic misgiving. Micaëla, however, is simple, sweet, and unimportant. It is not a great role, despite the popularity of the aria. Similarly, Santuzza is a great role, but her unofficial partner, Nedda, is not—though Nedda is a more intriguing character, with an aria (the Ballatella) unlike anything else in opera and a wonderful last ten minutes in which her professional and private lives collide and shatter onstage during an innocuous comedy. This sort of juxtaposition never fails in theatre; the tension between the foolish farce and the threatening jealous-husband realism (ironically mirrored in the farce) is the very spark of art. The rare soprano who understands this has found much in Nedda—Teresa Stratas, for instance: devastatingly earthy on her entrance, dreamy in the Ballatella, nimbly *dell'arte* in the *commedia*. Still, what star looks forward to a stint as Nedda? Stratas is exceptional; she likes what she likes. Most divas want to like what the public likes. They seem to prefer Santuzza—or perhaps Nedda is simply overshadowed by Canio, whose "Vesti la giubba" is the most famous tenor aria in all opera, and whose pose with the drum in Pagliaccio pajamas provided Enrico Caruso with one of his most resonant photographs. Whatever the reason, reputations are made on Santuzza, not on Nedda.

Some roles are ruled out of greatness because they belong to works that "no one" likes. Mélisande has an extensive performing tradition and attracts Kunstdivas eager to reveal new places for interpretive nuance, but the piece just doesn't sell. Incredibly, it was Mary Garden's idea of a fine debut role, even in a place like Chicago. This is a certain witness of her intoxicating stage presence, for debut roles as a rule are those loaded with diva materièl: if not high notes, then caressing phrases; if not lavish costume, then blunt plastique. Mélisande is neither here nor there. Garden triumphed—but no one since has inspired a substantial curiosity in the part.

Conversely, roles can slip from greatness because of performers' lassitude. In 1904 a La Scala revival of *Don Pasquale* with Rosina Storchio, Leonid Sobinov, Giuseppe de Luca, and Antonio Pini-Corsi nearly displaced the memory of Giulia Grisi, Mario, Antonio Tamburini, and Luigi Lablache (the "Puritani Quartet" with Mario replacing Giovanni Battista Rubini). Nor was this merely a local event, for extensive recording kept the performances alive; this was one of the first productions to reach a world audience through technology. Yet over the years headliners abandoned the work, leaving it to squally sopranos, tenorinos, buffos, and, eventually, Graziella Sciutti, an excellent Norina husbanding a shred of voice. Great roles, as a rule, are not those one talks one's way through.

There is another class of great role that can but doesn't necessarily provision stars. Lakmé is a "sometime" role that often doesn't pay off. Why? Because the Bell Song is a star turn while the opera as a whole is not. As countless Lakmés have painfully learned, the big number is embellished for high-note rat-a-tat while the rest of the singing needs a lyric's upper-middle-voice warmth—just where the leggiero is starved for tone. So leggiero Lakmés have only five minutes that work, while lyrics fail in the big exposed five minutes. Even Joan Sutherland hasn't made the work popular, though the chorus at her Philadelphia performance was so impressed it clapped for her Bell Song right along with the audience. One singer has successfully exploited Lakmé: Lily Pons. And she did it by playing the Hindu priestess as a cross between a Warner Brothers dance-hall "hostess" and Maria von Trapp.

Musetta, too, is a sometime part. Italian practice assigns it to a comprimaria, but the soprano possessed of a decent figure, a working high B, and a touch of ditz can steal the show.

At the old Met, in the terrible Rolf Gérard production, the role was carelessly cast and curiously costumed in one dress (for all three acts, though they span quite some time) in a lurid shade of John Gutman pink. Smart ears and eyes simply tuned the Met Musettas out. But, in one season in which eleven *Bohèmes* drew on at least six different Musettas, Elisabeth Söderström showed up in the inevitable dress and surged through a dull evening like electricity through wire. There's nothing like a Kunstdiva in an unsifted part.

Another possibility is the "turnabout role," in which a star tackles something out of her Fach, thrilling her fans and bemusing everyone else. Joan Sutherland's Marie in Donizetti's *La Fille du Régiment* is exemplary here, not merely for the novelty of Sutherland in a comedy, but for the suave aplomb with which the event was produced. Marie is not really out of Sutherland's habitual bel-canto arena, for all her lighthearted fun; and Dame Joan cannot be said to show the slightest spark of comic timing in the part. Still, Bonynge cannily brought out the original French version, for historical interest, and bolstered the excitement with the young Luciano Pavarotti, generally charming and, in the notorious cabaletta with the seven high Cs, startlingly game. Italian tenorinos had made the downward transposition by a whole tone a convention in this aria, and the difference in metal between Pavarotti and his predecessors was terrific. Annoyed that the production was a guaranteed international triumph before it opened, critics in London and New York impotently jeered and raged; everyone else had a fine time. Yet the part of Marie, *qua* part, is hardly the basis for a great role: cute, yes; touching, even; not great, not *imposing* in any way. It was a case of the silly writ huge, the world diva going off-Broadway.

Certain singers turn unpromising parts into great roles through force of personality. *Andrea Chénier*'s Maddalena di Coigny is seldom thought of as a big diva role, for the tenor's part is larger and overwhelms all their scenes together. Even Callas, at La Scala with Mario del Monaco, found nothing in it. Yet Zinka Milanov regarded *Andrea Chénier* as the soprano's opera, as did the Met public in the Milanov years. It became so much her piece that she made her farewell in it. Similarly, Renata Scotto reclaimed Adina in *L'Elisir d'Amore* from generations of acid-voiced leggieros of the kind who also ruined many a *Bohème* and *Don Pasquale* with shrill Musettas and insipid Norinas. Many star sopranos avoid *L'Elisir d'Amore* because the soprano has nothing to compete with the tenor's "Una furtiva lagrima." Applying her customary sharpness of character, Scotto took stage from the first moment, calmly restructuring the story around the romance where, always elsewhere, it devolved on the antics of Doctor Dulcamara. In a more advanced style, *Lulu*'s Countess Geschwitz can also go either way: into voice-rending shadow, as a strange walk-on who refuses to exit; or into the glamour of fulfilled humanity. It's a touchy part, that of a lesbian masochist, but Kunstdivas are attracted to it; Evelyn Lear did so much with it at the Met that it came off as something of a short star role.

What do great roles have that the others lack? Lotte Heinotz is tutorial here. A great role, she writes, "gives the diva a focus upon the self." Distrusting ensemble operas such as *Falstaff* and *Hänsel und Gretel* and emphasizing soloistic combinations like those in *Les Huguenots* and *Don Giovanni*, Heinotz warns the apprentice prima donna that staircase entrances, oaths of vengeance, and a really dependable velvet train—not good intentions—are what make a career. Is this cynical? Survival in opera depends on the public's taste, not that of performers, impresarios, and authors. Like it or not, the public loves a staircase entrance, not *Wozzeck*, no matter how many critics lecture them on its greatness.

Adriana Lecouvreur is central to this synthetic kind of great role, one that irritates those who see opera as the development of a leadership art. Adriana is backsliding. Even aficionados don't care for Cilea's opera, though they will go to it. Prima donnas adore it, for it is loaded with grateful business, doesn't have those exposed high notes that unnerve them in Aida's "O patria mia" or Maddalena di Coigny's "La mamma morta," and sets them off as if they were the only soprano alive. Adriana is a career of tricks rolled into an evening, a no-fail part (in an opera that usually fails), a prefabricated *Sternstunde*. Rosa Ponselle walked out of the Met when Adriana was denied her; and Tebaldi offered to do the same. Perhaps there comes a time when a little foolish glamour seems more attractive than *La Vestale* or *La Bohème; Adriana* then becomes the work of the moment. Besides the eighteenth-century costumes and the natural allure of the theatrical setting, Adriana has a highly focused entrance (one of those "La! Here she comes now!" anticipations followed by grandiose declamation, some warm-up recitative, and a first-rate aria that doesn't go above A flat), *two* confrontations with a vicious rival, yet a second declamation scene and second first-rate aria, excellent placement for all four curtains, and not just a death scene but an entire death act.

It's no accident that Adriana was the great role of Magda Olivero, for here was a diva of the oldest school, calculated in her tricks, yet mesmerizing in the way she brought them off. She habitually would hold and swell the G just before the first aria's final A flat to Olympic proportions. She would draw silly pictures in the air with her hands during a romantic interlude for orchestra in Act Two, her smile endearingly batty, as if all her teeth were about to fall out. At the end of Act Three, when a powerful rival has just insulted her in public, she would crumple to the floor, but *so slowly* that one strained one's eyes to see if she would quite make it.* And she sang part of the death act lying upside down on some piece of furniture, just to demonstrate that it could be done. None of this, no doubt, is high art or good taste; but all of it was tremendously exciting. The eventual discovery that Olivero performed the swelling crescendo, the finger mime, the crumple, and the upside-down position at least once in every opera she appeared in did not efface the bravura. Olivero simply sang every role as if it were great—and, at least, in *Adriana Lecouvreur* she held the composer's patent: Cilea declared her ultimate in the part.

Actually, few great roles lend themselves wholly to this approach, as Olivero discovered when she sang the Kostelnička to Grace Bumbry's Jenůfa at La Scala and hurt her back trying to sing upside down on a Czech banquet table. In fact,

---

*In Hartford, Connecticut, when Olivero made her northeast American debut as Adriana in 1970, she proved how well-packed this old-fashioned ham baggage can be. Mignon Dunn, as her rival, put her oar into the third-act finale by brutally crushing a bouquet of violets. Yet who watched Dunn? Every eye was on Olivero: sinking, gasping, yielding, falling, yearning, swooning, dropping, weakening, sighing, succumbing . . . yet never actually hitting the floor before the curtain did.

the same public that enjoys verismo theatrics in *Adriana* would be offended by them in Strauss or Wagner, for here the composition is of a vastly higher order. Some great roles, then, are greater than others—Sieglinde, say. One might for argument's sake reduce this character, too, to a rota of tricks, such as the coital scream Leonie Rysanek let loose at Bayreuth as Siegmund wrenched the sword from the tree. However, the list of sopranos who have excelled as Sieglinde runs to Lotte Lehmann, Régine Crespin, and Gundula Janowitz, and their route to triumph was a stand-and-deliver conviction devoid of artificial engineering.

Die Walküre is rich in great roles, counting five, including two for soprano. Yet Sieglinde may be the most compelling. Fine Brünnhildes are rarer, and Wotan must outrank everyone in force of personal authority. Yet in the right hands Sieglinde's pathos and heroism sweep one away. Taking into account the *Ring*'s epic span, how directly it speaks to us today, and how crucial Sieglinde is to its action—it is she who bears the hero whose death initiates the end of the corrupt worldorder—we get some inkling of how serious a responsibility the great role may entail. My jokes about Olivero should not obscure the earnest sense of involvement with which singers and spectators regard a portion of the repertory. Sometimes a role is great not because of its star-part structure, but because its composer bends the structure of the star part to the integrity of his conception. To put it another way, *Adriana Lecouvreur* cannot survive a dearth of good Adrianas; *Die Walküre,* in a poor season, would lure us still. A great composition is stronger than its performers. And, ironically, the *Sternstunde*—the moment of glory—is surer in Sieglinde than in Adriana. For Adriana is moments: Sieglinde has the glory.

Some great roles are so hard to perform that they seldom turn up on the list. Till lately, Norma was one; it was probably the most infrequently performed opera in the standard repertory. Perhaps Isolde should be less frequently performed, now that the era of Kirsten Flagstad, Marjorie Lawrence, Helen Traubel, Martha Mödl, Astrid Varnay, and Birgit Nilsson is past and so few postulants are worthy of their order. One role is perhaps even harder than these two—four roles, more exactly: the "heroine" of *Les Contes d'Hoffmann.*

Because Offenbach left his masterpiece unfinished at his death, the traditional *Hoffmann* is heard in a messy "edition" marrying the authentic and the spurious. One of its many problems is that while Offenbach wanted Hoffmann's four loves to be played by one lyric soprano, the parts as they stand demand an assortment of vocal gifts. Offenbach is partly at fault, as the heroine of the premiere, Adèle Isaac, wanted to display her top range in coloratura and Offenbach recomposed the Doll Song for her. Other hands fiddled with the score in its early years, and authoritative manuscript is lacking. So we of today have inherited an opera whose "heroine" must control at least three different Fächer: Olympia is a leggiero, Antonia a lyric, Giulietta a dramatic or even mezzo; and as for La Stella, her music has virtually vanished. The chance to portray a quintet of archetypes—the robot, the moribund sweetheart, the courtesan, and the opera singer—is obviously tempting. This sort of marathon diverseness would make for the most novel of great roles, and to succeed thereby in a spectacular production in a major opera house would be to reap réclame. But who has the voice(s) for it? Callas could have done it, perhaps in a Zeffirelli staging to Leonard Bernstein's baton, at La Scala in 1956 or thereabouts. It would have been the novel triumph of her career. Who else could tackle it? Sills, Sutherland, and Malfitano have done so, but none is a Giulietta, and a single weak link in the chain mars the idyll of the ideal woman factored into components. As it stands, *Hoffmann* is practicable only as a diva festival, an all-star round-up as *Les Huguenots* used to be.

Are great roles only for stars? The question begs for a universal notion of what a star is, and there are too many different possibilities. (We will address the question later, however.) Let us say at least that, whoever sings a great role, it can't be done as an exercise, a tryout, a workshop for stardom, except out of the cultural capitals in a place like Geneva, where, say, Gwyneth Jones would make a stab at Tosca (not to mention Scarpia). At the Met, Covent Garden, La Scala, and the like, great roles should be a proof of one's abilities, not a question of them. With the opera world's eyes on one, one doesn't hope for a *Sternstunde:* one schedules one.

A good way to do so is to select a part suitable to one's voice and temperament, then coach it with a veteran. Maria Caniglia studied Manon Lescaut with Carmen Melis and Minnie with Gilda dalla Rizza (Puccini's favorite, remember); Licia Albanese, Magda in *La Rondine* with Lucrezia Bori; Amy Shuard, Kundry with Martha Mödl; Régine Crespin, the Marschallin with Lotte Lehmann; Josephine Veasey, Octavian with Maria Olszewska. Entrusted with lore and expertise—and this may include everything from how Puccini wanted a line phrased to how to cheat on a clumsily placed low note by emphasizing the syllable's final consonant—the diva then attains flexibility. She polishes the details, enriches the conception, varies her approach through contact with enlightened conductors, directors, and colleagues.

Thus Callas' Tosca was, in her early tries in Mexico City and Rio de Janeiro, loud and coarse, as if such ungainly melodrama did not deserve the delicacy and ingenuity that Callas took for granted in Rossini or Bellini. Perhaps she found the character incredible. This would be, to put it mildly, ironical, for Tosca's tempestuous, jealous vulnerability is Callas to the nth. She must at least have realized that Tosca and Callas were a combination of highest connection, whatever the quality of the work, for it was one of her most constant vehicles—and one notes, even amid the loudness and coarseness, that those early Toscas caught something in her, especially at "Vissi d'arte," extraordinary in the passionate outpouring of voice.

The role was hers for the taking despite herself, and she retained it, working on it till she was ready, when she first recorded it in 1953, to portray it as few have done before and none since. She invariably scaled down her volume for the closeness of the microphone, but this is no mere lightening of her probationary Toscas. She offers textual nuance and a depth of color. If the highly respected conductor Victor de Sabata could lavish such care on this music, there must be more to it than ungainly melodrama. God and Callas knew, none of the routiniers with whom she had sung Tosca before made it sound so good. Even Herbert von Karajan, so canny in getting what he wanted from an orchestra down to calibrations on the heads of pins, questioned his ability to conduct Tosca's third-act entrance with the ecstatic sense of pulse de Sabata brought to it. With Giuseppe di Stefano stressing the ardor in Cavaradossi and Tito Gobbi raising up in Scarpia villainy of almost attractive menace, Callas at last found her imagination gripped. Now she could play with the part, test it. Jealous of her painter lover's model for a portrait of the Magdalen, she tells him to repaint the eyes to accord with her own dark ones: "Ma falle gli occhi neri." In her first performances Callas read the line maliciously, Tosca diva. Later she would sweeten it, implore, Tosca *amante*. To the venturesome singer, theatre is protean.

Alternatively, a diva might not experiment with a portrayal but rather eternally improve it. Birgit Nilsson's Isolde is a case in point. When Nilsson first assumed the part in the 1950s, she was a purely vocal phenomenon, the bright, steely instrument with the coruscating top. But it was all steel, the central love duet lacking in warmth and the characterization unformed. By the time of the Florence May Festival in 1957, when the already heralded Nilsson sang Isolde with Wolfgang Windgassen, Grace Hoffman, and Josef Metternich under Artur Rodzinski, distinguished company was not drawing anything special from Nilsson.

She was best in the Act One Narration, the surest section of the score for the tyro and trouper alike because of its inspiring blend of rage and regret; any Isolde who is dull in the Narration is a poor Isolde indeed. Nilsson was not dull. "Seines Elendes jammerte mich," on the contrary, was lovely, the voice falling into plangency at the moment when Isolde the warrior dwindles into Isolde the romantic. Still, this was a Narration in general, too much an expository recital, as if Wagner could think of no better way to introduce background matter than in a What Has Gone Before synopsis. In fact, Wagner opens his opera at the hour when, after months of irate, mortified silence, goaded beyond endurance by the mocking songs of Tristan's crew, the heroine at last opens up to her companion and pours out her tale. "Pale and speechless on the way" she has been, in the lovable old H. and F. Corder translation, "food rejecting, reft of sleep." Now, on fire, she speaks. If conductor and singer follow Wagner's many minute fluctuations of tempo, the atmosphere is that of an impulsive confession, spilling out in barely articulate fury.

In Florence, then, Nilsson was yet a promising Isolde. But she was clearly the rising Wagnerian soprano of the day, and took her Isolde (among other roles) to the world's prominent stages, unfortunately in spot appearances that took more from than gave to Nilsson. At the Met, one *Tristan* was so disjointed as to feature three heroes, one to an act. This was not a house tradition: the scheduled tenor was ailing, and the only two possible covers similarly begged off. The public, however, was keyed up with Nilssonmania; better this medley of Tristans than no Isolde. Still, the production itself was a black hole with the lights on, virtually undirected in sets that must have come in a box of Cracker Jack. Such events could teach Nilsson nothing.

Naturally Nilsson had taken her Isolde to Bayreuth, where, eventually, careful work with Wieland Wagner transformed Nilsson's accurate Isolde into an incomparable one. She would not defy the memory of Frida Leider in the love music, would never fully melt the steel. But she could temper it. She could also place the voice better: the high notes, an early glory, actually got bigger, and after several seasons of Wieland's rehearsals Nilsson's Isolde grew into text and music as if under the author's instructions. Certainly she came as close as one could to such tutorial, as Wieland was grandson to the Meister, heir to Bayreuth, and himself the co-author (with his brother, Wolfgang) of the "neo-Wagnerian" production style. Now her Narration was psychologically complete, the words flung out as if only now, this second, had Isolde framed them. "Seines Elendes jammerte mich" turned acid, as if the memory burned, and "Er schwur mir tausend Eiden" (He swore a thousand oaths), which in Florence was empty weight, now rang with outrage, telling us what Nilsson had not done before: that honor, Tristan's and Isolde's, is what the Narration is about.

Other important lines fell into place, all fixed within the conception, and when the new Met at length gave Nilsson a *Tristan* staging worthy of her, she was in a position to make the best of it, especially on the one night that she sang it with Jon Vickers, a performance already legendary. Now the aficionados of the work had their disputations before them, and a possible new all-time champion to cite. With recordings to focus the memory, the old hands filled young ears with eccentric tattle of Leider, Austral, Flagstad, Traubel, the Most Dramatic, the Most Beautiful, the Surest in High Notes, the Epitome in Diction, the Volatile, the Timeless, the Epic, the Greatest. Nilsson may have been greatest even in this gala company, but perhaps the point is not who is "best" but that much of the energy in operagoing rides on discovering and comparing. Opera is unique among theatre forms for its audience, informed, fledged, and committed. With a repertory work, half the house may know a goodly portion of it more or less by heart. Even Shakespeare cannot claim such expertise from his public, but then opera is too complex to speak to browsers. Thus, if the great role is, on the singer's side, a matter of expanding one's talent, it is another matter for the connoisseur, who digests, discusses, and indexes the talent.

Comparing singers is a set pastime. One compares portrayals and minute bits; the acting and the singing; the inventions and misjudgments. Perhaps the great roles are so rich that one compares different versions of them simply to understand the roles in their platonic essence: a host of performances frees the composition from too much dependence on performers, and disputation enlarges the perspective. It is showbiz shallowness to pinpoint the entrance, the aria, the thrilling note, the famous line; but such concentration does bring us closer to the work. Anyway, haven't composers themselves pinpointed? Are not the entrance, aria, note, and line in their varying possibilities the basis for distinction, opera to opera? Tosca's offstage "Mario! Mario!," fretting at the locked door behind which her lover may be cheating; or Carmen's sauntering entry into the square, timed to the "fate" theme, a few lines of recitative, and then the marvelously casual beat of the Habañera; or Turandot's appearance in Act One, silent and nearly personless, more an apparition than an entrance; or the two high Bs that cap Isolde's Narrative or the one that catches Kundry at her recollection of mocking the tormented Christ; or Santuzza's parting shot to her former lover, "A te, la mala Pasqua!" (An evil Easter to you!); or Zerbinetta's big showpiece, a little opera in itself: all this may be food for the grandstand, but it is also the material of character and the means by which authors mark their work as special. When, every so often, we encounter a heroine without these identifying elements—when repeated exposure fails to log an aria or a note—we have to try extra hard to care about her, about how she may be portrayed.

"Difficult" composition of the elitist kind is not necessarily a bar to popular interest in an interpretation. Lulu is unquestionably a great role, for all Berg's expressionist intricacy, and his "sweet beast" of a femme fatale enjoys more than a few of those certain moments that outline a role for us, recognize it, so to say. Her entrance is one of the most striking in opera. "He, Aujust!" cries the Animal Trainer in the prologue before the curtain. "Bring mir unsre Schlange her!" (Bring out our serpent!) And out she comes in her harlequin costume, carried by a stagehand and plopped down before us as the Trainer warns us of her corrupt power. She has a love duet, too, with Alwa—the son of the man she murdered—at the end of Act Two, closing in one of the most resonant lines in twentieth-century opera, Lulu's "Ist das noch der Diwan auf dem sich dein Vater verblütet hat?" (Isn't this the sofa on which your father bled to death?) That two people sing a love scene in *Lulu* does not betoken any mark of acceptability, as if only operas with love duets are good operas. The very term is meaningless—look at how different are the love duets in *Madama Butterfly* and *Tristan und Isolde*. Is the very dramatic and episodic scene for Raoul and Valentine in *Les Huguenots* a love duet? Then what shall we call the very gentle, settled scene for Fritz and Suzel in Act Two of *L'Amico Fritz?* Two such different pieces can't both be "love duets." For that matter, *Pelléas et Mélisande* has one, too. I raise the question because this is standard terminology in opera; the public looks for points around which to navigate, and—like it or not—it does make comparisons.

The most fertile area for comparing lies in the roles for Kunstdivas, for with them almost any line might develop an unhoped-for reverberation that illuminates the character in a flash. *Der Rosenkavalier*'s Feldmarschallin, Maria Theresa, Princess Werdenberg, is an ace the Kunstdiva longs to play; it may actually be difficult to sustain a reputation as a sopranos' soprano without securing this role. Its advantages are obvious: a superb text, grateful music, a sentimentalistic solo curtain for Act One, a middle act in which to rest the voice while the Octavian wears her lungs out, a stupendous *ancien régime* gown in the last act, and one of opera's most famous lines ("Ja, ja") for the exit. The part is especially useful in the years just before retirement, as it suits a mature woman and sits well, for the most part, on a deteriorated instrument. A great Turandot, Brünnhilde, or Norma will be in distress in those parts some time before her voice breaks down altogether, but great Marschallins can schedule *Der Rosenkavalier* for their farewells.

Elisabeth Schwarzkopf put this to the test at the old Met when she made her house debut at the very end of her stage career. For fourteen years Rudolf Bing had closed his theatre to any singer who had supported Nazism, which somewhat tangled casting in the Met's very active German wing. There were Germans like Lotte Lehmann, who left her country in disgust; and like Tiana Lemnitz, who startled British colleagues in the late 1930s at the start of a Covent Garden rehearsal by proceeding downstage (as was the wont in German houses) to give the arm salute and scream "Heil Hitler!" Forgive me for saying that there were also Germans like Ottilie Metzger, a Wagnerian contralto who died at Auschwitz. Where Schwarzkopf should be placed is not clear. The Allies officially denazified her, but Bing did not. He is supposed to have said of her, "I can forgive her for wearing a Nazi uniform and for taking an American colonel as her boyfriend right after the war, but I cannot swallow the fact that she then married a Jew." Mounting pressure at length forced Bing to invite her, quite late in her career, for *Der Rosenkavalier, Don Giovanni,* and *Falstaff.* But timing is everything and revenge is sweet: for after one disastrous Donna Elvira, Schwarzkopf canceled her remaining Elviras and Alice Fords and fled. Truth to tell, her earlier Marschallins were everything she had hoped they might be, filled with the devastating detail she was known for. Once her husband caught her . . . and in the middle of the night she stops all the clocks . . . and she views the mirror and weeps in her hand. It was a great role limned by one of the greatest—to the extent that one can ignore what a diva does when the Met audience isn't looking.

It might be argued that Schwarzkopf's, or Lehmann's, or Crespin's, or della Casa's, or Lear's, was the one true Marschallin, but there are ways of claiming a role without locking out history. Anyway, the charm of the great role is that any number can play, that opera's history never stops. Consider Butterfly, a role studded with entrance, aria, note, and famous line. Toti dal Monte distinguished hers by approximating the geisha's youth through vocal means. Rosetta Pampanini threw in what for a time became traditional ad libs in Italy: in the love duet, when Pinkerton, referring to collectors' mountain of butterflies, asks his wife, "Don't you know why they do that?" and tells her, "So they can't escape." The question is rhetorical; the authors gave Butterfly no line. Pampanini put one in: to "Don't you know?" she cried, "No!" and, to the answer, she gasped. Purists doubt, but Pampanini's was an immense Butterfly. Scotto, too, had her touches, as in her acerbic tone in "Ma senza farle torto," revealing her disgust for the unscrupulous Goro; or in the pillows she happily tossed around when Sharpless told her that Pinkerton was returning. Then he suddenly asks her what she would do if he never came back to *her,* and she dropped two pillows exactly in time with the orchestra's punctuating chord, exuberance astounded into horror.

Some great roles lend themselves to "treatment" more than others. Isolde has the least amount of possible touches, for it is entirely vocal except for the extinguishing of the torch that welcomes the love duet. Tosca, however, counts many singer's choices, from whether or not to enter with the once-traditional Bo-Peep staff, through the delivery of "Quanto?," to the science of leaping from the parapet of the Castel Sant' Angelo without looking like a rag doll. Tosca is filled with opportunities, some born of situation and some applied to it. Magda Olivero took the roof off with Tosca's final line in Act One, "Egli vede ch'io piango" (He sees that I weep): true to form, she held out the F on "vede" in an endless crescendo that beautifully scored the woman's sorrow. Maria Jeritza made headlines by singing "Vissi d'arte" prone on the floor. Callas made her Tosca history with the knife. Most singers pick it up early in the interlude wherein Scarpia prepares the safe-conduct, hide it behind their back, and spend the pantomime gathering courage for the murder. Callas spent hers hypnotized by it. Sipping from a glass of wine, she spotted the knife and utterly froze, as if the idea of killing instead of yielding to Scarpia had *just* occurred to her; and she was appalled by the idea; and she knew she would do it, all in the same instant. Slowly—but so slowly one scarcely saw movement—she put the glass down, her eyes wide, locked on the knife. Not till Scarpia approached her— "Ah, Tosca, finalmente mia!"—did she snatch it up, turn, and give him a taste of Tosca's kiss.

The urge toward great roles has given some divas their finest evenings; but it also presses young or mediocre singers who cannot live up to the requirements. After *Der Rosenkavalier* with Schwarzkopf, Jurinac, and Rothenberger, or with Söderström, von Stade, and Battle, it is difficult to tolerate a workmanlike cast. This in turn presses the major houses to produce a *Rosenkavalier* cast from the A list every time out. Worse yet, the great role has become debased through overuse in times when greatness is in short supply. About twenty years ago *Salome* became one of the most frequent items on European stages, because the public likes it, because its logistics don't unduly drain a theatre's exchequer, and because sopranos keep thinking they're going to have a sensation in it, as Ljuba Welitsch did in the postwar years. But Welitsch had long since abandoned the part, and her successors counted few important Salomes and more than a few bunglers. Some Salomes of the 1960s seem to have come forth, untested, from some Salome factory, for they sang no other roles that anyone knew of and this role neither well nor badly. Like Mimì, Salome became just another note in the scale—when it is more likely an elusive one, not to be reached by the neophyte.

The public, anyway, is divided as to what constitutes a correct Salome. The character is that of a teenaged girl, spoiled and trivial, sensual but virginal. Her extravagant Art Nouveau flirtation with John the Baptist and subsequent kissing of his severed head is not meant as hysterically self-dramatizing depravity, but as coolly self-important selfishness. It's shocking when it doesn't *act* shocking: Salome has no conception of what shocking might be. She operates outside of morality, simply takes what she wants. But the public often wants a lascivious psychopath, and the singer who attempts a less flamboyant and more appropriate Salome runs some risk. Helga Pilarczyk was booed at Covent Garden for a stunning, authentic Salome. Glittering high notes might have protected her, but hers is not that kind of voice. At the same house Inge Borkh covered a shrill and woolly reading with a portrayal that might have been coached by Caligula. This is the easy way to obtain a sensation. Does it "count"?

Did it count to be a Salome at all in times when Salomes are as common as corner houses, when some interesting but inexperienced sopranos burst upon the scene, sing their voices to bits in the role, and vanish after two or three seasons? In such times the work itself ceases to matter, becomes a statistic of repertory. The Salome of the present day is Norma, once the dare of a lifetime but now undertaken by any singer, mezzos included, who feel in the Norma mood. The role has lost its sense of *entitlement,* its formidable ban on all but the ultimate in technique and temperament. Beverly Sills says she didn't even find it difficult. Like the Marschallin for Kunstdivas, it has become the Stimmdiva's piece of cake: only it isn't. It remains *ne plus ultra,* but it has been debased. One soprano whom I'd rather not name began an evening at the Met with a "Casta diva" so ignoble that the cavatina finished in something almost never heard from a Met audience, flustered silence.

Actually, the Norma problem is decades old. The opera was already slipping out of reach in the early 1900s: Normas were becoming scarce, Polliones with the polish as well as the heft were scarcer, and the part of Adalgisa was suffering an awkward transition, from lyric soprano to dramatic mezzo, that disturbed Bellini's aural autograph. When Rosa Ponselle first sang Norma, in 1927, the Met had not been able to stage the work (at any rate had not done so) for some thirty-five years—and, as we shall see, even Toscanini, with La Scala's forces behind him, could not produce a *Norma* to his satisfaction.

The question of who deserves Norma answers to more than just who can sing it, even sing it well. Remember, the great role demands something grander than the merely legitimate; divas and great roles authenticate each other through an explicit rightness of personality. Sills knows Norma, but lacks the voice; Caballé sings it beautifully, but is not stirred by it;

and some have sung it with neither voice nor understanding. Two women have made this role theirs in our time, Callas and Sutherland. To hear Callas fold the vulnerability into the savagery as she moves from "Oh! rimembranza!" to "Tremi tu?"; or to hear Sutherland's effortless beauty of embellishment in the second verse of "Ah, bello a me ritorna" or her gigantic high D filling the auditorium at the end of the trio is to accept the breadth of opera's possibilities, the size and variety of its personalities. Its very size limits its potential for perfection—but can any other performing medium claim so many first-rate talents?

One advantage of the great role that the public seldom considers is the protection it gives singers from the chance calamities of a dull director, an insensitive conductor, a crazed designer. A great role is more than an ideal mating of character and artist: it is surething stage business, command of score, and your own foolproof costumes. A weird director might talk a first-time Marschallin, at her final exit, into some unflattering or anti-musical effect—a desperate, tearful run into the wings, say, or the slapping of Octavian's face. A veteran Marschallin, however, has gone through this scene in full true on stage too often to mistake the bittersweet and, above all, forgiving nature of the moment. She will resist. There is, furthermore, tradition's mandate, which prefers the Marschallin to follow von Faninal out, pause at the door, and extend her hand behind her, without looking back, for Octavian to kiss. The gesture is of such nuanced elegance that it is nearly de rigueur. And of course once one has achieved reputation in the part one can usually override a director who wants something less appropriate.

Relying on local talent in decor can be perilous. Evelyn Lear so relies—"I'm not a troublemaker," she says. But she can recall a Lulu outfit that made her look "like a baby elephant." It has happened to everyone. Montserrat Caballé once came on in the ball scene of *Un Ballo in Maschera* in a mask that looked like those gaudy sunglasses favored in Miami Beach. (Or were they Caballé's own, representing her notion of period chic?)

For most singers the first half of the career involves extending one's repertory, the second half trimming it. The extending is practical: one isn't famous enough to turn down an offer (even if it means singing for four or five times a role one will never sing again), one needs the experience, and one doesn't know which roles will be one's particular great ones till one tests them out. The trimming, later, is artistic: perfecting the parts that inspire one. Why waste time and talent on parts other singers do better? In retirement, Titta Ruffo told Walter Legge that, having sung "something like a hundred operas, if he could start his career again he would restrict himself to five or six parts, study and polish them in every vocal and dramatic detail, and sleep happily without fear of competition." Still, how was he to know *which* five or six till he sang them all?

Many singers do not trim their repertory, and thus take their chances with the hazards of modern opera production—hazardous especially in Europe, where a director who doesn't Interpret his classics may be drummed out of fashion. Those singers who do go on extending, at any rate, keep themselves in the news. There is excitement in hearing a diva for the first time in a new part, whereas cutting down to a few specialties can make one too familiar, even routine.

Leonie Rysanek is a good example of the ceaselessly daring singer, widening her repertory with a new role each season, nearly each a great one. Rysanek could easily have settled down with roles of greatest success—Senta, Sieglinde, Chrysothemis, Lady Macbeth, the Empress in *Die Frau Ohne Schatten*—with an Ariadne or Desdemona here and there. But as she passed into the 1970s, after two decades of career a presumed time for scaling down, she reintroduced herself to the public in difficult roles—Cherubini's Médée, Kundry, Salome, La Gioconda, Ortrud. Unlike the Abigaille she attempted long ago at the Met, these were exactly right for her, even the Gioconda, suitable for her Fach and temperament but stylistically a little racy. Rysanek triumphed; better yet, she became more famous, more exciting, and younger than before.

Callas exemplifies the trimmer. A secure musician and a tireless rehearser, she was willing in her youth to sing anything that suited her. But as her voice became more and more wayward, she retreated to Tosca and Norma, in neither of which, by then, was she of stature. She might have taken refuge in vocally less expansive parts; what a Carmen she would have been! She recorded it. But to sing a mezzo role onstage would have been admitting that the instrument was deteriorating.

How desperate and foolish her choices were at the end, and how she vacillated making them; yet how ruthless and certain she had been, years before, when planning her debuts at major houses in her great roles, or in roles she herself would make great. When Antonio Ghiringhelli, chief of La Scala, realized during a performance of *Les Vêpres Siciliennes* at the 1951 Florence May Festival that Callas' prowess was irresistible, he offered her the coming Scala opening night in *Vêpres,* with *Don Carlos, Norma,* and *Die Entführung aus dem Serail* to follow. Callas was not flattered, scarcely even seemed glad. She had deserved it before this, and was angry that it took so long. Ghiringhelli had coolly ignored her till then, most likely because she was Tullio Serafin's protégée—Serafin had been one of Ghiringhelli's outstanding enemies ever since their wrangle during La Scala's first postwar seasons, when Ghiringhelli was administrative head and Serafin musical director. Ghiringhelli had been so anti-Callas that he told Gian Carlo Menotti he could have anyone he chose for the Scala production of *The Consul*—except Callas, who of course was exactly Menotti's choice; *no,* absolutely not, never in this house! Maybe Ghiringhelli was simply afraid of Callas. She always lacked true self-assurance, but to the unknowing eye she could appear as resolute as an early Christian. When Ghiringhelli finally gave in, the soprano knew he needed her more than she needed him, and, admitting the honor of opening La Scala's season, made a counter-offer. Instead of Norma, she would play Violetta.

But Renata Tebaldi had recently suffered something less than success in this part at this house. To present a sure Violetta so soon after would offend Tebaldi. If only Ghiringhelli could employ both divas: but Callas was determined to run a competition of Stimmdivas, Callas versus Tebaldi, Callas *assoluta*. This could not be done by singing the leggiero and lyric-dramatic parts Tebaldi didn't sing. This could be done in a *Traviata* championship. That's what great roles are for.

Ghiringhelli kept his composure. What he was thinking has unfortunately not been recorded. He tried to work Callas around to his idea of things, full of promises ambiguously worded: managerspeak. Callas, always direct, said It is or it isn't. Which is it? When Ghiringhelli and two cohorts turned up at the Meneghinis' apartment in Verona, Callas went right to her point: *La Traviata* or nothing. Astounded and offended, the La Scala team mumbled its way out of the apartment; ten minutes later they returned. *La Traviata* it was.

La Traviata it wasn't, however, because Ghiringhelli wanted Callas but not as Violetta—not yet—and he was willing to prevaricate to get her. Callas haunted him with his promise and he said yes and no at once. Finally she confronted him in his office, and one does not fool around in such a scene, because if Callas gets angry enough she will kill you. She will: because you stand between her and her self-respect, and those who have been taught by life to have too little of the latter are inclined to defend that little in blood. "Caro Ghiringhelli," she begins—but don't be fooled. She very nearly smashed the intendant in Rio de Janeiro with a bronze desk piece for favoring Tebaldi over Callas, and, disarmed, kicked him in the stomach. Why cannot Ghiringhelli stage the *Traviata* he has promised?

"There are good reasons," Ghiringhelli blusters.

"Give me one," says Callas, perhaps eyeing the desk pieces.

"For example, the unavailability of Enzo Mascherini."

Mascherini was a second-rate baritone whose availability in any role was something less than crucial. Ghiringhelli paid Callas off for the nonexistent *Traviatas* and stalled her thereafter. Ultimately, she did sing Violetta at La Scala and had one of her greatest successes. Callas had been equipping and tuning her Violetta to be the supreme great role of the age. Norma is without parallel and Tosca more exciting, but Traviata is the acting singer's richest showcase.

Callas was so proprietary about *Traviata* that in São Paulo in 1951, bare months before the La Scala *Vêpres,* she was ready to duel to the death any colleague who threatened to usurp her leadership. The technicians were having trouble with the curtain after Act Two, so the stage staff asked the Germont, Tito Gobbi, to take a few extra bows to distract the audience from the mishap with the curtain. Callas' poodle of a husband, Battista Meneghini, lurking and watching as always, ran yapping back to his mistress, and the next thing Gobbi knew he was requested to face Madame in her dressing room. There, she told him that if he ever interfered with the success of "my *Traviata*" again, she would destroy his career. Gobbi treated this nonsense with the contempt it deserves. And he reminded her that it was not hers, but Verdi's *Traviata*. That is one problem with great roles: they emphasize the singer's commitment, not the composer's.

Notice, incidentally, that all the great roles are old roles: Mozart, Rossini, Bellini, Donizetti, Meyerbeer, Wagner, Verdi, Puccini, Strauss. Are no new roles great? "Beware the contemporary!" Lotte Heinotz warns, and Elisabeth Söderström agrees: "I hate all living composers." Yet, she admits, "Contemporary music can be killing to the voice but it's a duty to perform it." Once it was a privilege. In Viardot's day, divas were honored by premieres; that was before expressionism became the style and the music less fun to sing. Today the interesting composers are radical and the complaisant composers are dull. Callas, Tebaldi, Horne, and Caballé created no parts, and Sutherland did so (in *The Midsummer Marriage*) only when she had little choice. In Germany there is more pressure on a star soprano to meet her age on its terms; some of them even appear to like contemporary music. But it is a fact of operatic life that if great roles are made by composer and librettist and animated by singers, they are approved by ticket-buyers—and the latter don't heavily approve modern opera.

In any case, it is dangerous to run a career without great roles; one must be unique. Dorothy Kirsten, without question a Met star and a regular in Puccini, made no impression in any role and retired leaving no gap behind. It is not enough to be a trouper, not enough to be useful as Butterfly or Fiora. Opera is about the spectacular. Anything less is routine.

CHAPTER

6

ETHNICITY, POLITICS, AND GLAMOUR

*I had to represent German music,
and if the artist were to fail, it
would be at the cost of Mozart,
Beethoven, and Schubert.*
Wilhelmine
Schröder-Devrient

*Remember, Maria, you first
belong to your public, not to
your husband.*
Evangelia Callas

The social things make one tired.
Joan Sutherland

*How they all love to go out
and bow!*
Mary Garden

Fach and temperament one is born with, but a singer makes choices: in language, territory, historical style. A lyric might concentrate on French roles classic and arcane in the original and in translation; a dramatic might develop either toward Wagner or verismo; a mezzo with *agilità* might identify herself with the parts Rossini wrote for Isabella Colbran; or shall one consider making a name in contemporary music?

One could, alternatively, sing everything in any language, as Lilli Lehmann did, but it's difficult to establish oneself this broadly.* "You do a lot of things well," John Barbirolli told the young Michael Langdon, "but if you're going to get to the top in this business, you've got to *specialize.*" That Langdon then learned, polished, and sang Baron Ochs virtually to the exclusion of everything else might be too specialized; but that was his choice, and it did push him through to stardom. Other singers have specialized by repertory—Renata Scotto in Bellini, Leonie Rysanek in Strauss, Helga Dernesch in Wagner. Nor is this a postwar novelty, for Mary Garden similarly fa-

---

*It also calls for stupendously efficient muscianship. In her autobiography, Lehmann recalls learning the soprano lead in Lortzing's *Undine* in three days, despite being irritated by a carbuncle.

vored coeval French works, Conchita Supervia delved into Colbran Rossini, and Helen Traubel sang Wagner.

Years ago one was born to these choices along with Fach and temperament. In the 1800s it was a matter of geography. French singers sang French roles, in French, according to French methods of voice-training (admittedly Italianized), and meeting French standards of theatre production. So was it, in the respective ethnicity, for Italian and German singers. (British singers followed the Italian line, Covent Garden and points beyond being outposts of Bellini, Donizetti, and their interpreters.) It's typical that the Paris Opéra, undisputed in leadership of the music world, invariably presented titles in French, whether by Meyerbeer, Verdi, or Wagner, and with French singers. Opera, then, was regional, cultural, tribal.

Opera has steadily become international since then. Major houses respect composers' languages, including Russian and Czech, almost as a rule. The ancient local variations in the teaching and making of music have all but vanished. Entire repertories have fallen into disuse, the French and verismo among them, throwing their peculiar performing styles into the shadows. (Will we ever hear an authentic *Faust* again?) And the highly influential von Karajan approach, its finesse polishing all the sharp corners and personality off of Mozart and Verdi, urges opera's young impressionables to balance the contrasts into a kind of operatic Esperanto, one style for everything.

Still, a diva must choose her route, learn which styles and partners suit her, for some vestige of the old nationalities hangs on. There is the difference in how major theatres regard the major revival. At the Met, Covent Garden, or Vienna, an expensive new production is usually planned to impress, delight, and survive seasons of wear, and a relatively conservative public limits the scope of the staging to proved stars, realistically pictorial sets, and deference to tradition. In continental Europe—Germany in particular—radical reevaluation is the key to success (*de scandale,* at the least), with symbolistic decor and, often, singers who have no great reputation to risk if the first-nighters decide to whistle the thing off the stage.

Two productions of Meyerbeer's *Le Prophète* reveal the options most likely chosen in two different sectors of the opera world. The Met mounted it in 1977 with the best cast possible (Marilyn Horne, Renata Scotto, and James McCracken) in John Dexter's attempt to reconcile modern stagecraft with the old line in Peter Wexler's conceptual unit set. Whether one thought it successful or not, it was certainly earnest and handsome. It had presence. Eleven years earlier in Berlin, Bohumil Herlischka converted the piece into a scathing commentary on grand opera and the *ancien régime*. The principals were less prestigious but, by chance, all American, with Sandra Warfield (vocally weak but dramatically insightful), Annabelle Bernard, and Warfield's husband, McCracken. The text was sung in German, ensuring the public's comprehension—yet the stage was filled with towers and dwarfs, risking the public's confusion. The towers kept getting in the way; and why dwarfs? Clearly, a diva who has her eye on Fidès or Berthe must choose: which tendency in production would she be most comfortable in? A Met production loaded with dwarfs is unthinkable. Conversely, one gets few chances to sing Meyerbeer more or less straight and in French in Berlin.

Different national styles, too, guide the rehearsal process. In northern countries they are strictly timed; in France union guidelines can make an epic out of the placement of a tiny prop, and anyway if the chorus isn't on a wildcat strike, the orchestra is; in Italy time is approximate. British and American rehearsals lean to efficiency under one man, the director. German rehearsals may teeter between the director's and the conductor's authority, depending on their standing. Viennese rehearsals, till recently, didn't exist.* Italian rehearsals are anarchic. Any full-stage runthrough in Italy might involve, besides the performers: one, the conductor; two, the prompter; three, the chorus master; four, the director and his assistant; five, various staff personnel such as the designer, the choreographer, and their assistants; and, six, the "scene inspector,"

---

*It sounds sloppy, but the lack of preparation in fact helped create the oft-cited "ensemble style" of the Staatsoper regulars—a style known for its spontaneity, and no wonder.

who supposedly keeps order. At any given moment, half of the above are conducting (to different beats), the other half are chattering, everyone is addressed as Maestro, and the chorus isn't listening.

The public knows little of this. But the odd transmontane visit of a full company affords a glimpse of the national style. When the Rome Opera gives *Le Nozze di Figaro,* Rossini's *Otello,* and *I Due Foscari* in New York, or when the Bolshoi brings Russian classics to Montreal, or when the Dresden Opera takes Strauss to London, one glimpses stylistic instincts at work, language borne on melody, and personality reveling in atmosphere. Would not any diva long to be a part of such artistic authenticity? But sometimes it backfires, as when the Bing Met brought *Figaro* and *Il Barbiere di Siviglia* to Paris. Here were two Italian operas, one by a German, based on French plays and performed by unimportant American singers. Even when fresh the productions had been empty and stupid; one wouldn't want to take them to Passaic, let alone Paris. "Miss [Roberta] Peters may have had a bad night," said Bing in response to booing and catty reviews. "The Paris Opéra has had a bad century." Still, the Romans, the Russians, and the Germans offered singers proud of a cultural heritage. The Met offered culture adrift. Whose idea *was* this?

The difference in audience from country to country is momentous; this, too, may depress or stimulate the diva. All operagoers appreciate good singing in popular works, but Germans follow one's part in unfamiliar titles better than others do and truly appreciate a committed performance, while British and American audiences will most readily forgive a performer in chance difficulty. Italians and Viennese are the least tolerant of "modernism" (including works now half a century old), the British more so, and Americans will bear but detest it. If you were a diva, would you rather sing in Parma, where a theatre of aficionados whose experience dates back to Muzio will turn on you brutally if you miss a note—but will, surely, listen to you carefully—or in Houston, where a sporting public wouldn't dream of harassing you and hasn't the vaguest idea what you're singing about ? Nicolai Gedda warns young singers of the fulfillment of absolute communication: not in the vernacular, but in the utter sounds, note and word, that the composer laid down in score. "It's not just a matter of learning the meaning of words," he says, "but of learning a cultural heritage, a tradition." He wants Domingo or Pavarotti in Verdi, Vishnevskaya in Tchaikofsky, Fischer-Dieskau in Schumann. Where does this leave the American diva who aims at Aida, Tatiana, Genoveva? Somewhere in the boat Camilla Williams rowed when, carried away during a *Butterfly* in Italian at the Long Island Festival in 1963, she capped the flood of emotion at the sighting of Pinkerton's ship by crying, "He's coming!" Granted, one shouldn't ad lib—but it did provide the sole moment of theatre in an evening of music. The audience was thrilled.

Gedda speaks as an expert in this matter, for as a Swede of Russian family he had to internationalize himself to pursue a major career and thus learned the expedience as well as the disadvantages of the cultural crossover. Gedda is virtually native in German operetta, in Russian opera, and in all French styles from musical comedy to the grand monster shows of the Opéra. If his voice doesn't sound idiomatic in Donizetti or Verdi, still he knows his way around the *di grazia* parts like Elvino and the Duke of Mantua. Above all, his command of language and diction is amazing. As Régine Crespin proved in the Met's *Dialogues des Carmelites,* sometimes it is the foreigners who sing the best English.

Opera in English is a consideration the English-speaking diva must address, for it is a worthy controversy here and in Britain. Some opinion-makers demand opera in the vernacular, for the theatre of it; others want the original, for the culture Gedda speaks of. But when, for example, postwar Covent Garden had Elisabeth Schwarzkopf singing the Italian Violetta in English through a Germanic conception, opera is texturing its vernacular. Soprano Sheri Greenawald finds this contention favoring translation disturbing. Should art be "easily digestible" or retain its integrity?

Opera as a nationalistic condition is at its strongest in performances of national art. A *Tosca* in German with Anja Silja, James King, and Dietrich Fischer-Dieskau may be intelligible and spirited theatre, but it is not as authentic a *Tosca* as one might catch in the Italian provinces with a cast of unknowns, if only because opera has always been and remains fascinated by language. The lyric who hopes to grow into a Puccini spinto but who doesn't trouble to master Italian, or the dramatic with eyes on Isolde and Elektra who doesn't think her German need be any better than her public's, is cheating the art.

They've been arguing as to whether words or music count more heavily since the first rehearsal of the first opera—no, since before: it was a crucial question to the Florentines who devised opera. But it may be that opera's words and music are inseparable *once the composer sets them*. This must color our comprehension of various Mimìs, Marschallins, and Marguerites. It is not a question of pronouncing a language properly; it is a matter of singing on the words. In opera, language is the backbone of style, and not only in roles as verbalized as Mélisande or Jenůfa. I once heard Montserrat Caballé wander through a Met *Aida* vocalizing on vowels, repeating snatches of her colleagues' lines, and occasionally inventing her own. Except for the first words of arias and a few other phrases too well known to miss, the woman was not singing Verdi: she was humming his tunes. This is shocking: but this is opera today. Years ago a singer would not have gone onstage so ill-prepared. Nellie Melba may have been the prototype of the Commonwealth parvenue, but when she sang French opera she had the guidance—and the admiration—of Gounod, Thomas, and Saint-Saëns behind her. Melba's example assures us that a diva can select her musical ethnicity competitively.

In Melba's day, then, the center held. Since then the gyres have slipped. At the old Met, rehearsing for his debut as Scarpia, Tito Gobbi was astonished to discover that, despite the fearsome music Puccini wrote for the totalitarian police chief, no one on stage registered the slightest fear of him or his henchmen. Then, in Act Two, the Cavaradossi, following the "production book" as upheld by the usual shabby assistant, actually threatened Scarpia with a chair and advanced upon him holding it above his head. Everyone else on stage—Scarpia's armed bodyguard—just stood there. Gobbi stunned the tenor with a look so awful he fell out of character, stopped dead, and said, "Scusi, Commendatore."

Gobbi halted the rehearsal and questioned this absurd piece of business. In Italy, where everyone of Gobbi's time had had personal experience of totalitarian police chiefs, such a direction would have been as bizarre as flying Spoletta in on Peter Pan wires. The entire staging was incorrect, and Gobbi made the necessary revisions as he went along. His Tosca, Zinka Milanov, must have been impressed by the confrontation with, for once in that house, a genuine Scarpia: at best tolerant of her colleagues, she singled Gobbi out for unique commendation by leaving him alone at their curtain call—in defiance of house rules. Bing, himself a refugee from the Baron Scarpias of Austria, should have understood exactly what Gobbi was driving at: the people in charge of the Met *Tosca* had not the slightest knowledge of history, of Rome, of politics. Lotte Heinotz has a term for this: *Schlemieloper*. But Bing was not happy, and called Gobbi into his office, backed by his own henchmen, to reprove. If the Met couldn't stage an Italian *Tosca,* it was at any rate going to have a Bing *Tosca.*

The difference between the usual internationalized-stage *Tosca* and the one that Puccini had in mind was made clear at this same Met some years later, in the season in which Renata Tebaldi returned in a glowing *Bohème* after having surmounted vocal difficulties. A special, one-time-only *Tosca* was announced, with Tebaldi, Gobbi, and—less definitively— Barry Morell. Came the night, Bing stepped before the curtain, surely to announce an indisposition, and to growls of despair. But no. Timing it exquisitely, Bing assured the audience that both Tebaldi and Gobbi were fine. Morell was indisposed—and Franco Corelli was taking over. Sensation in the house: not the typical patient encouragement of the underdog that Americans donate to the substitute, but the excited revving up appropriate to a rare Met event: opera in the national style. For once, the Met gave the *Tosca* that Italians have been taking as their due since its premiere in 1900, Tebaldi's tenacious diva, Corelli's Byronic hero, and Gobbi's suavely louche villain singing the tongue of shared customs, character, and loyalties. In other places Tebaldi's Tosca was too much the Madonna, an aunt who had forgotten her bustle and was looking everywhere for it. Playing to "Italian" tenors who had no idea what she was singing, how could she extend herself in a love duet? "Have you seen my bustle?" she seemed to ask them. When a coarse Scarpia produced the fatal fan without knowing how it informs the intrigue, why should Tebaldi seize on it, worry it? "No," she might have told him, *"that's not my bustle."*

With Corelli and Gobbi, it was another Tebaldi, a tense, electric Tosca, the details of flirtation (with her lover) and loathing (of the villain) her spontaneous alchemy. The byplay between her and Gobbi on her first-act exit was an opera in itself, and their second-act battle might have logged ten years' rehearsal. Ethnicity *does* matter: it produces nights like this one. It must hearten divas (in a metaphorical audience) cn the question of culture, must hold Germans to Pamina, Agathe, Octavian; the French to Alceste, Valentine, Thaïs; and so on through the catalogues. Better to be born to the part—if you must acquire it, do so to the utmost. *Understand* the event.

Bing didn't. When his aroused Met public stopped the show after Tebaldi's "Vissi d'arte" and took over for an interminable ovation, Bing slipped out of a stage-right side door, surveyed this demonstration—offended, as if he knew that it implied that some Met nights are a lot better than others—and muttered, "Ridiculous!" No doubt it was, the audience trying to join the performance like *espontaneos* at a bullfight.* But this was a precious demented night of style, opera as documentary, and we had to pay it its due. For style is melting away.

What stylistic choice has an American soprano? Unlike the Italian diva, with her heritage in bel canto or verismo; or the German with hers in Singspiel or Wagner; or the French with hers in opéra comique, the American has no set operatic forms to indulge. The important American operas are each *sui ge-*

---

*Bing blamed the Met standees for starting and protracting all ovations; he and they never got along. They were indiscriminate in bravo, vicious in satire, and fat and horrible. They lacked the wit of the devotee or of Bing. Few of the thousands of retaliatory actions cf his Met régime must have delighted him as much as the sudden banning of standing room after some idiot had anonymously threatened the life of Leonie Rysanek. The logic that the threat might have come from anywhere in the house—or even from without it—was not entertained. Anyway, Bing could hardly close the whole house. He punished the standees, though he had to reinstate them in short order, unchastened. Rysanek's anonymous mail began to pick up *after* the incident.

neris, unlike each other—*Porgy and Bess, Four Saints in Three Acts, Street Scene, Regina, The Consul, Susannah, Elephant Steps, Sweeney Todd.* Except for *Porgy and Bess,* at length established as a classic, none of these has produced a great role—the sense of familiarity, of absorption within the normalized Western repertory, is lacking. These are still special works, culturally unconnected except in the very broadest sense.

True, American sopranos have built up a certain reputation in them, Catherine Malfitano in the Weill, Brenda Lewis in the Blitzstein (not least for her turnabout in creating the hapless Birdie in the premiere, then switching over to the heinous Regina in the City Opera revival), Patricia Neway in the Menotti, Phyllis Curtin and Maralin Niska in the Floyd. But it is arguable that the most authentic American operas are those that have grown out of or have borrowed from the striking theatricality of Broadway's music theatre. Of the eight works mentioned above, six were premiered on Broadway; note also that Lewis and Neway sang musicals as well as opera, Lewis in a comic role as the gritty theatre manager Lotta Leslie (in Sigmund Romberg's last show, *The Girl in Pink Tights*), complete with the unique Broadway "belt" Fach (which delivers an entire part in an extended chest register) and such ditties as "Love Is the Funniest Thing." Is it possible that American divas are neglecting their heritage by not singing more "Broadway" roles, including those in, say, *The Most Happy Fella, A Little Night Music, Show Boat, The New Moon,* and *Naughty Marietta?*—the last written for production in the popular theatre but with cast, staff, and even orchestra drawn from Oscar Hammerstein's Manhattan Opera.

There is, of course, the pan-cultural world of opera in English, counting British titles as well as a few by Stravinsky, Henze, and other internationalists. Sheri Greenawald has found a niche here, honing Anne Trulove in *The Rake's Progress* and the Governess in *The Turn of the Screw* into her great roles in places as diverse as Amsterdam and Santa Fe. But some Americans sound odd in the Hogarthian *Rake,* odder in Britten, oddest of all in Vaughan Williams and Tippett. The styles are dense in language and cut of melody, as foreign as Meyerbeer. How, then, to be an American soprano?

Rosa Ponselle's solution was to express nationhood by

reigning in her national opera house, singing that house's repertory. In effect, she became an Italian soprano, seeing such cultural transformation as the natural portion of American singers. "Just as I was destined to pave the way for American-born singers with no European experience," she wrote toward the end of her life, "fate chose Leontyne Price to open the doors of our own opera houses to black artists."

Italian by family and a native of Meriden, Connecticut, Ponselle came to the language easily, though she had to switch from Neapolitan dialect to Tuscan librettese, taught her by the coach Romano Romani. As the Met's Italian dramatic *d'agilità,* Ponselle sang classic repertory with Caruso, de Luca, Ruffo, Martinelli, Gigli, Lauri-Volpi (with a little French and contemporary work on the side). With such company at home, why dare foreign parts? She did sing at Covent Garden, upon which occasion Nellie Melba frostily warned her about a regional custom—applause after acts, not after arias. (The English revised the custom after hearing Ponselle's "Casta diva.") Then, performing Spontini's *La Vestale* at the first Florence May Festival in 1933, Ponselle was considering a La Scala debut until she took in *I Puritani* and heard the Florentines treat Giacomo Lauri-Volpi to a hail of booing for missing the high note in "A te, o cara." She cabled her agent, "FORGET MILAN. ONLY IN AMERICA." And she never sang anywhere else.

Maria Callas was as international as Ponselle was local. Their repertories coincide, and Callas, of Greek parentage, became thoroughly Italian in her early years as a resident of Verona, even taking on the inflection of the Veneto in her speech. Let Milanov, Gueden, Tebaldi, or Crespin try the company life; Callas led the new postwar style of vagabond stardom. She was rootless. Artistically, she had impeccable training, from such teachers as Elvira de Hidalgo, Tullio Serafin, Victor de Sabata, Antonino Votto, Carlo Maria Giulini, and Gianandrea Gavazzeni. But she came into tradition, not out of one; she had to derive her culture osmotically, as Ponselle did. Still, Ponselle had her berth at the Met, a form of cultural structure. Callas had no such defenses when, in the late 1950s, her series of scandals aroused public opinion against her. She could give to Italian opera, to the singing of bel canto and, in collaboration with Luchino Visconti, to the staging of it. But Italian opera gave her nothing to keep: she taught, briefly, in New York, lived for a time with a millionaire sailor as expatriate as she, and eventually took up residence in Paris, a city of chic exiles. Everywhere Callas went, she was either honoring the local strangers (as in Dallas, London, and her "hometown," New York) or insulting them (as in Edinburgh, Rome, and Milan). Culture *can* be derived. Ponselle knew nothing of opera when she was hired by the Met, and Callas spent her most impressionable years isolated in wartime Athens. But Ponselle at least retained national roots: "ONLY IN AMERICA."

The outstanding rejection of Callas' mode, closer to Ponselle's, yet more truly native, is that of Beverly Sills. Granted, Sills had a close family bond that did not impel Ponselle or Callas—the one married late in life and the other had no use (in any sense) for her blood ties and went off to destiny alone. Still, Sills' station at the old City Opera was unpromising, invested with those lyric roles that get one no place and coloratura roles that create furore only in more redoutable theatres than the City Center.

She might have tried Europe; most Americans of her generation were doing so routinely by about 1960. Sills stayed put, at last taking advantage of the company's move to Lincoln Center into a tabernacle encouraging furore under the now doting eye of the press. It was the moment, and Cleopatra, in an eye-filling production of Handel's *Giulio Cesare*, was the part. Sung to the nth embellishment, Sills' Cleopatra proved her first major assumption* in a series that would take her through many great roles and even give her a chance to assert her own rights in the bel-canto *riesumazione*.

Thus graduated into fame, Sills could have made her tour through the capitals; but she seems to be a company person. She did not even sing at the Met—Bing apparently didn't care

*It might be argued that Sills' Baby Doe takes pride of order, dating back to the mid-1950s and certainly finding Sills at her best. However, even having recorded it with the other City Opera principals, Sills did not become known for Baby Doe till much later. Then it became so associated with her that folklore credits her with having created it in its world premiere in Central City. No: Dolores Wilson.

for her voice. What she did was, all things considered, immensely loyal and smart as well. Rather than desert the City Opera (which needed her desperately), she made a few jaunts abroad, aiming to sing *just* the part in *just* the place. The first big new one hit the nail on the ace: Pamira in the famous "American" *L'Assedio di Corinto* at La Scala with Marilyn Horne and Justino Díaz under Thomas Schippers. The event kindled Sills' spark as a world star without her having to make more than a few more acute appearances and the usual recordings. She could return to her home house, secure in reputation and true to her ideals. She could do her guesting with American companies, helping provincial organizations to muster their subscriptions by promising a turn by Sills. She could turn up on talk shows, hosting her own, diva as public figure. And she could finally do the Met after all, when they needed her far more than she them. This is a truly national career.

Now that ethnic tradition is crumbling in polyglot superproduction and "festivals" that take on the cultural character of the presiding ego, opera is in danger of losing its cultural grip, of turning as rootless as Callas. One cannot blame Joan Sutherland for renouncing all claim on English opera; who wants to sing *The Bohemian Girl* time and again (or even once)? But here at least is a singer who did come out of a national movement, as maid-of-all-work at Covent Garden in its "interesting" times when opposing pressures of native and alien language, artists, and music were battling for control. As we know, except for Bonynge, everyone saw Sutherland as a dramatic soprano of no particular affiliation; but then the management had far more to cope with than settling Sutherland's Fach just then. Having put together a company virtually from scratch, David Webster and his music director, Karl Rankl, were busy enough filling out the repertory. When you have yet to secure sets and costumes for major titles by Verdi and Wagner, and you're worried about finding a decent Carmen, you have little time for the nurturing of national talents.

By the mid-1950s, with the hard-working but unfortunately uninspired Rankl edged out, the production catalogue swelling nicely, and the ideal of opera in English put by, Webster had discovered and developed a crucial talent in the

Canadian Jon Vickers. Dramatic tenors are rare today; one as sensitive and musicianly as this one is rare even in a golden age. While Vickers was to become international, in demand everywhere for his Siegmund, Otello, Énée, and Tristan, he grew up as Covent Garden's "own" Heldentenor, the only house singer Webster allotted a lead role when he went all out on the centenary *Don Carlos*. And note also that Vickers became an ambassador for English art in his unrivaled Peter Grimes.

Sutherland went the other way. She worked for Webster but sang on the side for Bonynge, and it was Donizetti of course who sent her into stardom, at Covent Garden, with Webster's support in the face of his board's misgivings, for *Lucia* had never been popular in England and Sutherland was not known for bel canto. Actually, she was not known for anything at the time, including English opera, though she created Jenifer in the world premiere of Tippett's *The Midsummer Marriage*. Came then the *Lucia;* and all the world had to hear Sutherland; and, as Callas had spurred interest in bel-canto archeology, Bonynge encouraged his wife to reopen the digging; and gradually Sutherland's connection with Covent Garden waned. Now her traditions lead her far from native art. Her Alcina and Lucy Lockit (in *The Beggar's Opera*) resound with London pride (Handel's opera had its premiere at Covent Garden, though not in the present building), and she has even recorded songs by Noël Coward. Still, for good or ill, Sutherland is no more Australian, or Commonwealth—or could one say Avalonian?—than Maria Callas was Greek.

Transnational stylistics are no novelty in opera. For centuries, singers of various nationalities had to "become" Italian on any major stage except that of the Paris Opéra. French music theatre was created in large part by the Italian Lully and Rossini, the Czech Gluck, and the German Meyerbeer. Bel-canto pedagogy was outlined most influentially by the Spanish Manuel Garcia, one line of descendance traveling through his son to the German Mathilde Marchesi through the American Estelle Liebling to Beverly Sills: nearly two hundred years of strict Italian style, and not an Italian in the company!

There is something admirable nonetheless, and patriotic, in advocating one's culture, in lending one's support toward its nurture. Janet Baker balances Sutherland on the ethnic side, as a diva especially identified with English opera and, in recital, English song. She has portrayed Purcell's Dido and Britten's Lucretia, Hermia, and Kate (in *Owen Wingrave*), sung continental works in English with the national companies, even crossed over—and simultaneously back again—to songs by Haydn and Beethoven written on Scottish texts:

> O! can ye sew cushions, and can ye sew sheets,
> And can ye sing balla loo when the bairn greets?

In such repertory a singer may influence her peers and incite the youngsters. This is, for an arrived star, a *Divagöttin,* a defiance of received wisdoms. Should a diva move so tightly within her birthright realm? Should she glorify not the international Festival but Scottish Opera? There are penalties to pay when one sticks close to home and asserts nationality. There is especially the company trap of being taken for granted for not being a transatlantic import. James McCracken might sit bonnie Baker doon and sing her balla loo on what it was like day to day at the old Met having Otello's voice but not his part; and Frederica von Stade could present her Wowkle.

Yet Baker made it work, perhaps with her infusions of Schubert and Berlioz; or perhaps she would have arrived just so without their assistance. Notably, she did rule out much of the Festival, limiting her stage appearances to the home isles, even turning down a chance to make headlines when Tatiana Troyanos apparently got nervous and missed the dress rehearsal of *Giulio Cesare* in San Francisco and Baker was invited to step in and triumph. Imagine the impact—Baker as hero in her sole American engagement! But she had a recital coming up at home and needed her prep time: commitment outranks headlines. She said no; she is one of the few who know how to. The sense of nation that has eluded many of her colleagues centers Baker.

Surely there is nothing political in her intentions; Baker makes art, neat. But it is very English to view opera as pure art, separate from the world in its magical theatre. On the continent the opera house has long been and remains a focus of political life, a kind of distilled town hall. One of the factors in the ascendance of La Scala was Milan's congregation of writers, politicians, amateurs of the nobility, and other opinion-makers. No other Italian first night could count so influential an audience, not only in music but in every aspect of culture, and the Scala prima became, by the late 1800s, the most important performance in Italy as much because of who heard as who composed or sang. With the invasion of industrialist money power, this holds true today.

Opera itself is inherently political and can also be politicized. In Rossini's Naples the republicans made performing dangerous for Isabella Colbran for her royalist associations. In Verdi's Milan a chorus of people dispossessed of home and culture would be cheered in rejection of Northern Italy's Austrian overlords, whose officers were sitting right there in the house. Auber's *La Muette de Portici* sparked a riot in Brussels that led to Belgian liberation from colonialist Holland. Anti-German sentiment expressed on toy whistles forced the Paris Opéra to withdraw Wagner's *Tannhäuser*. The Nazis disrupted performances of Kurt Weill and Bertolt Brecht's *Aufstieg und Fall der Stadt Mahagonny* as a test of the strength of Weimar liberty. One of the most essential repertory items, *Fidelio*, is an overtly political work, for the republic against the despot. How strange to find it solemnly and lovingly performed in Nazi Germany; but then it's popular in Soviet Russia, too. Italian vocal competitions—a regular feature of the opera scene—are judged entirely on a political basis, the juries drawn from union members, Party stooges, and the occasional retired prima donna. When, on one such outing, Maria Carbone was told that a certain young woman would have to win because of her family's connections with the mayor of Milan, the former verismo specialist bridled, and when she heard the woman's less than acceptable singing, Carbone rose and furiously suggested that the others on the panel inform the mayor that as Carbone doesn't advise his civic administration, he should stay out of music. And she took herself away.

One favorite tale of political demonstration in the opera house—actually of how a diva foiled one—reads somewhat like an opera itself. The diva was Marietta Alboni, a coloratura contralto of incomparable zest, one of Rossini's pets and the kind of singer all-star Meyerbeer was written for—and rewritten: the composer added a devilish showpiece for Alboni to use as the page Urbain in *Les Huguenots*. Alboni was utter legend, not a fair subject for heckling even in her sometimes brutal age; when critic Max de Schauensee took Emma Eames to hear the stupendously charming Conchita Supervia and asked for Eames' opinion, he got not the expected awe but, "Oh, my dear, I heard Alboni sing that music."

In Trieste for *Il Barbiere di Siviglia*, Alboni was warned that she was to be whistled off the stage, and somehow supplied herself with the names of the gang leaders and their favorite café. Disguised as a man—if this story isn't apocryphal, I'm Rigoletto—Alboni visits the café, joins the gang, and learns why Alboni is to be whistled: she has been singing in Vienna, and the Austrians are the Northern Italian's sworn enemy, as occupying overlords and composers of loud, unmelodic music. Then Alboni is issued a whistle with the rest of the gang and told that the fun will commence directly after "Una voce poco fa."

So, the curtain up on Act Two, Alboni begins the aria, and some of the gang, mistaking their timing, jump the gun and raise a clamor. The audience immediately senses an intrigue, and the contralto marches down to the footlights, displays her club whistle, and says, "My friends, you are ahead of your schedule. I understood we were not to begin whistling until after the aria."

Whereupon the house explodes in cheers.

English-speaking singers who stick close to home sense little of opera's political component, though they may have heard something of the fanatic politicization of Italian houses by the Communists, who hire only comrades or sympathizers and thus ensure the same partisan interpretation of the classics that has so bemused singers in German houses, where almost the only operas that come off as written are new works. Like it or not, opera is *res publica,* a public thing, and the diva a national, ethnic, or social symbol. Consider the case of Nellie Melba's unthinking anti-Australian outburst that became a *cause célèbre* and is still recalled today down under: the "Sing 'em muck!" story.

Melba, of course, was Australian, named Helen Porter, née Mitchell, married Armstrong, and renamed Melba after her birthplace, Melbourne. Like her compatriot Joan Sutherland, Melba went international but retained home ties, though she had no Sydney Opera House to coax along as the Bonynges do. Melba's Australia was for tours, ideally solo concerts but occasionally opera with an *ad hoc* company of respectably impressive second-raters so Melba would shine. (Once she miscalculated and took John McCormack along.) What does one sing in Australia? Melba reportedly considered the question when Clara Butt was about to tour there herself. Butt, a contralto who sang only one opera role, Orfeo, was no threat to Melba and therefore a sort of friend. Melba grew confidential:

> So you're going to Australia? Well, *I* made twenty thousand pounds on my tour there, but of course *that* will never be done again. Still, it's a wonderful country, and you'll have a good time. What are you going to sing? All I can say is—sing 'em muck! It's all they can understand!

Trouble is, the speech appeared in a biography of Clara Butt that came out in 1928 while Melba was in Australia. She was making her last of several farewells when a reporter accosted her with the book in hand. Outraged—but who knows whether or not she said it?—Melba promptly pressed the publisher into withdrawing all copies and deleting the questionable quotation. Butt was embarrassed and her biographer, Winifred Ponder, betrayed. However, word had got out around the world, and everyone wanted a copy of the book—only in "the 'muck' edition." This became a collectors' item and is seldom seen, but the story was told and retold. "Sing 'em *muck!*" An artist of Puccini, Gounod, and Verdi with no intrinsic musical heritage—Melba, in short—might naturally parse music (and people) into sections graded according to worth. Yet a diva's responsibilities take in more than raising a fancy noise and living in Sunday-supplement luxury. The diva is an avatar, an archon, a spokeswoman. A politician.

There are politicians noble and compromised, fearless and silent. Opera's best have defied oppression and worst collaborated with it. The area is so sensitive that many pasts have been left unexplored for fear of what the sleuth might find. Art, we are told, is distinct from politics. But a Leonore who delighted in the Nazi death camp is revolting, no matter how pure her portrayal. It is an earnest of the diva's symbolic obligations as a public figure—as a deputy of highest art, moral art, she should know better than the rest of us—that politics infinitely intruded into the ovations accorded singers in the direly relieved first days of peace in occupied Vienna of 1945. Recently, in the *The New York Times,* former American Intelligence officer Richard H. Goldstone recalled that there were cheers for Maria Reining specifically because she was known to have secretly aided Allied operations during the war, and the temporary intendant of the Staatsoper at the Theater an der Wien (the Staatsoper building, of course, had been destroyed during a bombing raid) told Goldstone that, even had Allied policy permitted the hiring of Elisabeth Schwarzkopf, the presence of a Nazi sympathizer "would have demoralized the company."

It is a sad commentary on opera's politicization during the first postwar years that a few completely innocent divas were smeared, by journalists who live by assault, by a public ready to believe the worst of anyone, and even by opportunistic rivals. Not surprisingly, it was Wagnerian sopranos who took the worst of it, as if singing in German betokened Nazi sympathy. Kirsten Flagstad was made victim thus, for, while she entertained no admiration for the Nazis, her husband moved in Quisling company—as an associate, indeed, of Vidkun Quisling himself. His fellow Norwegians knew what he was and, at the war's end, threw him into prison, where he died. But where is it written that one bears the sins of one's husband? Realization that the Flagstad instrument was intact led to a clamor to hear her again, and she returned to places of her former glory, the Met and Covent Garden. Yet the events were soiled by the protests of a few ignorant people.

More active protest—persecution, in fact—destroyed Germaine Lubin, the unrivaled French *Wagnérienne* at the Opéra. John Steane calls her "the sort of Brünnhilde who was also a good Tosca," unwittingly revealing her tragic flaw: her versatility enraged jealous colleagues. Outside of the lyric and leggiero roles, there was little Lubin couldn't do better than other sopranos in the insular atmosphere of French opera. More than thirty years after the end of the war, Lanfranco Rasponi interviewed Lubin for *Opera News* and found a woman consumed with the wrongs done her, a veritable Isolde in her Narration. Rasponi likened her to Hecuba, still at war after the fighting is over; Lubin thought herself an Amfortas: "My wounds," she said, "are destined to remain open."

Note that the similes prefer Wagner. The connection undid her, for what Frenchman could believe that so enthusiastic a Kundry, welcomed at Bayreuth and congratulated by Göring and Hitler, was not a partisan for the other side? Lubin had her Massenet and Gluck, her Ariane in Dukas' so very Gallic *Ariane et Barbe-Bleue*. But her sense of timing was atrocious. The late 1930s was not a recommendable era for the singing of Wagner at Bayreuth by a Frenchwoman, no matter how much she separates art from politics. If our artists cannot lead our resistance at a time when our very sense of civilization is threatened, art is worthless. Any diva who thinks herself "above" politics is a traitor, a stooge, or a fool.

Lubin was a fool. She loved Wagner and longed to sing his works in Germany, in state. She was no collaborator, but she exposed herself dangerously to those who wished to unseat her, not least in singing at the Opéra throughout the Nazi occupation—singing Wagner at that. One must remember that the drive toward retributive paranoia in postwar France outdid anything in McCarthy's America; even Maurice Chevalier, who made a very few appearances under Nazi aegis, entirely to preserve the health of his Jewish wife and her parents, was branded—Chevalier, France's unique *vedette du monde!* It happens. It happened to Lubin, as she tells:

> I kept being arrested and then released again, for the accusations—so outrageous that in other circum-

stances they would have been hilarious—always proved groundless. Except for having eaten the flesh of children, there was nothing I was not accused of. . . . Suddenly it turned out that I had been the mistress of everyone from Ribbentrop to Admiral Dönitz (I had never even met him!) and Hitler, who supposedly was impotent. . . . Every new anonymous letter brought new interrogations.

Her son killed himself, her career dissolved, her reputation stank, and she lived on, roiling at her treatment, guilty without trial. Of Lubin, *The Concise Oxford Dictionary of Opera* reads, "Her career was brought to a premature end after the war as a result of her collaboration with the Germans."

On the other side come the resisters of totalitarianism, though it is notable that standing up to the beast won't do as much for a career as collaborating with it will hurt one. That's an arresting favoritism. Galina Vishnevskaya is the brandname anti-totalitarian of the age, the postwar equivalent of Lotte Lehmann, cut off from her culture for her refusal to kowtow to tyrants. There are telling differences. Lehmann left Nazi Germany-Austria, while Vishnevskaya was dismissed from Soviet Russia (specifically for giving succor to dissident Aleksandr Solzhenitsyn); and Lehmann went off on her own, while Vishnevskaya had her conductor and cellist husband, Mstislav Rostropovich, for professional support. Most important, Lehmann could accept the change of venue more easily, for her language and culture were not as foreign to her British and American havens as is Vishnevskaya's Russian. It's one thing to be able to take your Sieglinde and the Marschallin to Covent Garden knowing the house is used to—and prefers—Wagner and Strauss in native style. It's another to know that you'll never be able to sing Tchaikofsky's Tatiana in Tchaikofsky's tongue except in the context of a costumed concert, true theatre swept out, the melody pleasing but the thought banned.

Being a public figure and a cultural stranger at once can be bewildering. Some years before their exile began, Vishnevskaya and Rostropovich had struck up a working friendship with Benjamin Britten, and Vishnevskaya was invited to par-

Sheri Greenawald (*as the governess in* The Turn of the Screw*)*

Maria Malibran

Mary Garden (*as Mélisande)*

Lotte Lehmann (*as Beethoven's Leonore)*

DEMENTED THROUGH THE YEARS

*First, "Melba
and Her Friends"*

*She's secure
with Colonel
Mapleson...*

*roguish with
playwright
Haddon Chambers
(her drama coach)...*

*dour with Mrs. Mapleson
(who knows why?).*

Then, "Taking Flowers from a Brownie Troop," with...

Rosa Ponselle philosophical, Kirsten Flagstad thrilled. Wouldn't you be?

Lastly, we have the semi-informal "modern style," with...

Joan Sutherland engaging, Richard Bonynge conciliatory, and Marilyn Horne dreamy.

The truly demented diva will own her own opera house:
Adelina Patti and her Welsh castle, Craig-y-nos ("Rock of Night"),
with its theatre set up for the "Garden Scene" in Faust.

The many moods of bel canto: as the heroine of Bellini's
La Straniera, *Renata Scotto displays crafty indecision,*
sage supremacy, and an intensely romantic despair.

THE UPS AND DOWNS OF IMAGE

Opposite above: Grace Moore on the dull side in her early films (here as Jenny Lind in A Lady's Morals *with Reginald Denny), then full of kaboum at Columbia in* One Night of Love, *and... a movie star is born.*

Opposite below: Helen Traubel as Isolde, then dancing ragtime with Jose Ferrer in Deep in My Heart.

Above: the young Leontyne Price breaks into the business as Bess, then breaks out of racial typing as Donna Anna.

TWO IMMORTALS

Janet Baker
(looking a
little like
Renata Scotto)
as Penelope

and Marjorie
Lawrence
(as Salome)

ticipate in the premiere of Britten's *War Requiem,* to be sung at the rebuilt Coventry Cathedral with Peter Pears and Dietrich Fischer-Dieskau as the other soloists, the whole suggesting an air of postwar shriving in international understanding through art. Britten's music, his choice of texts, and the setting combined to produce a comprehensive piety, an act of beautiful peace. The Soviets, who had withheld Vishnevskaya from the performance, allowed her to make the recording, but somehow little of the peace and shriving was conveyed to Vishnevskaya, who spoke no English. Told that Pears and Fischer-Dieskau would stand with the orchestra and Britten on the rostrum while she would be placed way above and beyond them in a kind of angel choir, Vishnevskaya resisted, could not understand or be understood, imagined she was being taken for a comprimaria, and so lay down on the floor and began to scream, more or less non-stop, right through the rehearsal.

It's an odd picture, for Vishnevskaya is a formidable woman, not at all the sort who would have to throw a tantrum to get her way. Interviewed in New York after she and Rostropovich left Russia for good, she had little to say of her various skirmishes with state authorities, but was clearly seething over her relationships with her colleagues at the Bolshoi. She still knew no English, and spoke through an interpreter, waiting with sharp austerity as each broadside was translated. Some of what Vishnevskaya said even surprised the interpreter, herself Russian. Vishnevskaya intimated—no; Vishnevskaya never intimates. She firmly stated that some of her fellow musicians were eager to see her dislodged, and her choice of words bore some rather expansive nuances. Could backstage jealousy have contributed to Vishnevskaya's political travail, as it certainly did to Lubin's? The implication is stunning: that opera is a life-and-death struggle, and that the theatre is no refuge of holy art but simply another arena of the war of life. "A grand profession, but a dirty business."

One wonders what antagonism the free-spirited Lotte Lehmann might have endured before she departed for free soil, for the Vienna State Opera was and still is a bastion of star-system vanity, always tending toward fame and favoritism. Vishnevskaya's Bolshoi, on the contrary, is operated so secretively that the elements of stardom as we know it in the West are scattered and suppressed. The company is resident, with rare guesting from abroad. The posters are unreliable and the season's schedule unavailable. The repertory is limited. New productions are few and old ones stagnant. Principal singers appear infrequently, often in the same few parts for years. Great roles are not shared: you sing it, you own it. Ovations are unheard of. Anyway, tickets are difficult to obtain except by foreigners and Party ghouls.

Even so, Vishnevskaya reigned as the house diva, the only soprano famous and in demand in the West. Such a talent might easily offend many another singer. Who knows what untold stories contribute to the making of a political symbol? Little of Vishnevskaya's Bolshoi battles got into the interview; I know because I wrote it, and did so deleting the underground matter because I find dissident heroism inspiring. I wanted to set it off cleanly. Still, a diva is a diva. When the interpreter left the room briefly, I carried on myself in college Russian, asking Vishnevskaya if there was any role the Bolshoi denied her that she might like to try. There was, she said— Salome. Would she perform her own dance?

"Konyechno!" Of course!, with an air of "How else?"

"That would be very interesting."

All she said then was *"Da,"* but she pronounced it to translate roughly as "Kid, you better believe it!"

Not every diva can take on the authoritarian state, but living with it uncompromised calls for ingenuity. Maria Caniglia foiled the beast with wit. In an Italy run by Nazis, opera singers were treated as prize slaves, useful in morale-boosting broadcasts to the Fatherland. After one performance Caniglia, Beniamino Gigli, and Tito Gobbi were ordered to hit the microphone for a program of arias. While Gigli and Gobbi tried to excuse themseves, Caniglia silently slipped away, borrowed a Mimì shawl from the costume department—what Italian house doesn't have a *Bohème* somewhere, all set to go?—and swept out with the cleaning women, no doubt chattering away in Napuletan', her native dialect.

This subworld of opera besieged by fascism is another aspect of the art that American singers have no ken of. There is one political situation unique to American opera, in the racist resistance to black singers that limited them to obscure all-black troupes or to careers as recitalists. Broadway opened up a stage for black opera before bigtime "art" houses did—typically, for opera's social pretensions would not admit of any revolutionary racial integration, while most of the leadership talent on Broadway was itself of outcast stock (mainly Jewish and Irish) and often politically motivated. The black baritone Jules Bledsoe found work in *Deep River* and the original *Show Boat,* and of course *Porgy and Bess* continued to provide a major source of professional stage work for black singers from its premiere in 1935, through the famous 1953 revival that marked Leontyne Price's first major assignment, on to the 1976 revival with Clamma Dale, Donnie Ray Albert, and Carol Brice. By the mid-1940s there was yet so little opportunity for important black opera that the outstanding performance of a repertory opera by a black cast was a Broadway project, *Carmen Jones,* virtually Bizet's opera with the original dialogue instead of recitative, sung in English translation and reset in the American south. Certainly mezzo Muriel Smith, a Curtis graduate, never had a more prominent chance to sing Carmen—nor a more instinctively theatrical atmosphere in which to develop her interpretation.*

The notable change in policy occurred at the New York City Opera in its old home at the Mecca Temple (renamed the City Center in the 1940s). Such singers as Camilla Williams and Lawrence Winters sang white parts to little socialist fanfare, for City Center was "popular-priced" opera. It didn't Matter. Not till the Met cast Marian Anderson as Ulrica in *Un Ballo in Maschera* in 1955 was opera's racial integration considered official in America, though Anderson only did the one part (at that some years after her vocal prime had ended, in a role for which she was temperamentally a little staid) while Williams had been a regular member of the City Center company, multi-

---

*Smith did sing Carmen on major stages thereafter—Covent Garden, for instance, in the mid-1950s—but nothing in the opera world quite matches the thespian flair and reputation (and recording tie-in) of a hit Broadway musical.

parted. By an odd footnote, Anderson was not the first of her race to grace the Met, as a black dancer, Janet Collins, had preceded her. Still, breakthroughs in opera are made by singers, not dancers, so a footnote it remains.

Anderson's Ulrica was greeted as a splendid event, even if it does demystify her underdog's legend somewhat to learn that she had been referring to herself in the first person plural for quite some time before. Under Bing, the Met pursued black artists throughout the rest of the decade—Robert McFerrin, Mattiwilda Dobbs, Gloria Davy, Martina Arroyo, and George Shirley in that chronological order. It was not surprising, but still relevant, to note that this little group displayed little racial identity, instead typifying facets of the singer confraternity in general. Dobbs was leggiero, Arroyo clearly meant for Verdi. McFerrin showed no distinction; Shirley revealed an acute sense of theatre and superb exploitation of text. Some came to the Met in small parts—Arroyo, appropriately, as *Don Carlos'* Heavenly Voice—others in leads, and Dobbs had European glitter to back her up, with credits from La Scala, Glyndebourne, and Covent Garden.

One black soprano, however, came Metward in a distinctively racial atmosphere, and has remained the world's resident black soprano ever since: Leontyne Price. In Price, artist and public figure merge, despite her personal distaste for PR projection. A role model for young black singers, Price is more broadly an example of how to do justice to opera and oneself, how to spend commitment and take one's time. Some of Price's saga typifies opera: the miscellany of parts at the start of the career, when one collects experience more than applies it; the enlightening mistake in overstepping Fach (that Met *Fanciulla*), not made again; the gradual emphasizing of great roles over experiments. But the unusual is more typical of Price: her Verdian timbre, so authoritative that it has become the sound around which modern Verdians navigate; her outstanding series of recorded aria recitals, spanning an amazing breadth of stylistics and always urging rarities on the ear—*Vanessa, Atalanta, Francesca da Rimini, Dialogues des Carmelites;* her identification with the Great American Voice-Eater, Gershwin's Bess, abandoned long ago, yet still a vital recollection and a uniquely American possibility in opera; and Price's lon-

gevity, that singing on the interest: "Don't use your principal."

Price is open and humorous on the subject of race; in this
she was somewhat ahead of her time, when everyone was sensitive on the issue, grimly looking forward to a lengthy transitional era of letting novelty wear into convention. With her
vocal endowment, she *had* to sing Aida, and assumed the part
in San Francisco as a replacement for Antonietta Stella. By
telephone the woman in charge of costuming, who knew nothing of Price, recommended earth tones, because the outfits
would have to be cleaned after each performance to remove
that dark body makeup. Price told her, "I've got that dark body
makeup built in." Wisely, she did not make her Met debut in
Aida. From the start it was one of her great roles; but that's
the easy way in for a black singer, not *transitional* enough.
Verdi was right for the occasion, but let it be something set
apart from the racial issue. Let it be a soprano's debut, period:
pure opera. The Met offered her *Il Trovatore* and she took it,
breaking one of the cardinal rules of sage soprano careerman-
ship: *never* make a joint debut with someone hot, because the
other debutant may grab the notices. Price's Manrico was
Franco Corelli—but if you have Price's talent, you aren't risking much in the end.

The ethnicity of the American singer is unlike that of any
other nation's divas in America's pervasive demotic praxis. As
an institution, popular music is more American than opera is,
if only because all of the popular operas (except *Porgy and Bess*)
are *not* American. And American divas, in concert or on records, must sooner or later get around to popular music. This
is not by way of proletarian solidarity, nothing so condescend-
ing. It is because this is the best way the American ear can
place a voice. Folk music is considered apropos, being neither
here nor there. Hot licks, however, can trouble one's reputation: the Bing Met viewed with a leery eye Helen Traubel and
Eileen Farrell for their engagements with—and, worse, loving
expertise in—blues styles. Christmas records are acceptable—
good "for the industry" (they sell amazingly well) and temper-
ing opera's crusty flamboyance with universalistic Christian-
ity, an informal piety. And of course American opera singers
have been recording the mainstream of American popular mu-

sic since the early acoustic era. Few sopranos, from Carolina White to Beverly Sills, have not paid their homage to Victor Herbert or Jerome Kern.

It is interesting when a diva defines the solemnity of her Kunst by pointedly avoiding pop music—Callas, for instance. Perhaps she felt that verismo was already pop enough as it was. It is more interesting when a diva explains her versatility by reveling in fine pop music—Price, again. Sutherland and Sills have played Lehár's merry widow on stage, Renata Scotto used "Send in the Clowns" as an encore piece when the ink was still wet on the sheets, and Teresa Stratas gave a recital of unknown Kurt Weill. It sounds like pieces of a submovement, perhaps, a cute little side-Fach one might call *Stimm-kitsch*. Yet how different these performances, each from another. Neither Sutherland nor Sills is a merry anything. Scotto's Sondheim is lovely but incorrect. And Stratas is so right in Weill that Lotte Lenya is no longer the touchstone in the style. Still, taken together, these and similar tries make a welcome note of ecumenical canto from otherwise Fach-demented divas—like, again, Callas, obsessed with opera, then obsessed with getting out of it, then trying to climb back in too late. A "popular" diva, singing, so to say, "our" music, tells us that music theatre is not mapped exclusively between Monteverdi and Zimmermann: tells that vivacity, the vernacular idiom, and lowdown amusement are musical. This is the diva as opinion-maker, an international archon promoting art in its widest variety. A diva can't make history but she can change your life.

One aspect of the diva's public image corresponds to those of the woman thespian, movie star, and even writer and television news-reader: the diva as glamorous figure, as fashion-setter, charmer, beauty. This is the far side of temperament, the opera singer in her offstage Presentations. "It's nice not to be a prima donna," says Janet Baker. Acting out in a day-to-day situation is "distracting from the job you have to do." Baker has no use for the frippery and fury of diva. She'll even ride the London underground. But, says Dorothy Kirsten, "I've tried to maintain the image of the prima donna all through the years." It's more than acquiring a look, throwing off a sure sense of style. It's demanding the star dressing room, the star entrance, the last curtain call.

Perhaps the difference between Baker's and Kirsten's views of stardom lies in the different views of opera, European versus American. In Europe, opera's dignity and glory are tacitly assumed. Opera is not "respectable," but a thing set apart on its own terms. It doesn't need respect: it is self-respecting. In America, opera cannot quite give up the notion that it must prove itself democratically, appeal to the greatest number possible, as if all song must be popular. Enrico Caruso, for instance, was inveigled before the silent cameras, though his experience projecting grandiose costume parts into cavernous theaters could hardly have served him well in the tight range of the camera, and though a silent Caruso was worthless in the first place. The money was good—over two hundred thousand dollars for six weeks' work—but the films were not. The second wasn't even released.

Oddly, one opera singer did become a silent star, a genuine one, with the swank of glamour and the gift of mime: Geraldine Farrar. She was bright enough to figure out how film worked and make it hers. For starters, she filmed *Carmen,* a sure bet. To continue, she played roles that would make use of what Farrar used onstage, great clothes and naked passion. And to end, she got out before the films grew too awful or the movie audience too used to her. And she pulled off the whole series with such aplomb that, instead of film's giving Farrar a boost in egalitarian likability, Farrar gave film a boost in high diva style. To rephrase Katharine Hepburn's summation of Fred Astaire and Ginger Rogers, Farrar gave the movies class and sex.

Of course Farrar was in any case one of those exceptional divas whose reputations expand well beyond the bounds of the music community. The "Gerryflappers" who made Farrar nights into outings of hero worship were the sort who would in later ages be screaming for Frankie the Voice or fantasizing a date with Ringo. No other diva of Farrar's day had such impact, not even Melba or Mary Garden. Melba's instrument was the finer; Garden was as famed as Farrar for acting. But Farrar had a glamour they did not have, a very particular glamour in which her remarkably intent singing, her extraordinary looks, and her charismatic plastique were inextricably merged. Too, she had a splendid sense of role: each one she sang—and she sang many—was a great one, or felt so while Farrar sang it. Manon and Carmen are proved vehicles, of course, and Farrar's Butterfly, for which she prepared by going around for weeks in kimono, tiny one-toe sandals, and shaved eyebrows, was regarded as incomparable.* Even odd and virtually unpopular items like Humperdinck's *Königskinder,* Leoncavallo's *Zazà,* and Giordano's *Madame Sans-Gêne* sold out with Farrar in the name parts, because they brought out a sexual vitality that her temperament fostered, both subtly (as Humperdinck's radiant goosegirl—with real geese, by the way) and overtly (in verismo). "Zazà in the role of Geraldine Farrar is a sensation," wrote critic James Huneker of *The New York Times,* noting in jest the strong identity Farrar gave her characters. Here is something more than musicianship and commitment: a personality so grandly intimate it can capture the gypsy hellcat and the village maid, the sophisticate and the saint. Another sensation in the role of Geraldine Farrar was Wagner's Elisabeth.

Opera stardom has a glamour particular to opera and its high requirements. Other performers need not be so accomplished as singers: actors needn't sing well and movie actors needn't even act. (Dancers are in another world altogether.) Still, a diva may borrow glamour from other performing mediums. Farrar, again, didn't derive luster from Hollywood, for when she made movies the cinema was not yet acculturated as a bourgeois pursuit.** A generation later, however, Grace Moore was able to exploit Hollywood when the first talkies,

---

*Puccini wrote as much on the photograph he gave Farrar, but in fact he thought her unsatisfactory; he liked more voice in this part. Farrar later said he may have been put off by her habit of marking at rehearsals, a survival tactic absolutely necessary for a voice that was, for much of its career, working well beyond Fach.

**Farrar's *Carmen* came out in 1915, the year of *The Birth of a Nation.* Before that, movies were primarily anonymous shorts made for a proletarian audience. D. W. Griffith's Civil War epic, so stunning that everyone in the nation went to see it, began the renovation of the medium as middle-class art.

unsure of their destiny but certain they had better be as musical as possible, were featuring Met stars. Moore's first films, for MGM, bombed: she wasn't ready for them and they weren't right for her—especially not the pseudo-biography of Jenny Lind, *A Lady's Morals*. But Moore tried again after a bit, at Columbia, saw her first entry there, *One Night of Love*, become a worldwide blockbuster, and instantly redefined the measure of glamour in opera stardom.

Before Moore, this glamour was elusive; Moore spread it wide, through a personality so dazzling that few realized that her movie career amounted to a program in Opera Reaches the Masses. Moore's Columbias had a lot of opera in them—in rehearsals and onstage in full kit—and this was not their least attraction. A very wide audience that seldom set foot in an opera house rallied for Moore, taking her earthy poise as a direct complement to the elegance of her music. The movies themselves were not glamorous: Moore was. Her earlier MGMs were lavish costume pictures, designed, as all MGMs were, to teach fashion and charm. Overburdened by the responsibility, Moore was wary and imperious, not glamorous. Columbia, however, was a studio halfway between the majors and the shabby genre factories of Gower Gulch, and Moore's Columbias were unpretentious modern-dress comedies, anything but lavish. That was the point: in these films Moore could relax and let her charm shine. And, of course, when she sang, one caught the glamour of life-loving, free-swinging art. She was known to be difficult—could one, in the 1930s, be an opera-singing movie star and *not* be thought difficult? There is a glamour in being impossible. But those who knew Moore thought her bitchiness was meant to cover for an inadequate education. Musicality she certainly had—this was what gave her films such ring and feeling in the face of ludicrous plotting and Columbia's theatre-of-the-absurd "high fashion" costuming, every hat a satin teepee trimmed with bell pulls. Nor were the supporting casts anything to turn out for. Moore and music carried these films. She knew music—or, rather, how to sing. Argot she lacked. So when Fritz Reiner and she were not coming to terms at a rehearsal for a broadcast, Reiner lost patience and pulled rank with one term too many and Moore lashed back, "Who the hell do you think you are to tell me how to sing 'Carry Me Back to Old Virginny'?" After all, the man was from Budapest, Moore from Tennessee. She's closer to the source.

Two more vignettes turn the key into Moore's appeal, factoring her breezy style, her informality of glamour. Farrar, lecturing during intermissions on Saturday-afternoon Met broadcasts, came off rather *grande dame,* not so much glamorous as regal—they're quite different things. But Moore was always the kid as diva. One of these two images, from *One Night of Love,* presents Moore singing "Ciribiribin" in a tavern. There have been hundreds of such scenes in film. But Moore's has something the others don't: Moore. The tune is irresistible, the crowd impressionable, and the diva at her best; she makes Pestalozza sound like Puccini. When she brings all present in for a singalong, the screen swings. This scene alone would have sent *One Night of Love* to the top—its infectious waltz tune actually had whole theatres joining in in Italy. The second image gives another side of Moore, one just as pertinent. On the Met's spring tour, womanizer Ezio Pinza is enlarging on some conquest when Moore's voice cuts through from a corner. "Oh, get off it, Ezio. Everyone knows you're the worst lay in the Met."

Perhaps glamour takes in a certain earthiness as well as a radiance: Farrar and Moore had both. And certainly the opera divas who tried and failed to equal them in Hollywood did lack their sensuality. Lily Pons' *I Dream Too Much* felt silly, and one couldn't make out her words through the French accent. Gladys Swarthout never got the hang of film; she seems to be forever trying to locate the conductor. Rosa Ponselle's screen test is a nightmare of nerves and uncertainty. "Show us Carmen," some churl orders; and she doesn't. She shows them an opera singer working a fan.

Glamour flipped over by the next generation, in the age of Callas. If Farrar had It and Moore had fun, Callas had fame: glamour was headlines. Callas was, like them, a form of Cinderella. Farrar was the Massachusetts kid who went to Europe, auditioned (for, among others, Cosima Wagner, who was looking for a legitimate virgin for *Die Meistersinger*), took a job *als Gast* with the Berlin State Opera, won a contract and the heart of the Crown Prince, and came home a star. Moore was the southern girl who cut through the nonsense from Reiner to Pinza. And Callas? It depends on which legend you prefer. She was the Brooklyn scrub who becomes queen of La Scala; or the klutz with the ankles of a Kraken who slims down to jet-set trim; or the extra mouth who makes herself irreplaceable; or the disregarded and even despised woman who had to make it on her own, and, having done so, realized that she was truly on her own: alone; and who eventually died of loneliness. And the only thing that isn't true of all of the above is that cliché of being born in Brooklyn. She was born in Manhattan.

Is glamour beauty? Callas became beautiful by force of will. Is glamour talent? Callas had it. Is glamour that . . . you know, that Something? Callas was unique. Is glamour the attraction of success, the wanting to know about winners? Surely: but the public likes the scandal of defeat, and Callas had plenty of this, too. Eventually, however, glamour in Callas became anything in Callas, from her irreproachable musicianship to an uncouth high note, from her diet to her acting, from a Scala triumph to a Scala debacle. The woman made news simply by being there, anywhere she was, at home, at an airport, at a party . . . even onstage in an opera. The news itself was the glamour. The fame begot more fame.

How different this is from Farrar and Moore, in whom glamour was locked into the art, the performances. It varied when they crashed the movies, or when anecdotes slipped out of a stormy rehearsal into the ozone; but still the fame always related to Farrar or Moore as an artist. Much of Callas' fame had nothing to do with her opera performances, her movie, her rehearsals. Since Callas, it is no longer clear what constitutes glamour in opera. Beauty? Old-timers speak of Maria Jeritza, but older timers say no one could compete with Lina Cavalieri. She was so gorgeous no one recalls what she sounded like because they were engrossed in staring at her. She retired to Florence and died in an air raid while relishing her jewels; and Jeritza died in 1982, without a successor, unless one counts the Europeanized American Anna Moffo, and few do. Moffo has the beauty and talent. But if Cavalieri and Jeritza created a kind of glamour, it was an *operatic* kind, whereas Moffo seems like a movie star who sang opera instead of making movies. So passes the notion of an entirely operatic beauty.

What, then, of vanity? That corner of glamour is gone. The things they doted on in Melba they excoriate in Scotto. Style? There's some left here and there. Moffo had her moments. Catherine Malfitano will attend Met performances in state, beautifully and distinctively dressed, with her singer's eyes and mouth. Even those who can't place her name nudge each other and murmur, "See: the diva passes." Style is rare, beauty defunct, vanity in disrepute. Where's glamour? And who wants it? Would *La Traviata* be less affecting if La Scala's ushers were not in livery? Does a Met *Rosenkavalier* lose presence because half the audience is underdressed?

The trouble is, opera is largely about glamour: about beautiful women in romantic disasters. One need not be particularly glamorous (in a physical sense) to portray these women, as Lotte Lehmann proved with her Marschallin, one of the most glamorous figures in opera. Lehmann's lack of diva bite hurt her Tosca; her mind just didn't grasp the externals that style glamour for the mob, the *cosmetics* of glamour. In Eugen D'Albert's *Die Toten Augen,* Lehmann played a blind girl who recovers her sight. As written, the character immediately asks for a mirror, but Lehmann didn't sympathize with such triviality, and asked the composer to change the scene: she, recovering sight, would want to see the sky.

This is the glamour of imagination, of ingenuous musicianship and impressive commitment. One imagines Pauline Viardot doing something of the like, Viardot the lover of and even advisor to some of the nineteenth century's remarkable men. Perhaps it is uniqueness of talent that makes opera's best glamour. This is true of Farrar, Moore, Callas, Lehmann, and many others who don't, as a group, share definition in any other quality. Opera's glamour is that of remarkable women, finding an outlet in opera that no other profession open to them (in Viardot's age especially) could provide. "I would not have found it possible," writes Janet Baker, "to give up my career for anyone or anything. There would have been absolutely no contest. All the people who have surrounded me, from my parents onwards, have understood and accepted this. . . . Music has come first and life second."

Baker managed to accommodate a marriage; Mary Garden did not even love. She thought men foolish, most so when they fell for her and began talking nonsense. Like Baker, Garden helps widen the meaning of glamour, reminds us that opera's glamour does not necessarily walk with that of other professions. No wonder then that its national-cultural concerns and political edge so impel the diva's responsibility, her sense of obligation as a public figure. Opera is big, makes its people big, and makes us feel big along with them. The scope of its subject matter in such works as *Der Ring des Nibelungen* or *Les Troyens* or *Norma* enters into it as well. There is a glamour in living up to the proportions of apocalyptic love and death. Mary Garden was so big that, over seventy years ago, long before it was the fashion to make fame by assassinating a celebrity, Garden was nearly murdered in Philadelphia by a fan, apparently just because she was Mary Garden. Her eagerness to get back to her ailing mother in New York saved her: to ensure a fast return she closed her dressing room to all visitors and raced into her car. The fan, a young woman, was furious at being turned away; as she moved off, a revolver fell out of her muff. Two days later the woman shot herself, naming Garden as her stimulation.

Garden called this act "demented." She takes the word right out of my mouth.

CHAPTER

7

THE MAESTRO

*If there is no trouble in a house,
then I make trouble.*
                    Erich Kleiber

*The most important quality in a
conductor? Humility, humility.*
                    Arturo Toscanini

*A good coach is like a good
psychiatrist.*
                    Catherine Malfitano

The maestro is opera's absolute point of contact between artist and art. Voice and musicianship, language and diction, expression and characterization—all inform his instruction. If opera has one superintendent leadership, it is that of the maestro. The stage director may say that if opera is theatre, he is most crucial. But no, opera is *music* theatre in which, throughout all eras, musical values have overridden dramatic values. Nor will it avail the director's suggestion that this is what has been wrong with opera throughout all eras: those who perform opera as well as those who attend it subscribe to the musical bias. Singers who can't act have always found a place in opera—but actors who can't sing? Never. Even Wilhelmine Schröder-Devrient, of Chorley's despised "nature-singing," was nevertheless a singer, however flawed. And a famous instance of "theatre" casting—Verdi's of Marianna Barbieri-Nini as the first Lady Macbeth because he wanted someone "ugly and malignant" with a voice "rough, hollow, stifled"—remains a matter of musical casting. Verdi wasn't asking for someone who couldn't sing. He was asking for a different sound—a certain kind of singer, not actress.

Designers, too, have laid claim to being the crucial quotient in opera production: is opera not spectacle? And yes, in certain instances a strong-looking production overwhelms direction and casting if these latter are weak, or become weak through seasons of half-hearted revival. Still, who wants to hear an opera that looks better than it sounds?

From the start, opera has been a business strictly for insiders, and the insiders are all musicians. Occasionally a poet or dramatist of polished sympathies stands within the circle, as did the librettists of the first *dramme in musica,* as much opera's theorists as its servants; as did Arrigo Boito, a musician who not only wrote librettos for other men but set a few for himself, besides presiding over the artistic life of Milan; as did Hugo von Hofmannsthal, a highly cultivated writer who knew as much about opera as many a musician; as did Giovacchino Forzano, librettist to Mascagni, Puccini, Leoncavallo, and Wolf-Ferrari, who abandoned a second-rate potential as a baritone because his sense of leadership in theatre was first-rate, empowering him to stage some of the most important premieres of his day, that of *Turandot* among them.

With such men, composers entered into vital, canny partnerships. But such men were few. Basically, opera comprised the composer and the singers in uneasy collaboration, the composer serving as his own conductor, coach, and troubleshooter (sometimes director as well) and the singers eternally playing their need for great composition against the public's need for great singing. Conductors who exclusively performed other men' music came late in opera's history, stage directors even later. Gradually, the composer's predominance as a technician of performance declined. By the mid-1800s a composer might superintend the rehearsals and conduct the first two nights of his latest work, as Verdi did for the world premiere of *I Masnadieri* at Her Majesty's in London. Thereafter, each piece would travel on its own to fare as best it might in other hands.

By the 1900s, when the acknowledged classics had survived their authors and could be excellently re-created without them, the use of the composer-conductor-director was neutralized, and specialists rose up to factor the job. Music directors would oversee the productions to the general and the specific, from matters of style to the portamento on Mimì's "Bada." Stage directors and designers would take each work from the rehearsal room onto the stage. House *répétiteurs* (or coaches) would drill the singers, taking them through their parts at the piano to consider questions of diction and phrasing, perhaps passing on crucial points of tradition, from Patti's way with a phrase to Boninsegna's. The conductor's commission includes all of the above, for the most powerful conductors run the companies, choose, cast, and stage the works, coach the singers, and edit the recording tapes. Opera is musical above all—but even if this were debatable, it could still be proved by the maestro's ubiquitous administration. He is, then, the diva's greatest asset, mentor, nurse, promoter, even lover—and sometimes bitter foe.

In a limited sense, the diva's first maestro is her voice teacher, though only Italians routinely apply "Maestro" to professors of voice production. (Similarly, "Dottore" might address just about anyone holding a university degree; Italian terms of respect tend to the expansive.) The distinction between the technician who trains the instrument in its formative years and the musicians who develop its musicological, musico-dramatic, and purely vocal-sensual perspectives in maturity is an important one. These are two jobs that, like the halves of the composer-conductor métier of ancient days, have been inseparably diversified. They are even mutually antagonistic, teachers attacking conductors for their spendthrift volume that forces a tender voice, and conductors impatient with teachers' dainty ministrations. Teachers care about singing; conductors care about music. So say the conductors. But the teachers say conductors are mystical where they should be technical, patriarchal instead of collaborative.

Teaching has its mysteries, too. Once it was a relatively severe science of internationally acknowledged "Italian" exercises; now it is a miscellany of traditional approaches, modifications, innovations, and wildcatting. The field is further clouded by the rumor that some teachers are good for some voices, other teachers for other voices. Nonsense. Each body is different, but there is *one* way to sing, and teaching against that way is chicanery. The best teachers are the ancient teachers—the devisers of the eighteenth-century exercise books. Master their exercises and one is a singer. A favorite opera legend finds the singer and composer but mainly teacher Niccolo Porpora training the castrato Caffarelli for five years on one sheet of vocal calisthenics, followed by a sixth year with added lessons in verbal articulation. The sixth year passed, Porpora dismissed Caffarelli in unique graduation as "the first singer of Italy and of the world." And so, to many ears, Caffarelli had become, installing himself in the indexes of the great in due course.

The tale is fanciful, but its point is well taken. Whether or not Caffarelli was truly and well trained without singing a single aria, to perform opera one must know how to sing, and to sing one must assimilate technique. Can one do so without a teacher? What would Caffarelli have been like had he pursued this course of study without Porpora—arguing (for they say Caffarelli was high-strung and restless) that he could have done? Surely one needs an extra ear, an editor, a don: a maestro. He or she wields the crucial influence on a young singer; but, given the vast enrichment of the repertory since Caffarelli's day, how is one to know when the voice is fully composed—when, so to say, one's Porporian six years are up? Was Caffarelli ready to sing, for instance, Janáček? Schoenberg? Handel?

This question of timing has as many answers as there are divas to ask it. One soprano assures you that once the voice learns how, it is there to stay indefinitely, like breathing. Another soprano wonders if the muscles "forget" after too long a period without a teacher's advice, or after sneaking into unfamiliar repertory. A third says she may not need lifetime study but that maintaining rapport with a teacher cannot hurt and —who knows?—might help. A fourth shudders at the very notion of teachers altogether, recalling her scrapes with some two or three "well-meaning charlatans" who nearly destroyed her instrument. A fifth soprano says a daily prayer for the teacher who put hers to rights when she encountered vocal difficulties in mid-career.

This raises a second question—how does a singer know whether her teacher is assisting or impeding her progress? It is not invariably clear at first. A certain pedagogy might liberate the voice rather quickly; another might tell gradually;

yet another might yield fast and delightful results in the always sluggishly developing middle range only to weaken the top in ways that don't become clear for years. Sadly, the days of the one, true Neapolitan academics are long gone; so, how is one to choose among today's various approaches, some contentiously "orthodox" and some innovative? "Look out for teachers with freak methods!" Mary Garden warns. "The chances are they are making you one of their experiments." And what was Garden's reading of "freak" in the methods? "No voice teacher," she opines, "has ever found anything superior to giving simple scales and exercises sung upon the syllables 'lah,' 'leh,' and 'lee.' " Well, that's that.

No, it isn't. Granting that scales on vowels are the prime component, still, different teachers teach different scales, hear with different ears, shoot for different goals. Then there is the worry that a teacher might be a failed singer himself; if a singer cannot *do,* can a singer teach? But there are reasons for "failing" that have nothing to do with the mastery of one's voice—a reprochable timbre, perhaps, or a dull stage presence. Until recently, tradition decreed that singers turned into teachers upon retirement from the theatre. Having proved their abilities, they were qualified to pass the wisdom on (or to pass on sloppy habits). And of course by this method one always knew what one was getting, for a singer who had just closed three decades of secure projection of the voice was clearly a good bet as a teacher, while a singer notorious for a wobbly top or wayward intonation clearly was not. Yet we are still not home free in the selection of a teacher, for a singer who knows how to sing doesn't necessarily know how to convey technique to others. Some who can do *cannot* teach: for teaching, too, is a gift.

Coaching is a gift of a different kind. The teacher assumes that the student's voice is there and only needs to be developed. The coach assumes that the voice is developed and now needs artistic direction. Some teachers can coach. The Italian divas of the verismo era who went into conservatory teaching regularly shared their theatrical expertise with their pupils, who were after all preparing roles that some of these women had themselves created, or at any rate were working on comparable parts. Renata Tebaldi's teacher, Carmen Melis, not only arranged for Tebaldi's debut, as Elena in *Mefistofele* at Rovigo, but also took her through the part in a ten-day cramming session and stood by in the wings to deliver official approval after it was over. Melis, one of the most delectable stylists of what was to her contemporary opera, was in one way more sage as teacher than as singer: having hurt her voice by falling into the verismo trap of giving too much, of singing on the principal, and of singing beyond Fach as Sieglinde and Salome, she could with authority warn her pupils against such follies. So, while she and Tebaldi shared such parts as Tosca, Adriana, and Mrs. Ford, Tebaldi avoided much of Melis' *carta* and kept her Tosca within certain limits, so much volume for each act, so much oomph on the famous lines, so much chest voice, so much on the high Cs, so much and no more. As teacher, Melis enriched the voice; as coach, she tamed the interpretation.

How precisely does a coach work? Catherine Malfitano terms her practice with Janine Reiss "creative stimulation," emphasizing coaching as collaboration. A rudimentary coach and an unimaginative singer may use their time to pound through a part for memory drill or language brush-up, but the Malfitano-Reiss duet is an evolutionary process of characterological explication. Reiss doesn't have to correct Malfitano's French or cry out "Five, six, seven, eight" as an aria begins. There is no "teaching" as such—rather, it is two musicians inspiring each other, a *personal* experience of trying and testing based on artistic empathy.

If the singer-teacher relationship is often that of the child to the parent, singer and coach are more like siblings or best friends, even lovers. Opera history is studded with backstage tales of divas and conductors who became so involved in the expounding of character at the piano that they went on to expound a characterful romance, like the pianist and violinist in the famous Tabu perfume ad, caught erupting into a fabulous kiss (during, one imagines, the Liebestod). A few pages hence we shall catch the eruptions of Toscanini and Mahler; for now, consider the better-known coach-and-diva teams of Elisabeth Schwarzkopf and Walter Legge and of Joan Sutherland and Richard Bonynge.

Just to name the two pairs is to reveal the breadth of the coach's personality and art. Legge was technically not a musician but the A-and-R man (in charge of artists and repertory) of EMI Records, while Bonynge was a coach who became a conductor. Legge imposed living tradition as his model, drawing on the recordings of the fabled great; Bonynge had to reach back to a vanished age whose exponents had not recorded. Schwarzkopf was versatile, as assured in operetta as in the grand style, sound in coloratura and ample of legato, tackling French, Italian, and Slavic music as well as German—and Legge celebrated this wide reach, till by the time her career was over she had sung just about everything but *Fiddler on the Roof*. Bonynge's Sutherland, on the other hand, was focused upon bel canto, stepping out of it with variable success—accomplished Massenet, sedative verismo. Moreover, Legge's powerful base in the recording industry allowed him to channel his wife's energies toward EMI's output, letting her cut her stage repertory down to a few great roles, whereas Sutherland and Bonynge kept adding to their catalogue, putting each new performance onto both stage and disc.

Legge, a record buff from childhood, must have been shocked to learn that Schwarzkopf owned no phonograph; she made her own music. They met just after World War II had ended, in Vienna, where Legge was collecting artists for EMI's repertory. He was quite ready to sign her, but she insisted on auditioning for him in detail, convincing him that he had not an interesting singer on his hands but a fascinating one. He recalled her saying, "I don't want you to buy a cat in a sack and regret it, and I don't want you to offer me less than you think I am worth." All this is valid; perhaps Schwarzkopf also saw the audition (for, remember, the head man at a world-class recording company) as a chance to impress upon him her adaptability. Till then she had been typecast as a lyric-leggiero, so she pointedly painted Legge a broad canvas at the audition. It was her moment of crossover, from Stimmdiva to Kunstdiva. Legge was so impressed that they began their coaching that day:

> I started to work with her on a very difficult little Hugo
> Wolf song, "Wer rief dich denn?," bar by bar, word by

word, inflection by inflection, a song demanding changing emotions often on one syllable, one note: it was the beginning of the way we were to work together for the next twenty-nine years.

Legge also took Schwarzkopf in hand to the phonograph, "to widen," he said, "her imaginative concept of the possibilities of vocal sound." Ponselle, Melba, Seinemeyer, Schumann, Leider, and others were played into Schwarzkopf's imagination, not for imitative duplication but, as Malfitano says, for "creative stimulation." As an example of the alchemy of the process, it was Farrar's Carmen that informed the undulating suave of Schwarzkopf's operetta style.

As coach, Legge broadened Schwarzkopf's foundation (in her recording assignments), centralized her imperious prestige (in his emphasis on the Marschallin, the *Capriccio* Countess, Donna Elvira, Fiordiligi, the *Figaro* Countess, and merry widow Hanna Glawari, all magisterial roles in which Schwarzkopf was incomparable), and enlightened the tact and thrust of her phrasing till she became, depending on private taste, either the most mannered singer of the postwar era or *espressiva assoluta*. It was one of the most influential coach-singer processes in opera, forging in Schwarzkopf's tireless renown as a recitalist a link between the subtlety of Lieder and the larger storytelling forms of opera.

This enhancement of the grand line with verbal petit-point is a phenomenon of the postwar age—the age of Legge, perhaps. In earlier eras Lieder and opera were more segregated, with, say, Elena Gerhardt, Clara Butt, and Marian Anderson on one hand, and Emmy Destinn, Rosetta Pampanini, and Zinka Milanov on the other. There was some crossover, especially from artists too intimate to neglect the recital platform, such as Marcella Sembrich (whose partitioned musicianship of soprano, pianist, and violinist provisioned unique concerts). Lotte Lehmann particularly was a model of the recitalist opera singer. But generally opera singers put on rather operatic recitals and Lieder artists avoided opera. An opera diva was larger than life, a recitalist subterranean. Schwarzkopf proved one could be both, profoundly textual in opera and momentous in Lieder. Similarly, such singers as Dietrich Fischer-Dieskau and Janet Baker have made the connection; if it seemed like a wondrous aberration in Lotte Lehmann's day, it has now become a cornerstone of Kunst.

Sutherland and Bonynge have been as influential as Schwarzkopf and Legge, in an entirely different way: to the general away from the precise phrase and to a few *spécialités de maison* away from the Schwarzkopftisch smorgasbord. When Schwarzkopf tried Hanna Glawari, Lehár style was set on an international level. When Sutherland dared the widow, it was dowdy boogie.

Yet Sutherland's voice in its instrumental potential is not as limited as Sutherland's repertory or her sense of genre turned out to be. It is intriguing to contemplate what different history she might have made if Bonynge had been engrossed in Verdi rather than in Bellini, or even in verismo. Sutherland has sung Verdi, but somewhat as a foreigner, more a leggiero picking her way through Verdi's relatively backward-looking parts (such as Gilda or Amalia in *I Masnadieri*) than a native Verdian. But surely this is the voice for *Ernani, Les Vêpres Siciliennes, Un Ballo in Maschera, Otello*. Sutherland's Aida would probably sound like the Aidas of Verdi's day—remember, Patti and Tetrazzini sang it—and with Verdian coaching might bridge the gap between their approach and that of our time. Verdi himself thought it sane practice that the embellishments of bel canto be retired in favor of a cleaner line, as witness his remarks on Jenny Lind, the original Amalia:

> If she would come to Italy I am sure she would sing differently and abandon her mania for embellishments, because she has a voice even and flexible enough to sustain a phrase simply.

If she would come to Italy: if the transmontane artist could realign her art at the source, ethnicize herself. This might almost be Verdi on Sutherland, on Bonynge's bel-canto emphases, on that quotient of their presentation that lacks Italianate elation. If coaching is, at its least, mere rehearsal and, at its best, a probe into opera's stimulation, it can also amount to directing an entire career: the Fach, the roles, even the bookings. As Sutherland's maestro, Bonynge provided the identity in which she arrived and continued; as Bonynge's diva, Sutherland enlisted major houses in the partnership by making Bonynge's conducting a perquisite of her engagement. Once Bonynge mastered stick technique, the deal proved salubrious. But the union is static, adding nothing to what Sutherland was able to show in those first world-shaking Lucias— in fact, showing less, in a sharply husbanded facsimile of character involvement. Holding back, letting the voice ring but seldom *urging* it unto dramatic situation, Sutherland supported an amazingly extended prime; at this writing she is nowhere near the need to sign out.

A distillation of the coach, both as Leggean expander and Bonyngesque curtailer, is the teacher of the master class, which, like youth, is wasted on the young. Usually taught by an acknowledged emeritus but to students who have no experience worth gauging, the master class is meant as edification on the level of highest artistry, more "vocal" than voice training and more musical than coaching, covering historical and stylistic and practical points, notes on everything. However, few students have the commitment and musicianship needed to absorb a master's lessons.Voice they may have, even temperament. But at the apprentice stage one is unable to encompass the master's perspective. Maria Callas underlined this when she canceled her master class at the Curtis Institute in Philadelphia after two days of wasting her time on novices. A bit later Juilliard mustered a quorum of tolerably promising kids, and Callas went to work.

Callas' Juilliard sessions are the most famous master classes in modern opera, partly because anything that happens in New York gets noticed and spoken of more than what happens elsewhere. The classes were supposedly open only to Juilliard students, but security was lax and, as Callas had not appeared onstage for seven years, pieces of an audience checked into the auditorium—critics, buffs, and fans. Those hoping to hear Callas actually perform were disappointed (though she did have a go at Rigoletto's "Cortigiani, vil razza dannata!"). But her eliciting commentary proved that great singing in-

volves self-knowledge (artistic if not personal) and historical
awareness more than "natural" aptitude or a mystical intui-
tion. Opera has its gifted primitives, but these are all Stimm'
personalities. A master class is for Kunst.

Callas couldn't have looked less the diva. Once she had
paraded the world in a state of near-blindness, nearsighted but
too vain to wear glasses; this was behind her now. Serene and
sleekly schoolmarmish, with that tart, charmless rationality
that had made her an interviewer's treasure, she asked, "Who
wants to sing?" and off she went, correcting, questioning, insisting, challenging. She was, in a terrible way, overqualified:
a woman who had ingested the wisdom of Serafin, de Sabata,
Giulini, and von Karajan trying to share it with kids who had
been nowhere and done nothing. Some barely knew their arias
at all. They were products of a television culture, muddled,
concentrated on bits of nothing, uninformed; she was music
itself. You must know the score. You must understand the
words. You must sing the notes. You must express. A mezzo
who went astray on the top note in Azucena's "Condotta ell'era
in ceppi" tried to defend herself by suggesting that the note
was "a cry of despair." "It's not a cry of despair," Callas snapped
back. "It's a B flat."

Yet, on the foundation of an austere belief in the black-
and-white of what composer and librettist wrote, Callas built
outward as each next singer presented some new problem. How
to feel the embellishments in Donizetti and Bellini—indeed,
where to introduce them and why. How to know one's Fach.
(Callas, who sang everything, didn't believe in it: "It is soprano, basta!") Which golden-age exercises to practice on. How
to stand, how to look, how to think. As maestra, Callas touched
every possibility, from the art of opera to the facts of its life.
Still, at the front and end of her course lay the dictum: Know
the Score.

So, again, the musician is paramount in opera, and the
conductor the paramount musician. Not only is he in charge
of the score on a moment-to-moment basis, he can, in its preparation, serve as its overwhelming leader—its coach, really.
Singers constantly refer to this in interviews. Janet Baker cites
John Barbirolli, Otto Klemperer, Carlo Maria Giulini, and

George Szell as generators of ideas: teachers. The best conductors do more than interpret a score; they nurture and incite it. They even coopt much of the job that in the spoken theatre belongs to the director, that of helping the performers realize their characters. Describing his responsibilities in an interview, Riccardo Muti once pointed out how much Verdi could write into a silence (and how much a singer should hear in it), in Aida's line "E quel sentier?" in the Nile Scene. This is the moment at which she must betray her Egyptian lover for her homeland, Ethiopia: at her question, meaning "And which route [will the Egyptian Army take in its attack on Ethiopia]?," Radames will reveal the troop movements to Aida's eavesdropping father, the Ethiopian king. Verdi set a tiny hesitation between *E* and *quel,* nudging Aida's reluctance in this squalid intrigue, and any soprano who sings Aida under Muti will be made party to Verdi's insight if she isn't already, at the piano through the maestro's explication. This is a case of character analysis, of scene structure—yet it lies in Muti's domain.

Nor is Muti poaching on the director's preserve. The conductor controls. He or she is the link between performance and composition, the one person in the theater committed to observing the authors' intentions. Singers are hungry for fame and harassed by the pressure to be succinctly brilliant, directors play around with concept, designers are more imaginative than correct, and audiences simply want an Important Evening. Only the conductor is obligated to the piece *as is,* as a fixed item in the catalogue of art, something that has not only a platonic essence but unalterable flesh and bones. Everyone else on the team realizes a work; to the conductor, it is already realized in black and white on the page and need only be played.

A lyric soprano might look at Leonora in *La Forza del Destino* and think, "I'll never get through it in full voice, but I spy cheating places, so I'll depend on temperament to get through 'Madre, pietosa Vergine,' pull out my pianissimos for 'La Vergine degli Angeli,' give them everything I've got in 'Pace, pace, mio Dio,' and croak through the Final Trio. After all, it *is* a death scene." A mezzo assigned Preziosilla might think,

"I can't get my mouth around all those notes in the 'Rataplan,' but then nobody has sung this part well since Ebe Stignani, so what have I to lose?" A director might see the piece as a metaphor for the futility of space travel and have the designer paint the action in *Star Wars* chrome, and the worst that can happen is: they tried. But if the conductor were to dismiss the woodwind for an act, or write a new part for the tympani, or introduce a piano into Verdi's nineteenth-century pit, he would be hooted out of town.

A conductor might institute cuts where "necessary" or make tiny adjustments in orchestration (though this has become much less acceptable since the reign of Leopold Stokowski, a devoted tamperer). But, in the end, the conductor holds the reins on the *quality* of stylistics: not only in how faithful a performance wants to be, but also in what excellence of execution it can achieve. "The conductor," says Zubin Mehta, "is often the only person aware of the entire expanse of a given work." And he must bridge the footlights, weld pit to voices, music to action. Janet Baker says singers call Charles Mackerras "Chuck-'em-up-Charlie" because of his sense of control:

> As the machinery of the performance is working, Charlie is always using his hands in the most extraordinarily helpful way to us singers. . . . There is a clarity of beat, a clarity of signal, and a particularly strong sixth sense for any mishaps, which gives you the impression that he is completely divided between stage and pit. And the rapport! . . . On a really good night, you feel as if the two of you are composing the music together there and then.

What if a conductor loses control? It happens. Karl Böhm once fell so under the spell of the *Tristan* love duet that he, Birgit Nilsson, and Wolfgang Windgassen began to float through the music as much as make it. German writers have expounded the mystical attraction of the *Tristan* love music as a love-as-death nirvana; inevitably these three *Tristan* specialists had, sooner or later, to forget their pacing, throat-clearing, and other parish expertise and fall into the magic themselves. Had Böhm not reawakened, the performance might have swooned into a kind of nirvana itself, leaving the audience feeling like shipwreck victims suddenly beached; but Böhm did reawaken, and his retrieved control is the ground-zero of what empowers opera. Control is epic and momentous, the whole idea and the minute-by-minute at once, and only the conductor wields it. He holds the greatest potential in opera in an evening's success or failure.

Some say that the notion of an opera house run by anyone but a conductor is lunacy. Even where informed administrators have run major companies, a music director has usually played a significant part in the proceedings. Typically, while the postwar Italian houses all submitted to appointed chiefs, the actual work of planning and producing the productions fell to the presiding artists. (Thus the photograph of Toscanini, de Sabata, Votto, and Callas consulting at La Scala—no Ghiringhelli.) Note also that in Vienna greatness in leadership ran to conductors, not impresarios—Mahler, Weingartner, Schalk, Krauss, Walter, Böhm, von Karajan, Maazel. It is especially notable that the emergence of Covent Garden as one of the top companies began not with the desperate, patriotic, and resourceful grinding out of repertory under David Webster in the 1940s and 1950s but with the at first controversial and at length stimulating leadership of Webster's music director Georg Solti in the 1960s. Even Rudolf Bing, an impresario quite capable of deciding What and Who by himself, did—to an extent—try to arrange something like a tenure for someone like a music director. As this would, however, have meant ceding his despotic rule to that of the musician, nothing came of it.

After all, the better the conductor, the tougher he is. Tough about text, about voice, about tempo, about casting. It is only the conductor who retains the right to "protest" a singer—i.e., demand a replacement. No designer can protest the way a singer fills a costume, and the number of directors who have had singers replaced for rudimentary acting ability is few despite a high proportion of rudimentary actors among the singing cohort. Nor do singers, no matter how prominent, protest conductors in their turn. It happens rarely and invariably creates a scandal, as recently at the Met, when Ileana Cotrubas made public her scorn for Eugene Kohn's conducting of *La Bohème*. There was feeling in the house that Cotrubas' complaint was in fact not professional but personal, and the sympathy of the singing community was not with her.

The conductor holds the power of ultimate approval because everything in opera, from personal attitude to collaboration of ensemble, from the look of the backdrop to the plastique of the supers, is viewed through a musical bias. It is why visiting directors from film and the stage never succeed in opera unless they are highly cultured persons with an amateur's experience of the technology of music. It is also why writers seldom include librettists' names when speaking of Verdi's, or Gluck's, or Britten's works, no matter how crucial those composers thought a master libretto was. Opera is a country unto itself, where music passes the laws.

It is no less so now that opera has caught up with the several twentieth-century revolutions in stagecraft. Around 1890 theatre in general was static and disjointed, a succession of pretty pictures, the principals gesturing imperturbably in the foreground. Catalytic developments in design and lighting, in pacing, in casting, and especially in portrayal had utterly reorganized the spoken stage by the time of World War II. Opera moved more slowly—then, suddenly, began to catch up, without in the least diminishing its musical authority. On the contrary, the rise of the modern music director exactly coincided with the modern theatricalization of opera, for good reason: the more sophisticated (in the literal sense of "mixed of many parts") opera has grown, the more it needs a superintendent.

Our notion of the opera-house music director—as teacher, patriarch, and tyrant—is nearing its centennial, deriving largely from the reigns of Gustav Mahler and Arturo Toscanini. In their various appointments, but especially in Mahler's at Vienna and Toscanini's at La Scala and the Met, these two urged upon their subjects an authorial idolatry that demanded practicality submit to utopia. By the practices of their day, their standards were nearly unreachable. Yet they upheld these standards and flew into rages if anyone failed to meet them—including the public. It was not lazy singers that finally drove Toscanini from regular work in the opera house, but lazy audiences; and Mahler, unofficially regarded in Vienna as a Jewish intruder, entertained no ambitions about becoming beloved either behind or before the curtain. It seems rather savvy of the five-year-old Mahler, asked what he wanted to be when he grew up, to have answered, "A martyr."

Martyrdom is the lot of utopian maestros, for opera is anti-utopian: unwieldy and fragile, mired in jealousies. To bind an entire company to one's will! The only reason today's music directors are *not* martyrs is that they have learned from Mahler's and Toscanini's mistake in unleashing incomparable eccentricities along with formidable musicianship. Tantrums and savagery belong back in the golden age, whence they live on as quaint anecdotes; today we prefer diplomacy. Or is it only through savagery that one subdues the sloppy vanities of that golden age in favor of the professionalism we now take for granted? Before Mahler and Toscanini, great opera was made on this night or that, but there was no overall program for achieving greatness, no policy of excellence. Mahler and Toscanini set such policies. It is true, as I have said, that singing is less spontaneous and personal than it used to be; but it is also true that rhythm is more aptly judged, the line clearer, and the ensemble in balance. Two reasons why are the martyrdom of Mahler and the transfiguration of Toscanini.

Both were curt, sullen, self-absorbed, fanatically devoted to music, and determined to clean away the encrusted indifference of business-as-usual. Mahler was obsessed with correcting inaccurate details of design, revamping stage traditions, and introducing contemporary work. Toscanini horrified Milan by digging an orchestra pit in La Scala's floor to clear the stage perspective, by enforcing the ancient, ignored ban on encores, and by doing away with cuts, even in Meyerbeer and Wagner. The two were demons in the coaching room; but under their care a good singer might become a great one.

Infatuated with Anna von Mildenburg in his Hamburg years, Mahler found himself more or less willingly encircling her. He inspired her art, gave her confidence, redrew her own picture of who Anna von Mildenburg was through the magnificence of the music she learned and relearned under him.

Without Mahler, von Mildenburg might have been another of the Lilli Lehmann all-Fach sopranos lacking Lehmann's dash, splitting the difference between the Queen of the Night and Brünnhilde while singing them both. Mahler reoriented von Mildenburg, separated Mozart from Wagner, terrified and thrilled her. "Start again." "Superb." "Atrocious." "Go on." No one else's criticism was so acerbic, no one else's praise as glorious. "You can't imagine," Mahler told his sister Justi, "how gauche and clumsy she was when she began! . . . I . . . demonstrated to her precisely every step, every pose, and every movement in relation to the music. . . . No one has ever been so zealous or so anxious to learn and understand." It's hard to remain on a purely artistic footing with someone who is literally teaching one how to be marvelous. Mahler and von Mildenburg became lovers.

Such a liaison of course suits opera legend, for just as all that love and death ignites us in the audience, so—if it is to mean anything—must it exhilarate its deputies. But such a liaison does not suit all divas: not all wish to be subsumed by a maestro or anyone else. For one thing, some of them think they're marvelous already; for another, some want less a Svengali and more a technician who will keep the backstage of their lives efficient and professional. One never thinks of divas as reigning geniuses the way one thinks of superconductors, yet a few may have more than a little to teach a maestro, or may entertain a view of a given score that is right for the composer, yet makes no kowtow to the conductor. Riccardo Chailly represents a more genteel but no less artistic approach than Mahler's all-or-nothing charisma in speaking of the "combustion of all of us working together." Mahler had the "sound" of a piece fixed in his mind, would hear it no other way. Chailly would let the sound of the production at hand enter his ear as he gathers the cast around the piano. "Singers need a lot of help," he says, "both from the purely vocal and from the musical, interpretational point of view, so I must [take] account of the realities of the situation. . . . To be a Mussolini and say this is it, this is the way you will do it, is not only impractical but hateful and terribly old-fashioned."

Toscanini was impractical and hateful, though in his early

years as a grand maestro he seemed very avant-garde. Singers under him either worshipped or loathed him, largely depending on how willing they were to let him dictate absolutely the terms on which they could exist as artists. Yet it must be said that his impracticality implemented an astonishing brilliance of ensemble execution and that at least some of his hatefulness was sparked by instrumentalists' inattention and singers' stupidity. Like Mahler, Toscanini took singers through their parts at the keyboard, explaining to Toti dal Monte that the staccatos in Gilda's "Caro nome" reveal the nervous anticipation of first love, getting Gilda dalla Rizza to weep real tears in Violetta's "Dite alla giovane," showing Tebaldi how to time her progress through an evening as Aida without straining. Like Mahler, he was feared, even by the most resourceful artists. Lotte Lehmann put off working with him for years, though she was one diva whose commitment rivaled his. In the event, they got on splendidly. Their partnership in several seasons of *Fidelio* in Salzburg shortly before World War II count among opera's lore-laden performances. Even so, Lehmann had to knuckle under to Toscanini's hair-trigger mettle:

> I saw how he suffered when something was not done exactly as he wanted to have it—not from caprice, but from a relentless pursuit of the very highest perfection. He demanded absolute precision and at the same time the most complete spiritual surrender to the music.

Again like Mahler, Toscanini had his detractors, especially among the disaffected singers. Even the enthusiastic Lehmann, who forever regretted having delayed their collaboration, called working with the maestro a "fearful pleasure." Iva Pacetti was one diva who dared stand up to Toscanini's rages. Rehearsing Dukas' *Ariane et Barbe-Bleue*, Toscanini drilled Pacetti in the lengthy scene of the opening of the six treasure rooms as if deliberately to exhaust her, and, in front of the full company, screamed at her, "You are a sheep! For this role a lioness is needed!" Pacetti took a walk—out of Toscanini's La Scala, which in the 1920s was like walking out of Italian opera altogether—and as much artistic blackmail and flattery as diplomacy was needed to lure her back to the theatre. It was simple: either Pacetti sings, or the entire production must be canceled. Pacetti gave in, Toscanini was "icy but correct" (as she recalled it), and the show went on. Of course Toscanini immediately dropped Pacetti from La Scala's roster—this was the hatefulness, not only abusive of colleagues but vindictive toward those who resented abuse. Pacetti found steady employment at other houses, as much for her gumption as for her frankly rather acid instrument; except for Vittorio Gui, Antonino Votto, and other Toscanini disciples who supported the maestro at La Scala, humbly or else, Italian opera turned out to be manned by conductors offended by the Toscanini cult who were glad to employ one of its rare critics. Three years later, when Toscanini departed La Scala, Pacetti happily made her return.

Iva Pacetti is not one of the few divas Toscanini fought with; she is one of the few who fought back. Like Mahler, Toscanini was insensate of any feelings but his, though, also like Mahler, he sustained powerful romances with some remarkable women, among them Rosina Storchio, Geraldine Farrar, and (it is suspected) Lotte Lehmann. The widely hailed Toscanini might eventually have suffered what one might term a change of press for his implacable self-righteousness, good notices turning into dismay at his greed for backstage geschrei. But his disgust with fascism, which drove him from La Scala, from Italy, and from Europe altogether, made him symbolic in the same way Lehmann, Vishnevskaya, Baker, and Sills have been, as personifications of sociocultural forces, the musician as world figure. Mahler died too early to compete with Toscanini in PR terms; besides, anti-Semitism expunged his legend where it was most potent, in Vienna. But Toscanini passed into myth. Leading his NBC Symphony Orchestra on its weekly broadcasts; photographed with his left hand trembling over his heart, the fingers stretched into a web, as is typical of string players turned conductor, *canto vibrato;* trumpeted in news and apocrypha as the lovable but strict emeritus, Toscanini became more than a cult figure. He became the world's most famous (therefore greatest) conductor and thereby reaffirmed his policy for excellence in running an opera company. To be great, one must want what Toscanini wanted.

Granted, some of his legacy has been put on hold—the hatefulness, certainly. No one could get away with such aggressive behavior in this age of union negotiations. And, as Chailly points out, conductors don't assign singers their performances, as Toscanini did; they help shape them. What of Toscanini's standards? Can—or should—they be met? I have asked numerous sopranos what they think of Toscanini's famous recording of *La Traviata*, from two NBC broadcast afternoons. "Interesting," they reply. "Would you like to sing Violetta," I go on, "in that performance?" In the two or three seconds it takes to think up a tactful negative, their eyes swell in terror at the fearful pleasure of trying to fit Violetta's emotional ebb and flow to that Procrustean diagram of Verdi.

Riccardo Muti, the nearest thing to a replica of Toscanini, if one has to have one, upholds his predecessor's textual authenticity, his disgust for unstimulated audiences, and impatience with what Mahler called *Schlamperei* ("sloppiness," referring to the traditional opera-house "options" not part of a composition as writ). Yet Muti is not known for the perfectionist scandal that Toscanini dealt in. Muti's most ruthless act to date is the "disinviting" of Marilyn Horne to an *Orfeo ed Euridice* because Muti wanted to perform Gluck's Vienna original (with a mezzo replacing Gluck's castrato) and Horne wanted to perform a virtuoso amendment thought to be by Bertoni. The act of barring a headline virtuoso for wanting to sing a headline virtuoso's aria is shockingly Toscaninian, and the controversy became such a scandal that Horne felt compelled to set forth her side of the case in *The New York Times,* explaining that the questionable aria is in fact not Bertoni's, but pirated by him from Gluck. "Anyway," she concluded, "if one really wants to be truly pure and faithful to the original, then one must find a castrato to perform *Orfeo* or not perform [*Orfeo*] at all."

Even more Toscaninian is the act of protesting an entire production. Carlo Maria Giulini took such dislike to a Holland Festival *Don Giovanni* he was conducting that, at his insistence, the production was scrapped and the piece given as a costumed concert. At least the piece *was* given. Toscanini protested *and entirely canceled* his Scala *Norma,* immediately after the dress rehearsal of the first act.*

Mahler seems to have nursed something of a death wish. He died young, an apparent semi-failure, and left no recordings of his conducting, a martyr to racism and the public's coarse taste. Toscanini entered contests to win, and did. He lived long, enjoyed incomparable success, baited the totalitarians and won, and remains a required study in monaural sound, a one-man mythology. A great man. Where does this leave the diva? Is she to seek out some modern version, or avoid him? No one, surely, would argue that someone other than the maestro should hold ultimate authority in opera. The question is how much authority should the maestro have; and how will it affect the rise and fall of diva?

Lotte Heinotz tells us, in perhaps the most sage passage in *The Prima Donna's Handbook.* "Face yourself honestly," she urges, I think a little sadly. "Know what you can do. Is yours a precious talent, a sumptuous voice? Have you a lovely way, or do you merely support the adventurers?" Heinotz warns that a brilliant maestro is invaluable to anyone, that even a dullish Kapellmeister can cultivate one's talent beyond fair expectations:

> The diva looks at opera and sees only her roles, her colleagues, her company, her public. The maestro knows all operas, all the composers who wrote them, all the singers who sang them. The maestro penetrates history. If you are truly second-rate, the maestro will make you irreplaceable, for there are just so many adventures to give and no house can go dark between them. The maestro will tutor you in the unique art of the dependably workmanlike, so that the music may always be heard. You will serve the art. If yours is a fine tal-

---

*Once again we encounter *Norma* as the utter work, most splendid and most difficult. If Toscanini could not give a first-rate *Norma,* he would give none— an arresting example to the more expedient conductors of today.

ent, the maestro will make it finer. And if yours is a precious talent, the maestro will make it priceless.

It is ironic that we must take such good advice from a comprimaria of such small potential that she could only assume lead roles during flu epidemics. Or perhaps it takes a bench-warmer to frame the broad perspective that the adventurers are too busy to note. Certainly Heinotz' view is fair. Did not Legge make the precious Schwarzkopf priceless? Did not Serafin secure the precarious Callas? What might Kirsten Flag-stad's Isolde have been like if some potent maestro had taken that heavenly instrument through the character and inflamed her instead of just beating time?

True, the sword cuts two ways. There were plenty of fine singers whom Mahler and Toscanini treated with contemptuous negligence, and in our time Karl Böhm was known to most artists as a tyrant concerned only with raising a din in the pit with his Straussian host. Perhaps the diva, too, must course between extremes of martyrdom and transfiguration, avoiding the former while making a feasible entailment upon the latter. Malibran, Muzio, and Callas, each for her reasons, won martyrdom; Lotte Lehmann, Nilsson, and Price, again each differently, achieved transfiguration. It is notable that no one maestro contributed to any of these three downfalls, and none, decisively, to these legends of success. For the maestro cannot create a diva, only perfect her, through a process of collaboration that—up to a point—engulfs a singer's liberty.

Nuns fret not at their convent's narrow room, we have been told; but a diva wants air. Opera is too broad a world to tighten, however much its inhabitants celebrate specialization, belabor the simplest scales, interrogate an aria, a phrase, the microscopic inside of an eighth-note. The cult of the maestro is one of the paradoxes of diva, then: she gains and she loses. At least the transaction is made in the language of music, sure terrain. It is another paradox of diva that opera is theatre. We are now in an age of superdirectors, whose language is not necessarily musical, and whose ability to hurt a singer is considerably larger than that of any musician. Now the fearful pleasure really begins.

CHAPTER

8

THE STAGE DIRECTOR

The creative power of the singer-actor is the major contemporary factor in the development of realist musical theatre.
Walter Felsenstein

Stage directors . . . have drained all personality from the singer.
Maria Carbone

Back in the days when music theatre was more music than theatre, and back in the house where everybody liked it that way, from the stage door to the boxes, Margaret Webster decided to inaugurate rehearsals for a new *Aida* with a reading. Literally: Webster handed out librettos and asked the singers to read their parts, from curtain rise to curtain fall.

This was the Met in early fall of 1951, with Zinka Milanov, Elena Nikolaidi, Mario del Monaco, George London, and Jerome Hines. The reading was standard practice in the spoken theatre, where the first rehearsal is traditionally given over to the full cast, on chairs and in street clothes, making one faltering, experimental, energizing trek through the text. It is the moment in which the performers join as a company, a chance to defer to tradition.* It's a charade for the peacocks and an initiation for the violets. It's the indicated time for the director's lecture on period, customs, textual confusions, and

---

*Actually, the playwright used to read his work, solo, before the assembled thespians; still, the communal reading is virtually the last association the modern stage may make with its past. The sense of sacred rite has impressed even the avant-garde, who make a point of profaning their first rehearsals with discussions, improvisations, and other revolutionary offerings—*anything* but that traditional Reading of the Play.

the like. Most practically, it's the director's one way to be sure that everyone in the cast has gone through the entire play at least once. Webster, a director and actress of extensive experience in classic repertory, was herewith making a valiant attempt to turn opera upside down: to challenge performers theretofore concerned only with music to reckon as characters rather than as notes on a staff.

Some of the singers were attracted by the instructive novelty, but Milanov and del Monaco exchanged a dubious glance and cooperated no more than minimally. Del Monaco recited his lines in Conehead monotone; to such as he, words were meaningless without melody. Milanov was ingenious. She stared at the page. She held it to the light, held it again. She went into little trances after each phrase. She stumbled over the words of "Ritorna vincitor," which she had sung hundreds of times. She fumbled in her handbag for glasses, shifted her weight in her chair, stared at the ceiling, didn't know the role, didn't know Verdi, didn't know opera. And finally announced, "Wrong glasses." Recounting the tale in her memoirs, Webster concluded, "I know when I am licked."

In that time and in that house a diva could confidently stonewall the director—not only because Webster's dramaturgical technique was outlandish in an unstimulated house, but because opera is almost always compromised as theatre. The maestro, not the director, heads the college, we know. But the director, in charge of the storytelling department, has only lately become important, and to do so he had to battle a generation of singers.

Everyone says opera is theatre, but everyone knows that opera singers are not necessarily actors who sing. They are singers, period. Milanov perhaps regarded Webster as an interloper—imagine coming into Milanov's world; her turf, in fact—to tell Milanov how to deliver one of Milanov's great roles! What a risible invasion! Yet the director is crucial in the presentation of diva. He can teach her to understand her character's subtextual drives, to present not only the singing but the living person; as Wieland Wagner did with Birgit Nilsson. He can cover her inability to act in a production in which all elements are pitched to *her* deepest level of involvement and no more deeply than that; as Franco Zeffirelli did with Joan Sutherland. He can even help her fix her position in music history, style her revolution; as Luchino Visconti did with Maria Callas. By the time she met up with Margaret Webster, Zinka Milanov had frozen her Aida. How much more gripping it might have been had she let the director introduce her to the role. Milanov sang a great Aida, no question. *Sang* one. But did she know the character or the tunes?

The director is crucial in another way, as the master of that awkward time between the laboratory preparation at the piano and the performance in full true with orchestra, when all one's careful groundwork is vexed by backstage exigencies—the weight of the costumes, the heat of the lights, the action of story, and the tension of facing the public. Suddenly the cumbersome ephemera that turns composition into living experience falls upon the diva. And, however much the maestro superintends, it is the director who escorts her through the ordeal. She *must* undergo it: for the age when the public expected no more of a Milanov than she was content to give has passed. Try to imagine Joan Sutherland or Renata Scotto segregating herself from a Websterian reading. Impossible: Sutherland would be tacitly leery but, the game professional, would do her best; Scotto's pride would insist not only that she go through with it, but that she read better than anyone living.

It is more than being, as Evelyn Lear says, "a good sport." Singers are under pressure to adapt to the enaction of character, and divas are, especially. When the gyres shift and one epoch cedes to the next, it is usually the sopranos and mezzos who lead the revolution, another reason why demented is woman territory: Schröder-Devrient, Malibran, Pasta, Farrar, Muzio, Callas. Even in the echelon of the counter-revolutionary, women uphold a higher level of attainment than men. Going back to Webster's aborted *Aida* reading, del Monaco was a great voice without a shred of imagination or nuance, the operatic equivalent of the "white noise" that sound men turn on at the end of rock concerts to eject laggards. But Milanov, for all her resistance to theatre, was a musical and subtle singer. Divas, then, retain what publishing calls "first refusal" in the negotiation of a theatre-oriented opera.

Besides, so many operas are written around a heroine that the collaboration of diva and director can be explosively superb. I say *collaboration,* however. For if the great acting singers are not autonomous, not complete in themselves, still they are self-created and, after composition itself, opera's essential ingredient. Even if the director only serves to generate a sense of a work's naturalism, the apprehensions of its time and place, its persons as they are and as they present themselves; even if the director only impresses upon his cast the minute facts of the narration that few of us consider; even if the director only asks his singers to think about making a few "actor's choices"—if the director only goes this far, with alert performers, this is far indeed.

It is certainly a deal farther than many of our modern star directors go. Lothar Wallerstein, one of the first such, directed by rote. A fixture in the interwar years at Vienna, Salzburg, and (during the war) at the Met, Wallerstein arrived at La Fenice for a *Rosenkavalier* with Maria Carbone as the Marschallin and Gianna Pederzini as Octavian. Chalking numbers on the floor, he told the singers to navigate arithmetically, this phrase on number ten, that on number fifteen, and so on. Carbone was flabbergasted. "Either you rub out all those numbers or Carbone does not sing the Marschallin," she told him. "I happen to be a singer and not a numerologist!"

Directors can be a hindrance. Many of them are idealess hacks, others too ambitious for their good, with half-digested Concepts that obscure as much as enlighten. Do they constitute a profession at all: opera director? The most famous of them have come into opera from elsewhere—Visconti from film and the spoken stage, Zeffirelli from design, Wallerstein from the conductor's desk—and the maestro, we have seen, regards directing as his subturf, at his option. Even choreographers have directed, as for example in 1973 at the Monnaie in Brussels, where Maurice Béjart devised a flamboyant *Traviata* set in a joke-shop rendition of the Monnaie itself, with dummies at Violetta's party, the suburban villa a garden of Rodins (Vi-

oletta a sculptor in pants), the deathbed a ship, the whole decorated by a mysterious and at times nude dancer billed as A.D.
(Alexandre Dumas?), whom Verdi and Piave would have had
trouble placing. A fascinating entertainment—but was it *La
Traviata*, really? We know the maestro's imperatives, and his
responsibilities. But the director is still defining his. In fact,
opera has only lately installed its first generation of directors
not drawn from some other medium, men and women who
raised themselves on the challenge, inspiration, and love of the
musical stage.

A sense of vocation is not a sign of talent. Which is worse
for the diva, a vapid director or an overbearingly imaginative
one? Paltry guidance can dilute her portrayal, intimidating
Concept drown it. The Béjart approach of ignoring a work's
inherent naturalism and authorial style amusingly rehabili-
tates operas that predate or otherwise fail to satisfy modern
ideas of theatrical verisimilitude—we do not stage Lully or
Handel as they were staged when new, nor should we hope to.
But one wonders how much Béjart's Violetta, Vasso Papanto-
niou, grew in the role through exposure to Béjart's kaleido-
scope of cultures. In such a production, a Violetta learns the
value of independence conversely: through being the toy of a
master showman, not unlike her Monnaie party guests a
dummy herself.

Directors like Béjart might contend that opera singers are
not actors, that for each one who can dissect character there
are twenty who can't and forty who won't. Having renounced
integrity, they don't deserve independence, can't be trusted with
it. They *are* dummies. But ever since Schröder-Devrient's revolution in thespian plastique, the annals have filled with reports of spectacular portrayals, of compelling Leonores, Donna
Annas, Normas, Isoldes, Toscas: in short, of divas intuitively
projecting the qualities of the elemental and the singular that
together nourish the fascination of the great role. In Schröder-
Devrient's day, that also of the actor-manager's egotistical
heroism and subordinated ensemble support, such portrayals
must have been heavily mannered; nearer to our own day, that
of Stanislafskyan naturalism, the grand style is sometimes
tempered with realism. To opera's benefit and misfortune, the

outstanding directors do not thus compromise but attempt to rival the wizards of contemporary theatre, where a tradition stemming from the brilliant Max Reinhardt worships a conceptual Gestalt of devices, tics, coups, and feats in which acting is subordinated to production. Is this dummy opera, on a stage of chalked numbers, with the lighting plot getting more rehearsals than the actors?

It can be. Franco Zeffirelli's oversized Met *Bohème* does rather distance the principals, dwarf them as if in cinematic long-shot. Zeffirelli dwarfs the very opera itself, a romantic comedy about two couples here played in tableaus the size of *Aida*. Similarly, some of the many "updated" productions that reset old tales in anachronistic surroundings throw too much attention onto the novelty of the stunt, thus too little on the action. Worse yet, many composers, impressed by the prestige of such events, have taken to *writing* dummy operas, works that are supposed to be overproduced. Singing the world premiere of Hans Werner Henze's *We Come to the River* (1976) under the composer's stage direction, a baffled cast kept trying to make intelligent actor's choices, asking Henze to explain his turgid allegory or to simplify the multi-nucleate stage pictures so the audience could concentrate on the main action. No luck: the composer defeated them as much as the production did—composition and misdirection were, in this case, inseparable. At one point, told to exit through the auditorium making up their lines, the women of the ensemble chose such ad libs as "Money back at the box office," a possible check upon the rise of dummy opera that has yet to be put to practice.

In the right hands, enterprising production can be refreshing and enlightening rather than perverse. The passing of the storybook stage with its artificially lifelike "views" (as out of a stereopticon) has put more of a burden on the performers, not less. At the Met, John Dexter's stagings of *Les Vêpres Siciliennes, Le Prophète,* and *Dialogues des Carmelites* present each title in conceptual trapping: a stark black-and-white melodrama phased onto a huge staircase for *Vêpres'* "with us or against us" rebellion; a miracle-play context for *Prophète's* pageant of holy war; convent plainness pressed upon a gigantic cross for *Carmelites'* parable of martyrdom. The sets frame the atmosphere, but do not overpower the principals. On the contrary, the sopranos tackling Hélène, Fidès, and Blanche must carry the weight of narrative: with nothing to look at for four acts but stairs, *Vêpres'* audiences will be watching the characters closely.

It is surprising how much even the most overweening directors depend on the ground-zero of character portrayal. Zeffirelli has been quoted as saying, "In my productions, the principals are of the least importance," as if making rubric for that controversial *Bohème*. But Callas adored working with him (at the end, her friends thought that the one person who could lure her back to the theatre was Zeffirelli), so perhaps his statement is mere picturesque overspeak. Certainly the *Falstaff*s that Zeffirelli left along the international route during the 1960s all emphasized the work and its players far more than they did decor or capers. No director who works regularly in opera can afford to high-hat singers' input. And, while they don't like to admit it, many of them delight in an unexpected aperçu—as, for instance, when Frank Corsaro and Patricia Brooks were rehearsing the New York City Opera's *Pelléas et Mélisande,* seeking a line into Mélisande's state of mind in the first scene, when Golaud finds her in the forest. Brooks recalled a family holiday in the country when her little boy had got lost; when found, he was shivering under a tree like a frightened animal. Corsaro immediately set Brooks to capturing that feeling, and it made for a thrilling start to an often underpowered scene.

Sometimes the singers themselves are surprised at how well they collaborate with an apparently uncompromising director. Working on *Jenůfa* with Götz Friedrich in Stockholm, Elisabeth Söderström felt he was placing an interpretation upon her rather than letting her develop one. She wanted to enact her Jenůfa, not pose as his. "I don't even know her yet," she told him.

"But I do," Friedrich answered.

Resentful but helpless, Söderström fell into step:

Not till I saw the finished production, with the whole cast, decor, lights, and orchestra, did I give way. I re-

alized then that I was nothing but a small piece of a
gigantic puzzle, and I was so impressed that I swal-
lowed my objections to his interpretations of some of
the scenes in the third act. . . . But it seemed cowardly
and false, and I was very worried on the first night that
the audience would unmask me. I will never for one
second forget the moment when the curtain went down.
. . . It was deathly quiet . . . then came an ovation that
was quite deafening! . . . I fell into Kerstin Meyer's arms
with tears of relief pouring down my cheeks.

When working with a drudge, the diva is at her most exposed;
with a master, she is both protected and defenseless: by his
imagination and against his power. Perhaps the modern diva
must learn to balance her own ideas with the elaborations of
modern opera stagecraft—as, in a more primitive era, her predecessors did not have to do. As opera has become more interesting—in the Chinese sense—the performers have had to enlarge their responsibilities.

One of these is the obligation to meet a more adult view
of the sensuality that was written into opera from its first day.
Isolde, Violetta, Manon, Nedda, and many other roles have been
liberated from the phoney eroticism that haunted them in ages
past. Not that no soprano of old could play sensuality realistically and becomingly. But the Calvés, Farrars, and Boris were
exceptional, whereas today's divas are expected to play a cred-
ible romance, passion, or seduction. The day when sopranos
might portray practiced courtesans or barbarian princesses as
if they were the chairmistress of an unusually rowdy bake sale
are long over.

Consider *Don Giovanni,* with its three great roles, Donna
Anna, Donna Elvira, and Zerlina. The work is a cornerstone
in the edifice of diva, a classic within a generation of its premiere, promising at its best an evening counting a Stimmdiva
(Anna), a Kunstdiva (Elvira), and a devilish soubrette (Zerlina), luring self-promoting divas to leap from one to another
or even to take all three into their repertories, and, finally, inviting mezzos, as Horne, Berganza, and von Stade try Zerlina
or Christa Ludwig tackles Elvira. Here are three roles that have

changed remarkably under the advice of the contemporary director, Anna turning from a cold aristocrat to a woman in search of a dream lover (and it isn't Don Ottavio); Elvira going Bacchante; and Zerlina shifting from flirtatious to earthy. "Là ci darem la mano" was once a duet for wolf and coquette; today's directors commonly stage it as a seduction, at times edging it past Mozart's suavely bantering tone but making it certain that Giovanni wants to take Zerlina to bed and that Zerlina is willing. (At the New York City Opera in 1972 Frank Corsaro had them embracing on a bale of hay when Elvira interrupted them.) Some operagoers regard these shall we say psychologically reconstructed productions with horror. But Mozart in fact needn't be reconstructed: everything is already in his music, and no matter how much more we think we know about the human spirit than Mozart's contemporaries did, Mozart's operas comprehend all the data. Thus the evergreen glamour of the Mozart heroines: each new age wants to see its divas test the parts with the "new" information.

There is a trap in this proposition, though. Each new generation of directors wants to take the classics further, dare more than the last generation. We judge our directors as much by their arrogance as by their talent, and have thus helped to create the superdirector, now confronting the maestro for supreme power in the opera house. This is bad for the diva's independence: one will get her coming and the other get her going. Superdirectors' bonuses include high production budgets, plenty of rehearsals, and tons of PR; but superdirectors' drawbacks include the pressure to be innovative rather than stylish.

This pressure has provisioned the current incursion of fancy directors from other mediums, not all of whom are conversant with the workings of opera as a system, from the physical fittings of the voice to the implications of orchestral narrative. Hal Prince, after thirty years as a producer and director of Broadway musicals, has made a satisfying entree into opera, not least because his long collaboration with Stephen Sondheim gave him profound exposure to the subtleties of musical theatre as musical as it is dramatic. After *Pacific Overtures* and *Sweeney Todd,* how can *La Fanciulla del West* stump

Prince? Nay, he can invigorate it. In his staging Minnie does not "ride" in on horseback to save her lover from a lynch mob, a dashing image invariably ruined by horse-shy sopranos perched nervously atop a drugged mount led onto the stage tethered to a trainer. This is opera at its silliest, a cup of sherbet afraid to stay hard. Prince had his Minnie truck herself in on a railway handcart, keeping the suspense realistically taut and, by the way, yielding a neat entrance for the diva. But some other Famous Directors who happen opportunistically onto the opera scene—especially those who arrive from the cinema— have achieved some truly ungainly disasters, bad for the singers, bad for the composer, bad for the public. They don't do opera much good, either.

PR is self-affirming, self-replicating; once famous, one inevitably becomes more famous. Thus the superdirector is now virtually out of control, even by maestros and company intendants. Then, too, a superdirector's pet stars will tout him, putting the stamp of backstage loyalty to his credentials. At root of it all is the uncomfortable truth that opera, like any business, loves success and dislikes failure. So even professionals and other insiders would rather flatter the emperor on his new clothes than let the kingdom know what fools are running the court.

The fame of Boston's Sarah Caldwell is an instance in point. She is an uneven conductor, an imaginative but uneven director. Yet, again, fame is impressive: reviewers cheer Caldwell, buffs look to her for leadership, Beverly Sills champions her, and singers and staff will stand still as statuary when Caldwell suddenly dozes off in the middle of a rehearsal, waiting patiently till she reawakens and never referring to the incident.

Why such forbearance for a director-conductor who is patently erratic? Perhaps Caldwell is being mistaken for her own good intentions. In a profession often wired into what is feasible, Caldwell is idealistic. She forced an opera company upon a city that thought it had no use for one; sought out alternate versions of, among others, *Madama Butterfly* (the original, longer score) and *Don Carlos* (complete, in French); staged *Les Troyens* because nobody else would; and disdains the lazily traditional cuts. It is admirable to retain one's ideals against high odds; but good intentions are not, of themselves, a form of talent. Maybe we are simply looking for an American diva, genus *maestra Bostoniensis*. Latest in a line of independent New England women (some think of Amy Lowell), Caldwell answers to some Aristotelian compound for demented in a separate-but-equal echelon, a New England demented, serene rather than boiling, but no less committed.

Caldwell belongs to a one-person category; unlike the superdirector, she also serves as musician and impresario. More typical superdirectors only direct, or also design their productions, for the look of the piece has become the superdirector's imperative of prestige. This emphasis on design stems from "neo-Bayreuth," the style pioneered by Wagner's grandsons, Wieland and Wolfgang, at the family theatre in the 1950s. Neo-Bayreuth purges decorative clutter, centering the view upon the interaction of principals. This is a refutation of dummy opera and, to many, the source of some of modern opera's most absorbing experiences. It is notable that the Wagners worked— had to work—with the most gifted *and independent* Wagnerian singers of the day, and worked as thespians, raising up the ritualistically compelling narratives that their grandfather had envisioned as antidote to the delicatessen revues promoted in Parisian grand opera. Wieland and Wolfgang despised the mediocre that much of repertory opera flourishes on. Wieland's program might serve as the diva's all-basic query sheet in preparing any part from Euridice to Mrs. Lovett: what are the essentials of the story?—"who to whom," as Lenin put it.

Neo-Bayreuth is extreme, not because of its unrealistic decor but because it so thrusts attention upon the actors. Herein the diva who could realize Isolde, Brünnhilde, or Kundry came into her day: reaffirmed the educated independence that is the singing actress' great hope. This would be the great arena of Martha Mödl, unexpectedly biting in Isolde's "Frag' deine Furcht!" (Ask your fear!) when Tristan inquires as to what she means by the word "foe," and shockingly strangled in her "Ha!" at Tristan's death. Or of Astrid Varnay, rapt in her virginal ecstasy as Senta, a fearfully sensual Brünnhilde, an almost pragmatically evil Ortrud, startled to see mere goodness winning out over spells, nasty acts, and a foul temper. Mödl and Varnay were superlative performers from the start; Bayreuth gave them opportunity and confidence. But, as we have seen, even Birgit Nilsson found her workshop with Wieland in Bayreuth, her sense of self gradually shaped into a sense of the Wagnerian universals, so that her portrayals became as authentic as Mödl's and Varnay's but unlike theirs.

It was an uneasy collaboration at first, for Nilsson had already sung Isolde under brother Wolfgang, and Bayreuth's nervous diplomacy forbade the two Wagners' sharing of stars. Perhaps Wieland also took offense at Nilsson's prestige as Isolde, for neither Mödl nor Varnay had enjoyed such vogue. Nilsson had the fame, Wieland thought, not the greatness. As she recalls it, he only turned to her at last because he was crazed to stage *Tristan* and no one else could or would sing Isolde. Even when she offered to work with him with utter openness, he was leery. She had sung eighty-seven Isoldes by then; inevitably, she would have discovered what worked for her and what didn't and wouldn't likely imperil her security. He was wrong. After a week Wieland and Nilsson were a team heading for one of Wieland's greatest (and, to him, most satisfactory) triumphs. "He took the best things out of you," she says, "and molded the role so it would fit."

This, then, is opera for acting singers, opera that glorifies production, yes—but not at the expense of the communicative humanity at the heart of musical storytelling. If one can in part identify a superdirector by the quality of diva in his collaboration, the Wagner brothers stand high in the lists, especially Wieland, who carried on through the generations to guide the young Anja Silja, an astonishingly honest and detailed actress who has never submitted to the tyranny of superproduction. Working with Silja on a Met *Wozzeck,* director David Alden would stagger out of the house like an athlete who places third: in there, but not winning. An experienced Marie, Silja fought Alden on everything, even the age of the child the Met used. "This is not in Berg!" she would cry. "This is not in Büchner!" Somehow each elicited from the other, traded knowledge, and *Wozzeck* scored a success. One feels, though,

that Silja's training with Wieland perfected her beyond the
resources of repertory opera, that she has moved so far ahead
of the anti-intellectual pictorial overload of polite presentation
that only the most rigorously prepared and insightful directors can function in her arena.

And it *is* hers: the acting singer, once fledged, is opera's
salient element. Truly great performances are triumphs not of
design but of emotional imagination, and great roles are more
than portraits. But to what extent must a diva supply her own
greatness for the role? How can she resist being made dummy?
Where, in other words, stands the diva to the director?

Who is the true auteur? One keeps trying to parse the
Callas-Visconti collaboration for the syntax of originality, to
learn who of the two sponsored that extraordinary series of
Scala revivals, along with Wieland's Wagner the most influential of the postwar era. If no diva was more independent than
Callas, no director was surer of his power than Visconti. It is
hard to believe that the two got along at all, but then supreme
egotists mesmerized Visconti, as mirrors will, and Visconti's
brutal elegance mesmerized Callas. Battista Meneghini denied it to his death, but everyone in Milan knew that she had
in some way fallen in love with the director. Neither one, then,
held total power. The collaboration ran on intense mutual fascination.

There were five Callas-Visconti productions, all for La
Scala: *La Vestale, La Sonnambula,* and *La Traviata* in the
1954–55 season; and *Anna Bolena* and *Iphigénie en Tauride*
at the end of the 1956–57 season. As *La Vestale* went into rehearsal, Callas was a disputed name, one of several who might
open a season or sell out a house, probably to mixed reception.
When, three years later, *Iphigénie's* curtain rose on the sight
of Callas plunging pell-mell down a baroque stairway in the
midst of a tempest through a crowd of priestesses, her robes
flying and their arms upraised to assuage the uproar of nature, Callas was the queen of divas—still disputed, yes, but
now only by bitter idiots who knew, for all Callas' curdled notes
and wobble, that the entire music world was laughing at them.

The difference between Callas famous *(La Vestale)* and
Callas unique *(Iphigénie en Tauride)* lies in Callas' talent—

but it was Visconti who presented that talent so that no one could miss it. As with the Wagner bothers and their generation of Isoldes, Visconti and his Callas prove the value of the diva-director partnership, of making history in splendid, one-of-a-kind productions. Who but Callas could have sung these parts, worn those costumes, been so rightly framed by Visconti's bewildering archaic beauty? Arriving as they did by accumulation, first to general amusement but quickly enough to awe and unbearable anticipation, these five revivals condensed a career's headlines into three years—just as well, for Callas' career was condensed in any case. Most sopranos can count on such triumphs once every few years, and some—Flagstad and Milanov, for instance—got along in productions of no particular quality.

Flagstad and Milanov, then, had to invent themselves basically singlehanded; Callas had Visconti, timing, variety, and a theme. The timing was perfect, attuned to a public that craved new works and was willing to rediscover old ones in default of any contemporary insurgence. The masters of verismo were dead or dried out, and no one of popular appeal had replaced them. So Visconti invoked the elders: Spontini, Bellini, Verdi, Donizetti, Gluck. Except for *La Traviata,* the pieces had dropped from the repertory, *Vestale* and *Sonnambula* partially, *Anna Bolena* and *Iphigénie* almost entirely. But they were eminently capable of revival in Italy as not elsewhere, because, being composed in Italian or performed in translation, they had the immediacy of new work in the native tongue.

The variety was acute, for each work is different, *Vestale* a forerunner of Parisian grand opera, *Sonnambula* a *semiseria* piece,* *Traviata* an intimate bourgeois romance, *Anna Bolena* a bel-canto "noble house" tragedy, and *Iphigénie* one of Gluck's revolutionary "reform operas" that challenged the supremacy of the Italian style in the eighteenth century. Thus, Callas could exploit her versatility within her chosen Fach of early-middle demented Kunstdiva, Malibran's heiress, *singer*

Semiseria genre lies somewhere between *melodramma* and opera buffa, borrowing the former's musical intensity and the latter's middle-class or rustic characters, lightness of touch, and happy ending.

of scores from the remote classical sunset to the Risorgimento. (Note the avoidance of the detested verismo of the grouchers and moaners—Visconti seems not to have admired verismo any more than Callas did.)

The theme was Visconti's, that ottocento opera had lost its clarity of style over the years and had to be redesigned, reblocked, and remimed from scratch. Attacking the exercise with a modernist's eye but a penchant for antiquing, Visconti distilled a carefully anachronistic look to revive opera as the rhetoric of the leadership classes, self-advertising works of heroic grandeur outfitted in archival costume and set against the feeling of faded postcards. The action was now naturalistic, now mannered, a daring sophistication of plastique. But then this was exactly how Callas acted—the grand manner propelled by realism. Visconti refreshed the outdated, sometimes as historian, sometimes as mad hatter, and always as a design director, obsessed with the way it all looked (though he didn't take a program credit for decor till after his Callas period). His *Sonnambula* heroine was a ballerina out of *Giselle,* but his *Vestale* headdresses seemed an inadvertent spoof of imperialism from Caesar to Cortez. His Iphigénie was a resplendent high-baroque icon in velvet and pearls, but his Violetta tried to dress for Alfredo's last visit and was supposed to die with her hat on, to guaranteed popular dismay. Thus Visconti erred as well as advanced, but the verve of his conception outweighed the miscalculations. The great empty halls of royal England, the sumptuously overdressed Paris of the soirées and gossip, the delicacy of the Swiss pastoral, and the sweeping architectonics of the grand operas that opened and closed the series provided a stunning format for Callas' own antiquing, her revival of golden-age canto. Thus was launched the *riesumazione,* the exhumation of bel canto as a style rather than as a mere string of dead works tossed upon the stage like dice, in ignorance of the outcome, pure gamble. The theme was Visconti's but the variations were Callas.

Their collaboration was tempered by his belief in her and her trust in him. They must have known from the start how valuable the deal would prove for each, though Visconti's obsessive concern for tiny matters of decor exasperated Callas and Callas' independence infuriated Visconti. The *Traviata* hat, for example: it seems an imaginatively naturalistic touch to have Violetta hoping to celebrate the reconciliation with her lover by leaving her shabby sickroom for a return to her demimondain Paris. Of course she would dress, and women wore hats in those days. But the picture of Violetta crumpling to the floor in a hat offended Callas, and when the moment came, she unobtrusively lost it just before she died.* And Visconti cried, "Ah, that miserable woman! She will pay for this!"

Genius is always interesting but not always chivalrous; in this, Callas and Visconti were a match. It is sometimes forgotten that he was as controversial a figure as she when they began, patrician but a Communist, suave but vicious, brilliant but impractical. Visconti could offend anyone, and by the time he staged *La Vestale,* his first opera, he had alienated all Milan. In a letter to Callas he speaks of putting himself "on the line with all the pointed rifles and submachine guns we both know." *Both:* a match; and they knew it.

It's hard to say which was quicker to quarrel. It was Visconti who inflamed Callas' feud with Serafin over his recording *Traviata* for EMI's Scala series, made with Antonietta Stella instead of Callas. This was a grievous offense, for it was the *Traviata,* after the rousing but disliked *Vestale* and the semisensational *Sonnambula,* that put Callas and Visconti over into history. True, Callas had already taped the role for Cetra, and would not be able to record it again for a few years. Still, for EMI to issue a "Scala *Traviata"* just after this without Callas' participation (worse yet, *with* that of Giuseppe di Stefano, who had abruptly abandoned the production after conductor Carlo Maria Giulini sent Callas out for a solo bow) was at the least a stupid blunder, not unlike Deutsche Grammophon's releasing the "Von Karajan *Ring"* conducted by Fausto Cleva. Visconti treated it exactly as Callas did: as *casus belli.* This primary sense of themselves as abused heroes' may have strengthened the collaboration, may have tamed the natural

---

*Witnesses recall her trying a hatted death at the prima, to rebel thereafter. Meneghini says she fought Visconti on this from the first and never attempted it.

animosity of two powerful forces sharing territory. Together, Callas and Visconti were a form of auto-da-fé.

Obviously, divas cannot count on meeting up with a Visconti. His *riesumazione* with Callas depended on unique conditions in repertory, house facilities, language, and on Callas' tautly incipient fame, which promised to pay off the experiment in an inflamed atmosphere of Great Occasion. Lotte Heinotz had little to say about stage directors, possibly because in her day they were an amenity, to use or ignore at will. Today they offer a diva everything from salvation to perdition, from the development of a great role to dummy opera, or (even worse) insipid cliché, so one must be prepared to fill in the blanks when sentenced to a hack or to stand hard when assaulted by a superdirector. "The growing—and now, in my opinion, excessive—importance attached to the [director] can only be attributed to the waning power of the actor."

So spake one of the era's most mighty directors, Walter Felsenstein, of East Berlin's Komische Oper. To Felsenstein, salvation comprised an integration of collaborators, "an authentic collectivity which is responsible for working out the conception of the production." In his heavily subsidized eyrie on the border of the Iron Curtain, Felsenstein was so famous he was left free to integrate and conceive at his leisure, admittedly with a strictly resident company of second-rank voices but in a rare laboratory of pervasive artistic interconnection. Typical of Felsenstein's searching definition of music theatre was his program welding Verdi, Mozart, Offenbach, Janáček, and American musical comedy, all staged within the same plant with the same artists. A veteran of a single season with Felsenstein would be stylistically prepared for nearly anything worth doing that music theatre does.

However, Felsenstein's utopian prescriptions are not readily realizable without the irreplaceable director-impresario himself, not to mention his coddled preserve.* It is also worth not-

---

*A typical Felsenstein idealism: no double casting or understudies. To keep his productions pure, those who rehearsed them performed them, no substitutions. If a singer was indisposed, the show was canceled and the house sat dark.

ing that the Komische Oper has not produced much in the way of international opera celebrities. It is a closed system, too integrated, admirably and unlikably perfect.

Which returns us to square one: where stands the diva in regard to the director? Better, how can she arm herself to deal, in equal confidence, with the different kinds? One way is to cultivate an impressionistic background for each role, a sense of time, place, and culture. Yes, everything we need to know about Violetta is in the score. Yet why not supplement one's coaching with a reading tour of the era that produced *La Dame aux Camélias?* Flaubert, Zola, Baudelaire, de Maupassant? Why not browse through Verdi's letters, a trove of opinion, to learn how he saw the piece? Why not take on fewer roles and use the extra time to conquer them from every angle, thereby to be better prepared than any director?

A smart diva will cultivate also an interest in theatre, in all its kinds from classic repertory to the avant-garde, as spectator, reader, theorist. "It is only soprano, *basta!*" Callas said; on another level, it is only actress, from Sophocles to Strauss, Shakespeare to Verdi, Büchner to Berg. An offbeat but useful study may be made in the acting-in-opera classes, such as that given by Frank Corsaro in New York in the 1970s.

In a rented hall, on a small stage outfitted with a table and two chairs, to piano accompaniment and the criticism of their peers, young singers investigated thespian possibilities in music. The students prepared arias and ensemble scenes on their own and presented them to the class, and the most frequent questions were, "What were you trying to show? What feelings were you playing; what happens just before the scene; just after?" Newcomers were forced to vent their shyness, vanity, and other impedimenta in a "hostility exercise"—for example, by delivering "Pace, pace, mio Dio" in a rage directed personally at the "audience." The intent was to thrust aside the tension of a hit-or-flop profession for the clumsy luxury of the workshop, where mistakes won't hurt you. Strangely, some feel even more exposed in such an arena. One mezzo went behind a screen to ready herself for a snippet of *The Medium* and was unable to come out, so pronounced was her stage fright, even in the schoolroom.

There were the dunces, too—a Musetta using her silly hands as semaphores of coquetry, the kind of performance that goes best with a Ruth and Thomas Martin translation. Those ready to use the class drew on it impressively—Elsa's Dream sung entirely in a chair as a study in the immobile purity of transfiguration, or Tosca and Scarpia actually listening to each other. Nothing could have been less like the Callas-Visconti compound or the Felsenstein *Gesamtkunstwerk*. This was the American approach, an informal do-it-yourself under benign supervision. Yet the principle is the same in all three: the word-music tells something and the singer must learn what that is in order to sing the words. Voice is everything—but the singing must inform. Or: Stimm' is total, but Kunst is irreplaceable. Or: the conductor controls, but the story must be told.

Most important, divas must retain their independence, must, as Felsenstein recommended, reassume their creative role, as Schröder-Devrient, Viardot, Garden, Lehmann before them. When they do not—when they let directors make all arrangements—they can be, at best, no better than he is. What does that make them, when he doesn't know his job?

Dummies.

CHAPTER

9

THE
IMPRESARIO

The public has but little idea
of the difficulties by which
the career of an opera manager
is surrounded.

Colonel J. H. Mapleson

Your successes are my successes.

Giulio Gatti-Casazza
to Geraldine Farrar

Don't be misled—behind that
cold, austere, severe exterior,
there beats a heart of stone.

Cyril Ritchard
on Rudolf Bing

While the maestro in his various incarnations heads one of opera's oldest regimes, and while the stage director has only lately come to power, the impresario is all but extinct. As a maximum leader who is not himself a contributing artist, he survives: as corporate booking agent, as personal manager, as administrative director of a company. Even the word "impresario" has hung on. But the old-fashioned "promoter" who collected and organized a troupe, presided over in-house seasons or extended tours, and handled everything from advertising ploys and dispensation of box-office receipts to rehearsing the claque and courting the swells in the boxes—the true impresario, in short, has long vanished.

This golden-age impresario was a major figure in the diva's history, for his operation concentrated on the hiring of stars to the near-neglect of all else. Today's administrations have a great deal to juggle—the stylistic and historical texture of the repertory, the esprit de corps of component performing forces such as the orchestra, chorus, and ballet, the maintenance of amiable public relations, the custody of financial investments, for example. But the old impresario's opera was more a hand-to-mouth operation, depending on the availability of renowned sopranos (and the odd sensational tenor) and subject absolutely to their art, fees, and whims.

Such an impresario was James Henry Mapleson, a chronicler's favorite for his volubly gruesome memoirs. Colonel Mapleson, as the day knew him, was by his admission "student, critic, violinist, vocalist, and composer, concert director, and musical agent" before he took opera's ultimate leadership position. As impresario in England and America during the middle and late 1800s, Mapleson encountered the cabals, miscalculations, and acts of God that plague managers today, including contentious stars, striking orchestras, disloyal associates, negligent audiences, and theatre fires, even an earthquake in San Francsico. Still, his opera lived outside of the idea of history, looking neither behind nor forward. It thrived on a cluster of contemporary (or recently late) composers whose style hung in the air and whose characters, therefore, could be sung in one of two ways: correctly or badly. New works chimed in, but these basically respected rather than insulted audiences' perception of what constitutes pleasant operagoing. When Mapleson did go out of his way to introduce a risky novelty to England against everybody else's judgment, it was no *We Come to the River,* but Gounod's *Faust.* Already we see how basic life was then—and remember that stage directors of the time had no power whatsoever. In Mapleson's world, contestants for authority were he and his soprano of the moment. It was a rougher and simpler world.

What makes the outdated Mapleson useful in understanding the modern diva's world is his reliance on singers, not any singers but stars, not any stars but those who elate and move us: on whom one could build a season. It is the impresario's view of who elates, combined with how the public takes to her, that informs discussions on casting and repertory. If we schedule *Aida,* who is our first choice? Conversely, should we schedule *Aida* if great Aidas are lacking? Such questions can censor or inflect the repertory quite influentially. Though the impresario is by nature of his job exploitive, he can aid a diva in her development, for the greater her artistry, the more profitable and personally satisfying his operation. If he sees her as a supplementary figure, however, a workhorse, he will not develop but drain her. If one thinks of opera as the only sport in which the athlete is expected to *improve* as he or she gets older, and last into his fifties at top form, one realizes how easy it is to get drained and how fast it can happen. Thus the importance of the impresario in the establishment of diva.

There is no place for a Mapleson today; now only the artists freelance. His métier, moreover, has broken into its constituents, yielding one profession for the drafting of singers' schedules, another for the guiding of singers' careers (these two may combine, or the voice teacher may play guide), and a third for the artistic and/or regulating steerage of the resident companies. All work together in unending symbiosis, the administrators disliking the agents' demands and the agents denouncing the administrators' lack of vision, each side certain the other has too much power for opera's good. Only one person has thought it useful or amusing to build the three jobs together again, the American agent-plus-manager-cum-impresario Matthew Epstein.

Epstein swept up through the ranks in the 1970s, first as an employee in concert management, then as an agent specifically oriented to opera, always insisting that his clients retain a strong sense of direction in their careers. By the end of the decade, when he left Columbia Artists Management to consult and produce on his own, he had by his example realigned the profession of artists' representative away from agenting (i.e., negotiating the fees and keeping the books) toward guidance (the creative side: planning the rise and forestalling the fall). Throughout, applying an almost mystical knowledge of opera from core repertory to potential rediscoveries, Epstein was, as agent, the most demanding; when guide, the most insightful; then impresario, the most comprehensive. He rightly sensed that this would prove the age of the young Americans, and his code in their care and training might be stated thus:

> You must learn the great roles of your Fach, even if you won't sing them for a decade.
>
> You must work with the best coaches.
>
> You must be first-rate in the first place; or get out of my office.

It is never too early for a lyric to begin work on Violetta, or for a mezzo to consider Charlotte or Périchole, or for a presumed dramatic to investigate—by piano—Isolde. And shouldn't a singer strike up a collaboration with a tutorial maestro as soon as possible? If an impresario is interested mainly in what he can get out of you, a good agent is there to put in, to guide you from the first auditions and debuts right into the assumptions of the great roles.

How does one enter opera? The musician of course starts with the lessons and the director logs experience in apprentice situations. Where does an agent begin? Epstein, with a squatter's sense of territoriality, invaded the greenroom as a teenager after the performances, to meet the artists and taste of the profession. Feeling his way in, he would expand, advise, and correct the mighty and humble alike, divas of personality like Marie Collier and divas of voice like Marilyn Horne. So he nosed in. At first it may have seemed impromptu to be getting mid-career diagnoses from a stranger in the cluttered backstage of the buffs and autograph hounds, but singers quickly realized that what they were hearing was more sensible than what they heard from impresarios and agents.

In short, the people in charge of the operations don't necessarily know more or have better taste than those in a supplementary capacity. What *are* the qualifications of the general director of a major opera company? David Webster gave his thusly: "I don't want to conduct, I don't want to produce, and I don't have a mistress who wants to sing." A gift for assembling a potent blend of talents and letting chemistry carry them onward without intervention is helpful; but the facetious Webster omits other gifts that he in fact had in some measure: tact, authority, loyalty, a love of the repertory, an instinct for recognizing potential in recruits, and the willingness to calculate a wild risk every so often.

After the Second World War, when Covent Garden was reinstituted and a company marshaled, Thomas Beecham felt betrayed and insulted that Webster had won the appointment. Had not Sir Thomas brought opera to that glorious theatre long since, at personal expense—ambitious opera at that? In Strauss alone, the first British *Salome, Elektra,* and *Der Rosenkavalier* were Beecham's, *Salome* with Aïno Ackté and

Rosenkavalier with the original Dresden Marschallin and Octavian. Did Beecham not welcome Supervia for Rossini, distinguished refugees from Nazism for Wagner? Had he not, long before it was popular, brought Russian opera to Drury Lane? He was Beecham the magnificent. Who was Webster? A businessman!

However, for all his importance in the history of English opera production, Beecham lacked the qualifications. No one would doubt his love and knowledge of opera, nor his authority and daring. Beecham's risks were the wildest, as a rule. But his scornful wit overwhelmed any possibility of tact, and he preferred the established genius to the developing one, which would have tangled Covent Garden's postwar finances irredeemably. Beecham would have been a famous choice, but Webster was a careful one, and sound. Yes, he was a businessman at the time he came to Covent Garden—he turned down an important commercial position to do so—but there was some opera tucked away in his past; and, after all, Antonio Ghiringhelli, at a similar point in La Scala's history, gave up the law to oversee the reformation of his company.

Anyway, experience in musical administration does not guarantee opera-house expertise, much less the broad vision a leader needs. Opera is not a day-to-day deal. Opera is preparing great roles one will restudy for decades, or advising singers on such roles, or knowing which singers will inspirit them; opera is disinterring classics of long-dead eras and commissioning future classics; opera is four hundred years' worth of art. Interim procedures of making do and shoveling productions onto the stage are destructive.

Clearly, a knowledge of opera as art and practice, from sublime nights of collaborative intensity to the workmanlike nights that keep the music going, is no minor credential. What does the diva want from the impresario? That's simple: the honor of the first night, all the new productions and primas (conducted, moreover, by her husband or lover), her choice of colleagues—and a little greenroom flattery would be nice, too. What can the impresario give the diva while taking, for the good of the art? The best he should do is exploit her—not stupidly or disloyally but sensibly, to channel her endowment into its most deliverable areas. A diva in her element is good for

opera: a diva wasted or miscast or bedeviled by inept technicians is good for nothing.

How simple; what truism. Then why have so many impresarios failed to see it? What service did Ghiringhelli perform
for La Scala in barring Callas? Why did it take Webster so long
to discern Sutherland's forte? Why did Bing sign undistinguished singers to heavy schedules while ignoring many acknowledged talents till they were pushing their dotage? His
resistance to Beverly Sills was preposterous. By the time Bing
had left and Sills at last made the Met, she was a veteran
within a decade of her farewell; Bing might have snapped her
up at the time of her first City Opera sensation in *Giulio Cesare,* plopped her into whatever was appropriate and handy,
meanwhile readying some new production for her, and a loose
national strain in the webbing of American opera would have
been tightened. Bing says he "did not care very much for her,"
and feels that an intendant must run his house by his, not
popular, judgment. Maybe. But not caring for Sills so much
that you can't even bear to let her sing a few performances on
your stage is questionable taste, especially given the quality
of some of the performers Bing did care for. Bing did make
Sills some offers, but halfheartedly and somehow always for
times when she was busy elsewhere, leaving her no choice but
to refuse.

Bing was one of the few modern impresarios whose reign
recalled the querulous vitality of the golden age. Webster of
Covent Garden was laconic, Ghiringhelli of La Scala a top hat
with nothing under it, Liebermann of Hamburg very earnest,
Adler of San Francisco skilled but turbulent in the *mitteleu-
ropäisch* manner, von Karajan of Vienna seldom seen. Bing was
articulate, characterful, suave, and omnipresent, as colorful as
Colonel Mapleson. However, where Mapleson's regime derived
its quirky rhapsody from the didoes of his selfish stars, Bing's
featured his own escapades, especially his unsentimental view
of difficult singers and his masterful sense of humor. Then, too,
Bing inherited a position endowed with an unbroken conti-
nuity of traditions. Webster and Liebermann were building
companies, Ghiringhelli (and Liebermann in Paris, after
Hamburg) rebuilding, Adler sharpening, von Karajan redefin-
ing. Bing came into the House of Voice, where Caruso, Pon-

selle, and Flagstad had flourished, where Knickerbocker aristos gently set rigid fashion, where the most outmoded staging conventions prevailed. Gatti-Casazza had tried to balance sensation with musicianship; under him the Met had personality. But after him Edward Johnson, a former tenor, aimed for an average in everything and locked the house into mediocrity. Singers ruled, their great roles uncontested and their good opinion the house's first imperative. It was the 1930s and 1940s, but it might have been 1900, everything old-style. When Flagstad struck one of her six poses, the dust was glad.

Bing did not subvert the Met rule of vocal glory. To his credit, he attempted to rescale the house along the high European standards in stagecraft that he had helped set at Glyndebourne and the Edinburgh Festival, to graduate the House of Voice into the modern world. The theatre revolution had begun; the public was beginning to notice (even care) who the stage directors were. When Bing took over the Met in 1950, only Paris of major houses was more *passéiste*, conservative in the worst way: unenlightened.

Paris, at least, had the excuse of being a national house, at the mercy of tenured voices, uncooperative unions, and deadly routine. The Met was an old name riding out a reputation made decades before, Edward Johnson's clubhouse for his old comrades (backstage) and the socially persuasive (out front). Not unlike the Mapleson-era impresarios, the Met was centered on its star names, so much so that but for Flagstad and Melchior's Wagner, Milanov and Warren's Verdi, and Sayão's French elegance, the house would have been dropped from the roster of magical places.

Bing brought in directors from the theatre (Webster, for instance; and there were others), drummed up headline business for a lively *Fledermaus* in Howard Dietz' Broadwayesque English, sought out other possibilities for opera in translation (Dietz' *Bohème* came off as vapidly heartless and was junked; *Così Fan Tutte,* in Ruth and Thomas Martin's High Middle Cockamamie, was atrocious, but for some reason Bing retained it), and generally earned a showman's image—meaning, to some, that he was cheapening the company with a popular infusion. On the contrary, he was trying to put zest back into the comedies and conviction into love-and-death. Unfortunately, many of the divas Bing inherited upheld Johnsonian practice: just go out there, open the mouth, and do it.

Also unfortunately, Bing would countenance theatre savvy only within his set structures. We have seen, on one hand, Milanov resisting Webster and, on the other, Bing resisting Tito Gobbi's attempt to Italianize, *naturalize,* a wrongheaded *Tosca.* Thus the Met was slightly progressive but mostly strait, not a place in which any singer could grow. Divas came to the Met to exhibit their accomplishments, as Tebaldi and Callas would bring their great roles already placed, resisting the production at hand. True, Bing did try to interest Callas in some projects that would have expanded her repertory—Poulenc's *La Voix Humaine,* for instance, or the world premiere of Samuel Barber's *Vanessa.* (How absorbing it would have been to hear Callas, for once, singing in her and our native language; reportedly she would have done it but for the competitive size of the second woman part, Erika.) Still, the exceptions are so few they praise the rule, and basically the Met was a revolving door for stars: in, do, and out.

But house artists had a hard time rising from comprimario or sidekick parts. When a very young Roberta Peters made a last-minute debut as Zerlina in the first weeks of Bing's first season, it seemed to augur well for the growth of a new American roster. However, Peters merely hung on, a canary in a red-and-gold cage, to sing Zerlina's sisters Rosina, Susanna, and the rest, frozen in the least interesting Fach in opera. Who knows for sure that Peters and the public would have profited from a more expansive program? We never will; by the time Peters turned up on an off night of the Met's *Sonnambula,* the effect of fifteen years of incarceration was saddening.

As with the maestro and the director, the diva can be either the impresario's victim or beneficiary. The agent is nowhere as influential (unless he or she really knows his business and loves his art, and few do), and advisors are early supplanted by maestros and directors. But the impresario affects the diva's career till it ends; indeed, he is often the major reason why it doesn't work out as well as it might have done, even why it ends: because the impresario does the hiring.

This brings us back to the issue of the impresario's taste, his sense of art, his personality, which can color every aspect of company life, from the steely back David Webster would present to importunate singers as he gazed out his office window to the sardonic eyes of Bing, everywhere, always in focus, brightly cruel as a retort gathered in his head. (It is said that when trouble broke out at the Met, Bing could get to it within fifty seconds and handle it in ten. Trouble was his kind of party.) The true impresario doesn't merely preside over a battery of assistants; he is the genius of the place. He can favor a diva with the best of his resources, a Visconti or Zeffirelli, a Serafin or Mackerras. He can thrust her into a half-decent production with rudimentary rehearsal, to electrify or fizzle entirely on her own energy. He can plop her into dreck. At such moments impresarios and agents could not be farther apart: for the one wants expedients for his house and the other wants justice for his client. If the word of old-timers be taken, they used to be the same thing: what was good for a company was good for the singers, and vice versa.

No longer. *Norma* is good for a company, not for most of the singers who tackle it; dummy opera makes headlines; and there's a shortage of everything needful. So one makes accommodations, such as hiring singers to "sing a few performances" of something—meaning they cover for someone else and get a grudging one night on stage without preparation, appreciation, or honor. Even a handsome invitation may hide a trap. The Paris Opéra offered Sheri Greenawald her first try at Manon in the new production's second airing; what Manon wouldn't want to perform for a public who can actually understand her, word for word? But Matthew Epstein advised her against it. Her rehearsals would consist of little more than a tour of the stage and, besides, Paris is not the place in which one tries her first Manon.

This gaming with careers is the thing singers most resent about the impresarios they do resent. Speaking for the other side, Bing might reply that he had to call the shots as he saw them; but why did this include the importing of an apparently inexhaustible supply of third-raters from Yugoslavia and Rumania? No doubt Bing was trying to show these captives of the East the pleasures of life in Western democracy so they could return, tell their friends, and so undermine Communism. Still, the constant irruption of Biserka Cvejic, Milka

Stojanovic, Ion Buzea, Nicolae Herlea, and others such considerably lessened the pleasures of democratic life for Met audiences.

Of course, if a diva should conceive an artistic understanding with a top impresario, she is made, for the company diva counts many a privilege. If opera's backstage can function as a workshop, a learning process in which canny singers absorb an input for personal development as acting singers, that workshop needs the stability of a steady address. True, the style of the modern star is travel: to Milan for Verdi with Abbado, to London for a controversial new production of who cares what, to Salzburg for festival spectaculars with Ponnelle. But travel means racing over, leaping through it, and racing off. It's good for fame but bad for the mind. Besides, travel is inconvenient, especially for a woman alone: suspicious hoteliers and restaurateurs, strange doctors, dizzy tailors, and hairdressers without references. Worst of all, travel fatigues. You can't sing well when you're tired.

Luckily, there are plenty of opportunities for divas to join a company and settle into a learning life. All the cultural capitals maintain "second" houses like the New York City Opera, the English National Opera, or the Vienna Volksoper, and such houses conserve the residential equilibrium that the old Met, Covent Garden, and the Vienna State Opera used to, everyone in constant ensemble interaction. The advantages a Bori, a Melba, a Jeritza knew as house soprano in such places were phenomenal, amounting to first dibs on everything that matters in diva: great roles, tutelary maestros, primas, and a loving public. One can thus launch one's career, as Sutherland did; reimpose it, as Flagstad did; see it to its close in high style, as Farrar did; all in collaboration with the best talents the house could produce. True, the house diva can be overbearing in her greatness—Farrar got touchy when Gatti let someone else try *her* Butterfly and gloated when it failed to draw. To miss out on being top in the house, as Claudia Muzio did at the Met in Farrar's time, is to see splendid opportunities lost, one's aces shuffled to the back of the deck. But for those with influence, the impresario becomes something like your reputation's best friend.

Who needed whom more, Gatti or Ponselle? Gatti could offer her a gala entree into opera; and, when she had made the most of it, Gatti could present her with a contract and further challenges; these met, Gatti could keep Ponselle comfortable and stimulated in the house of her choice. As long as Gatti ran it, the Met was Ponselle's heaven. But Ponselle could offer Gatti, it turned out, the Stimm' of the century. Who of the pair came out ahead?

Consider, too, the case of Beverly Sills and Julius Rudel of the City Opera. The company was ignored by all but the philanthropic foundations and a few dotty buffs when it inhabited its old barn on Fifty-fifth Street. But on its move to Lincoln Center next to the haughty Met, the City Opera became a thorn with which journalists needled the big house. Suddenly they fell all over themselves praising the little company's sense of adventure (in its repertory) and democracy (in its audience and home-grown singers). Suddenly the Met was pretentious and the City Opera was cute.

At the same time the smaller company began to establish an autograph in production style: in the use of projections, in Ming Cho Lee's jungle gyms and uncluttered downstage area, in Frank Corsaro's abradant naturalism, in Tito Capobianco's manneristic charm. Lo, the city took up the City Opera and, just then, intendant Rudel unveiled Handel's *Giulio Cesare* with Sills and Norman Treigle, adding to this triumph of nationalist casting the look of Capobianco and Lee and the atmosphere of the Latest Collectible.

Opera always looks to the diva, so the most potent factor in the sensational *Caesar* was Sills. Her loyalty to Rudel, everybody knew, would prove strategic to the company's fortunes. As with Ponselle and Gatti, Sills became Rudel's rarest wine, decanted in her newfound Fach of bel-canto beldame— a wonderfully lurid Elisabetta in Bette Davis grumping, a wiggy Lucia as true to Sir Walter Scott as to Donizetti; and, to complicate her art, her great role was Manon. If Ponselle was incomparable, she had competition in the house, for her eminence if not for her particular parts. But Sills was undisputed house diva in her house, and, as Lotte Heinotz puts it, "the house diva is the local sweetheart, the favorite princess, and the patron saint. She is everything for everybody."

It's nice to be chosen, but only for high stakes. The other

side of the company diva is the soprano on all-purpose re-
tainer, without Fach, without glory, often without rehearsals,
scarcely a diva at all. This is often the lot of the singer whose
gifts include neither temperament nor that immediately recognizable timbre that Walter Legge noted as essential to
greatness. For all her musicianship and theatricality, the singer
without an imposing instrument may end up like the Met's
Mary Curtis-Verna, an estimable artist whose dramatic bent
led her into Verdi and verismo, but whose Met career took in
almost everything, on call—a student-matinee Mimì, Aida
subbing for Renata Tebaldi (which can't have been fun), Turandot, Santuzza, a last-night-of-the-season Adriana, even Gutrune and a Norn in Gothic toupées. Curtis-Verna's versatility
gave her the range a house fixer needs; she was too useful. No
matter who became ill, Curtis-Verna could take over a Tosca,
a Mistress Ford, a Leonora (did it matter which one?). It's good
for a company, not for a singer.

Similarly, Bing retained Lucine Amara for these assignments, launching her—quite incorrectly—as the Heavenly Voice
in his opening *Don Carlos* and thereafter asking her to cover
virtually the entire schedule. One thinks of Sutherland in her
early years at Covent Garden; but Sutherland had a phenomenal voice and a guide who led her into an imposing specialization. Amara deputized, waited, sang countless Liùs—more
miscasting—and at great length won Ellen Orford in a new
production of *Peter Grimes*. By luck, it happened to be one of
Bing's best efforts, and if the occasion devolved entirely upon
Jon Vickers' extraordinary Grimes, Bing did defend Amara
when Georg Solti protested her.

Ironically, Ellen turned out to be Amara's great role, the
smalltown schoolteacher's spinstery pathos combining impressively with Amara's unglamorous voice and underdog
plastique. Such shining moments can revise one's view of an
entire career; still, this is no way to run one. Amara's Ellen is
remembered in New York, but so is the cruel joke about the
"Lucine Amara Gala." It seems that, on her retirement, the
Met would give her a sendoff in Melba style: one act each of
any three roles of her choice. No, she wasn't scheduled to sing
them—she was covering the entire evening.

CHAPTER

10

RISE

I wanted to do it on my own.
Catherine Malfitano

*If you love music enough to
serve it humbly, fame will
come automatically.*
Maria Callas

I adore the unusual.
Jessye Norman

*Once I was very near death. . . .
During the last minutes before I
was saved, I had but one thought
in my head which ground on and
on and on: "Oh, how marvellous,
now I never need be reviewed by
that . . . critic Nyblom again."*
Elisabeth Söderström

*The press always has
the last word.*
Geraldine Farrar

Where does a career begin? There are the years of first exposure, perhaps to one's parents' opera recordings or to some school project. There are first lessons, first coachings, first stage experiences in college or conservatory workshops. One tries one's first Pamina, Musetta, Micaëla, or even roles beyond the standard repertory, roles such as Sapho or Anna Maurrant that one might never sing again. One crashes the cultural capital, finds a job, hopes. One meets other singers, musicians, agents. One auditions. One picks up jobs here and there, bits and leads in the provinces that cannot take one anywhere but do swell the résumé. Through it all, one thinks of the first *Sternstunde,* the moment when all one's work and tenacity and rehearsals come front and center with major eyes upon one.

The Break, the Company, the Part: given a break with a solid company in the right part, one may be set for life, though many of the grandest careers began ignominiously in some part that gave no hint of promise. Helen Traubel got to the Met in 1937, in the world premiere of *The Man Without a Country.* This had to be the right company for an American born to sing Wagner, but no one wanted to hear the new work and Traubel had to wait two and a half years before asserting herself on the same stage, this time as Sieglinde.

Lotte Lehmann enhances such lore in her Hamburg debut. This was her first night onstage in opera, and it was surely the right company, for her Hamburg apprenticeship led directly to her legendary reign in Vienna. However, when Lehmann first stepped forth it was as *Die Zauberflöte*'s Third Boy, her unique timbre and delivery buried in three-part harmony.

There are debuts and Debuts, though it's probably safe to say that the sooner a diva makes hers, somewhere and somehow, the sooner her reign may commence and her legends collect. It is an article of faith today that singers debut too early, but they used to debut even earlier, in their teens or a bit over at the latest. Wilhelmine Schröder-Devrient first tried opera (after debuts in ballet and Shakespeare) having just turned sixteen. Maria Malibran reached the stage at seventeen, as did her sister Pauline Viardot. Giuditta Pasta was eighteen, Giulia Grisi seventeen, Jenny Lind eighteen, Marcella Sembrich nineteen (this after Liszt urged her to set aside the piano and violin for opera), Adelina Patti (billed as Little Florinda) sixteen, Lilli Lehmann seventeen, Ernestine Schumann-Heink seventeen, Luisa Tetrazzini nineteen, Celestina Boninsegna fifteen (following the most elementary studies), Elvira de Hidalgo sixteen, Geraldine Farrar nineteen, and Rosa Ponselle (the slowcoach in the group, though of course she had already been active in vaudeville) twenty-one. And most of these debuts were in major roles, some on major stages.

They don't debut too soon today. They spend too much time learning nothing in conservatories and debut, in their twenties, in worthless bit parts with other singers as unseasoned as themselves, utterly at the mercy of maestros and directors. No wonder Felsenstein thought singers' lack of independence was opera's biggest problem. They debut late: but they build too early, taking on too much without having put in the *Lehrjahre* under a propulsive maestro or two, as the women listed above did. A major difference between launching a career then and now is the absurd interference (in the English-speaking countries especially) of some form of higher education, which supposedly rounds out a singer's professionalism but which in fact delays its start. In Malibran's day one learned to sing, mastered repertory, and materialized. They didn't throw you a bouquet because you had earned a degree at some school run by musicians who couldn't make it in the professional world. Nor do they today.

What incipient divas need less than academies in opera is good advice on what moves to make; what music, which styles, to make one's study; what hopes to entertain; how to prepare. "I was ready," Mary Garden warns them. "I was ready, and that's what half of them aren't today." Not all newcomers need be ready to start where Garden did, spang at the top as Louise a few weeks after it had become the sensation of Paris. One wonders how well they would do in such a moment. Going Out There a Youngster and Coming Back a Star is a standard trope of the Broadwayite's ambition (however much promulgated in Hollywood), but does any youngster today make a contingency plan against such a stroke of fate? Garden, as early as 1951, thought not:

> They rarely have a goal nowadays, or when they have, they must get to it in a few weeks or months. I have always stressed three years of hard, unremitting work. I have emphasized my three don'ts: no drinking, no smoking, no men for those three years. After all, three years are nothing in the life of a young girl. When she gains her name, she can do what she likes. Then everything she says and does is news.

Lotte Heinotz offered her own prescription, emphasizing the need to specialize as early and thoroughly as possible. As Mary Garden had her French premieres, Carmen Melis and Gilda dalla Rizza their verismo, Helen Traubel and Martha Mödl their Wagner, Sutherland her bel canto, Marilyn Horne her Rossini, Leontyne Price her Verdi, Margaret Price her Mozart, so might the next generations present facets of themselves in such special series, a personal repertory. Specialization also has the advantage of centering one's availability to impresarios, discouraging the wildcat offers by the logic of reputation. Excel in a Fach or even a role and you will be asked to continue in the same vein, as those several Queens of the Night were, those Salomes, those Mimìs—as, right now, Susan Dunn is, for her promising Verdian soprano. The catch is that a dangerous repertory inspires dangerous offers. Dunn has already been pressed to try Turandot, though she is barely thirty.

A lack of specialization can serve as a specialty in itself, for versatility is so rare that it seems admirable in itself. Jessye Norman became famous not only for her lovely timbre and statuesque figure but for her connoisseur's interests—Berlioz and Mozart, Stravinsky and Wagner, Purcell and Strauss, Meyerbeer and Mahler. Here the danger is that a miscellany of expertise yields a miscellany of offers. An unguided innocent starting out at Berlin's Deutsche Oper, Norman sang the *Tannhäuser* Elisabeth and found herself urged into everything from high coloratura to dramatic and verismo parts. She said no; smart woman. "I had no intention of ruining my voice," she says, "by the age of twenty-five."

Besides recommending specialization, Lotte Heinotz also advised, a touch frantically, against taking chorus work at the start. This is perhaps the bias of a supplementary personality, obsessed with the terror of anonymity. Elisabeth Schwarzkopf and Janet Baker both began in the chorus; for all that, many divas took work in the secretarial pool or so while collecting their first musical credits. A job's a job: temporary. Only the opera work counts. Rosa Ponselle came out of vaudeville, Evelyn Lear and Reri Grist got started in musicals,* and Patricia Brooks made herself ready for the New York City Opera twirling a parasol in the chorus of the off-Broadway revival of *Leave It to Jane.*

Having a goal is essential and specialization can be usefully identifying. But perhaps guidance is most important—the wisdom of the expert who knows career-building as the maestro knows music. Such wisdom is hard to find, unfortunately, which explains why many sound plans are ruined by false moves. The driving need for guidance also explains re-

---

*Lear's first job, fresh out of Juilliard, was the ingenue lead in Marc Blitzstein's bizarre trip through a night of Manhattan's lower depths, *Reuben, Reuben,* which closed after a week in Boston. Grist played Cindy Lou in *Carmen Jones*—this is virtually Micaëla in English—and sang "Somewhere" in the original *West Side Story.* She was also the girl who prefers Puerto Rico to the United States, to Chita Rivera's disgust, in "America."

tired divas' popularity as teachers: they teach not only how to express but how to *become,* how to move through the profession. However, the opera world has changed considerably in the postwar years: the familiar impresarios and maestros have been replaced, the agent has become primary, the recording contract is salient, and the company ideal has given way to the freelance opportunist. How wisely can a Cigna or Milanov expound to her pupils on the current scene?

When precisely does one make entree? As of the first audition? The first *major* audition? These can be wrongheadedly discouraging. Half of the successful singers alive can tell of a crucial evil encounter with alleged authorities, including a few that ended with the assurance that the singer would never have a career. Or there is the revolving-door audition, such as the one Judy Kaye got when up for the City Opera's *Merry Widow.* Kaye looks great, acts suave, and sings a spectacular Vilja-lied. And when she had done so, out boomed the voice of Beverly Sills—"Thank you!"—and that was the end of that. Is there such a thing as being too good for a role?

Some few singers might date the initiative moment from the first major liaison, the meeting that changed one's status. For Rosa Ponselle it was the meeting with Romano Romani, the coach who put her on to William Thorner, the agent who put her on to Caruso, who put her on to the Met. For Joan Sutherland it was her chancing upon her old Australian comrade Richard Bonynge in London. For Maria Callas, typically, it was a perverse liaison, with neither a musician nor an agent, nor yet with anyone connected to the opera world. For Maria Callas it was Giovanni Battista Meneghini, the businessman who gave her sustenance while she blazed at the barriers that stood in her way.

You'll never find this method of launching a career in any handbook. Depending on how one reads it, Callas either used this Don Pasquale of a Meneghini because she was friendless and penniless and had no engagement on the books except the Verona *Gioconda*s that had brought her to Italy in the summer of 1947 at about sixty dollars a performance; or Callas threw herself into Meneghini's arms because, for the first time in her life as the ugly daughter with the pretty sister whom their mother preferred—and as the so-old-she-was-new singer with the voice no one could like—she at last found input of personal affirmation.

In the Italy that Callas arrived in for her debut, women were attractive or ignored. Overweight, silent, eyes cast down, and dressed in camouflage black, Callas was ignored by all but Meneghini, a man-about-Verona on some minor level and therefore a suitable escort for prima donnas in their offstage hours—dinner, coffee out on the piazza, perhaps a walk back to the hotel. The single moment of meeting one's Romani or Bonynge should be indexed; Callas and Meneghini met over a veal cutlet. He had happened upon the opera crowd in the Pedavena restaurant, and Callas offered him her plate. Meneghini was hungry, Callas was not, and, anyway, she had the last of the house cutlets. Serafin then introduced them. Their eyes locked, one supposes; maybe not. In any case, Meneghini squired Callas around, even, beyond duty's call, on a side trip to Venice, to show this American with her Empire State Building and Brooklyn Bridge the unequaled beauty of Italy.

Meneghini does not recall the Callas the rest of us know, strenuously rational, sure of herself and her art, sure of Bellini, Donizetti, Verdi, doubtful of everyone living, and keeping an enemies list. This Verona Callas was vulnerable and unknowledgable. Her Giocondas at the Arena were meant to be institutional, not just a debut but an explosion. It was a first test of talent that only she, at the time, knew was supreme. If no one else agreed, she might never get another job, much less crest the summit. She was so poor she hadn't wanted to go to Venice because it would have meant appearing in the same outfit she had been rehearsing in. She was, literally, without friends and without support. Had she never found anyone to help her? Meneghini asked.

"But who would be interested in me," she replied, "with my shape?"

Meneghini told Callas not to underestimate herself.

Callas told Meneghini she never underestimated, and she was dead right. She knew what she was worth unknown and what famous; it was the difference between a slight incline on a back street in Athens and Mount Olympus. Meneghini was the man who could connect the mean height to the elevation for Callas, and in the event her Giocondas were mere success, no sensation. How could they be, so early in the career? *La Gioconda* was Callas' first professional sortie, a tricky part to boot. She needed time in which to develop, without having to scramble for a living. Meneghini, then, would provide.

Callas' rise—as public fable, in the mythology of Callas—comprises her taking every acceptable job and letting the fame spread while tightening her talent. But there is this other, private rise in the Meneghini "romance." No one can analyze love chemistry. Maybe Callas did love him, or wanted to; maybe she was touched by his affection. Or was she in the end smart and hard and intent upon advantage? We'll never know. She married him, took his name professionally (between her two, albeit), lived with him in his hometown, absorbed him into her career, made the pledges women make to men. And, till she met Aristotle Onassis, probably kept them.

To the outsider's glance the Callas-Meneghini marriage was, aside from the great difference in their ages, not hopelessly unlikely. Her love letters to him, with which he pathetically documented their relationship in his book about her, reveal a genuine bond. But when her career began to hit its rhythm, when opinion-makers began to hail the strange voice as the sound of a new age, when the black-clad Rubens dwindled into chic trim in high style, Meneghini looked out of place. Callas must have begun to feel so; maintaining image was one of her obsessions. The liaison no longer useful, Callas disposed of Meneghini. Whether she had always meant to, at the appropriate time, or whether she had genuinely fallen in love with him in Verona and genuinely fallen out in love's good time is reader's choice.

One might also date a career from the first major offers, signals that the big houses know the name and need the talent. For many divas this is the all-moment in which the rise is felt most fully and abruptly, the instant in which one's ambition and the needs of the opera houses come together. It can be a trap: if one is invited into a "subsidiary" opera, a part without réclame, or an unsuitable great role. One might have a role of choice in a gruesome production or with an underpowered company. Can one say no? Many divas fear to—if they play it high-hat, they dread, they'll never be asked again. This has been given as one reason why sopranos tackle big roles before their time: fear of not flying if one doesn't fly *now*. They should take a lesson from Callas, who, at the very start of her career, said no to the Met.

It seems incredible, especially in the context of Callas' odd look, lack of exchequer and contacts, and questionable experience—largely student performances in wartime Athens. She had little more in her favor in 1946 than a distinguished teacher and her astonishing self-possession in audition, a directness of aplomb that measured out the parts of diva as the offstage Callas feared to. Clearly, she was born for the stage: for she was but half-alive off it, distracted and scheming. Somehow the untried Callas got an audition with Edward Johnson. (Or so the tale runs; it's in the biographies, and an audition card survives, but the story has the feel of apocrypha.) On the spot, Johnson offered her a contract, for *Fidelio* and *Madama Butterfly*. Callas turned him down, though she had sung Leonore in Athens and though she must have known that Butterfly was a role she of all sopranos was equipped to sing. Doubtless she also knew that—whether she liked it or not—the Wagner-Mozart-*Fidelio* field was a possible area of specialization for her, one to be exploited for entree and disposed of thereafter. Yes, Callas was bound for bel canto, ultimately—but she could, in her paradoxical way, be pragmatic when necessary. Anyway, the Met had no resources for bel canto at the time. It carried a drab *Norma* for Milanov and a shabby *Lucia* for Lily Pons, both productions utterly wrong for what Callas had in mind for Bellini and Donizetti.*

What could Callas have wanted from the Met other than Leonore and Butterfly? Could this be a lesson not in saying no but in defining one's goal in cultural, ethnic, imagistic terms? Imagine the unknown standing under the proscenium arch

---

*Ironically, these were the productions Callas sang in (plus *La Traviata* and *Tosca*) during her Met visits. In Dallas, holding proclamation after Bing fired her, Callas laid them out to filth—a buff's favorite moment in the Callas documentary occasionally aired on television.

plated with the names of Gluck, Mozart, Beethoven, Verdi, Wagner, and Gounod, on the stage of Caruso, Farrar, Bori, Martinelli, Tibbett, and Flagstad, facing the general manager of what was at the time the greatest house in the world, realizing that the Met wasn't what she wanted at all, that her history would reorient the public that had worshipped Caruso and Flagstad and that she could never do this in the complacent candy-box opened by a former tenor who was pals with his artists. If the story of Callas' audition is true, it is notable that Callas was not afraid to say no. It's ironic as well, for, fifteen years later, with her history writ bold and her career in disarray, she drew back in fear of failure, afraid to say yes.

Saying yes, learning when to seize the chance to impress, is one of the most crucial judgment calls a diva makes. "Timing," Lotte Heinotz wails, "is the first need! Timing and Fach, timing and role, timing and public. The variables must all be in season, ripe for picking." Less colorfully, Heinotz means that so much rides on a newcomer's debut that she owes it to herself to control as much of uncontrollable opera as she can. The casting must be genuine, the role right for the audience. A decent Butterfly might thrill Houston, with that town's limited opera history, but will not thrill an Italian assembly familiar with great Butterflys from Toti dal Monte and Rosetta Pampanini to Tebaldi and Scotto. Similarly, one might raise a sensation as *Wozzeck*'s Marie in Berlin or Zürich, but not in Rome or Lyons. Paris? Maybe. More likely New York. Then, too, it is decisive where in a season you make debut. First weeks are better than last weeks, last better than middle. Dead weeks are best of all: when there are no new or revived productions, no local favorites trying a new part, and no other debuts, *then* is the time to appear. Unfortunately, houses arrange their schedules without advice from singers—timing is a personal, not necessarily a house, need.

Being terrific in a good showcase of a part is the essential aim. Callas was dejected when her Verona Giocondas did not erupt in a hail of offers for the fall, even with Serafin, *Gioconda*'s conductor and immediately Callas' mentor, recommending her. Perhaps Callas just wasn't terrific at this time—beginners almost never are. Serafin finally edged Callas in at

Venice, Genoa, and Florence as Isolde, Turandot, and Norma, roles available to beginners because so few sopranos can handle them. But what an entrance fee! Veterans avoid these roles for three good reasons: the first is that they are not good for the voice, the second is that they damage the voice, and the third is they will devastate your voice. If old grads with their practiced equipment cannot master them, think what they must do to a tyro.

Why did Callas give her yes so freely? She needed to work. And note that by the time her reputation had begun to collect into the minor legend of a dangerous woman who sang everything, still the debuts were not the *Sternstunden* that hindsight thinks they ought to have been. What, in the welter of dire South American tours and guesting amid the dreary chaos of Italian provincial houses, could have promised a more explosive sensation than learning *I Puritani* at the last minute to replace an ailing colleague just after singing Brünnhilde on the same stage? And Callas' Venetian coup, masterminded by the ingenious Serafin, did make opera news. Yet, unreasonably and infuriatingly, it did not sweep Callas to the summit. It seemed a stunt. No one who hadn't heard Callas in both roles believed she could be good in more than one of them. Even her first visit to La Scala, in an unheralded—virtually unannounced—substitution for Tebaldi as Aida, generated no excitement. And this was Milan, soon to be Callas City.

Her first London roles were well chosen—Norma, perhaps her greatest role and by then securely within her command; Aida, if not a great part, a popular one; and the *Trovatore* Leonora, a great part. Yet, again, most of the audience was slow to comprehend and most of the critics were embarrassingly unknowing. (Covent Garden ought annually to decorate its program books with reprints of the most obtuse reports on Callas by those critics still sounding off on Covent Garden performances; it might warn a little perspective into them.)

Debuts are hazardous, then: even the apparently controllable elements can't be controlled. We can formulate one rule about debuts, going back to Lotte Heinotz' statement that voice is absolute in diva: when on the rise, a pretty sound will succeed more easily than an interesting sound. In other words, Stimmdivas go over better than Kunstdivas.

Thus one of the most radiant debuts of the century was Rosa Ponselle's at the Met on November 15, 1918—her first night in opera altogether. A gifted primitive, Ponselle had no background in opera, no repertory, and no spectator's experience, just the voice of the century. "Born to sing," she calls it. In vaudeville with her sister, Carmela, at the Met, on records at home for the parlor concert, even, decades later, at student auditions, singing a mini-program to give them a taste of the golden age, Ponselle had it all. True, she made effortful entree. Consider: *La Forza del Destino* is a great piece but in that place and time a novelty. She had colleagues of undisputed brilliance in Enrico Caruso, Guiseppe de Luca, and José Mardones; they might overshadow her. She had as well a rival woman newcomer in Alice Gentle, albeit in a role—Preziosilla—that no one gets noticed in. At least Leonora is an ideal Ponselle part, needing the velvet, dexterity, and power that Ponselle among few others had. All in all, it was the right debut, the stupendous debut—just not an easy debut.

Ponselle was a fiasco of nerves by the afternoon of the day before. "What in the name of God have I gotten myself into?" She tries to take a walk; cannot move. She crazes a companion into calling a doctor for a sedative; it doesn't take. She thinks she'll try a brush-up march through the score and pulls that special diva-*in-extremis* bit wherein she cannot recall half the notes. Backstage at the Met on The Night, she discovers she has Completely Lost Her Voice. She envisions a heart attack, complete with headline: "VAUDEVILLE SINGER DIES AT MET DEBUT." It has a ring.

This is one event in which the facts live up to the legend. Ponselle blessed herself with Christian totems, took Caruso's *sotto voce* "Coraggio!" in the first scene, was carried away by the beauty of Mardones' line in the "Vergine degli angeli," took heart from an ovation or two, relaxed enough to play music-lover in the wings during Leonora's long absence from the show between Act Two and "Pace, pace, mio Dio," and, in general, sang the hell out of the part. The house went wild, Otto Kahn gave her a thousand-dollar bill, and manager Gatti-Casazza groaned with relief. In one night, in one debut, he had assured the Met of an amazing talent. There is nothing as gala as a debut that *does*.

But there follows the second major debut, the big night that succeeds the big night—in a blaze of anticipation. What in opera is harder than meeting great expectations?—as Joan Sutherland realized when she attempted her first Violetta a few months after her historic Lucias, on the same stage before the same public. Though Sutherland had been a Covent Garden regular in big roles for years, this was the equivalent of a "second appearance," for not till those Lucias did she wield an image as artist and personality. The *Lucia* had been a surprise; the *Traviata* would be a sure bet. Or so the public thought.

In fact it was risky. Violetta is the lyric's *Norma, summum bonum* of singing as expression of character. Any soprano who can field line and high notes can sing Lucia; Violetta has a dimension, intimacy, and concentration Donizetti's heroine utterly lacks. Doubters may compare Lucia's conventional duet with her tenor lover with Violetta's flirtatious, ambiguous *conversazione* with her tenor suitor, each in the respective Act One. Or set Lucia's duet with her authoritarian brother against Violetta's interview with Germont, both in Act Two. These two scenes treat the same material: the baritone tells the soprano she can't have the tenor for family reasons. But how individually Verdi treats it compared with Donizetti; how characterfully. Lucia essentially pleads and weeps and gives in; Violetta does, too, but more rationally, then with greater despair, and at last with a strangely contemporary nobility, an Empire-salon Portia. As Sutherland was no actress, tackling Violetta just after her first sensation was foolhardy. Moreover, Lucia had been Sutherland's own production, staged around her by the ingenious Zeffirelli. This *Traviata* was house inventory. If it had ever been good, it wasn't now, especially not with unimaginative house Germonts *père et fils*. Added to this was the unforeseen: an attack of laryngitis which threatened the first night and pulled Sutherland out of the second and third.

Not surprisingly, the evening felt embarrassingly disappointing. Sutherland is said to have improved considerably in later performances; still, the event marked the first realization that she would always be more a Lucia than a Violetta. This is the "yes, but" technicality that jeopardizes a reputation, especially after retirement: "Yes, Sutherland could sing, but could she act, even passably?" As the years went on, excitement at hearing her technique and musicianship enlighten each next part fell into an orderly satisfaction, reexcited into jubilee more recently, when she had outlasted virtually all her coevals and become the ranking diva of golden-age trademark.

Still, no one expects anything *independent* from Sutherland. She has the prowess of demented, not the zeal. Perhaps it doesn't matter that Sutherland might have chosen a more appropriate part for her second big night, or that Zeffirelli might have staged that *Traviata,* or that she had been ailing. Every soprano who possibly can gravitates to Violetta sooner or later, and by rules of opera Sutherland had to. It's not a great part for her, but it's a Sutherland part: of the Fach and style she has claimed. It was a self-defining role, an "image" role, a Callas-challenging role. Except for Tosca, Sutherland's great roles were Callas', and the sooner Sutherland laid out her lines of operation, the sooner she could be most correctly perceived.

Selecting debut and follow-up roles for one's foreign jaunts are as crucial as excelling at home. One rises: the great roles develop, the glamour of the special productions heralds one's name, the PR collects. Long ago one became famous in one place, preferably Milan, Berlin, Vienna, Paris, or New York. Today one travels. Opera is an infinitely interconnected network of singers, great roles, superdirectors, and superconductors; linked by hype, paranoia, and nerve; harried by miscasting, flu, radical stagings, and conservative spectators; mitigated by commitment; and planned three years in advance almost down to the latecomer's cough. Thus the rise can come more slowly than it should and the fall take its time: for who can say what wondrous new talent might not turn up tomorrow, or what heavily booked star not run out of voice? Let a lyric come forth in Modena or Spoleto with a special reading of Mimì and she'll find the big houses have cast all the *Bohème*s for the foreseeable future. On the other hand, once a newcomer has Arrived, she can reserve as much as four or five years' work on major stages to find out—at audience expense—if she is a major talent. With the PR machine and records helping her along, she will sign up for any great role an impresario presses upon her: yet not till the curtain pulls up do we learn whether she can hold it. "Opera," James Levine has said, "is a victim of its own success."

In the old days a house could schedule extra nights of a surprise hit and cancel a disappointment days in advance. Now opera moves hesitantly, but rigidly. Some singers are hired simply because they are too famous not to show up on the rosters: we took the trouble to bring in a name, so you'd better show up. Wilhelminia Wiggins-Fernandez enjoyed a distinctive debut in the French film *Diva,* her timbre nicely suiting the movie's "theme song" (more or less), "Ebben? ne andrò lontano," from Catalani's *La Wally.* Quite young and still tracking the provincial circuit in America, Fernandez was invited to the Paris Opéra-Comique to present her Violetta. Fernandez accepted, to the cinemaphile city's delight. Alas, Fernandez did not have a Violetta. It is not clear what happened during rehearsals, but at the dress—public, as usual in Europe—the performance was canceled after Act One and Fernandez headed for the airport.

Conversely, Hildegard Behrens rose up on the German provincial circuit in the mid-1970s to become von Karajan's Salzburg Salome and, immediately, the debutante of the decade in roles ranging from Mozart and Puccini through Wagner, taking in *Wozzeck*'s Marie, Strauss' Ariadne, and Janáček's Katya. Behrens certainly knows how to say yes; with this broad a catalogue, the only thing she might turn down is Alberich. You want to record *Tristan und Isolde* and all the good Isoldes have done it? Behrens will learn it for you, even tape it act by act in public concert. Is she a good Isolde? Many reliable commentators think so, though nowadays fame has become its own rave review. And fame has a piquant way of corrupting some and exalting others. Behrens is an estimable artist, whatever her hazards in Fach, and if the Isolde she re-

corded for Leonard Bernstein sounds underpowered, her Met
Isoldes two years later were dynamite, even stupendous. Has
Behrens found a way to bend fame to artistic ends, to per-
sonal fulfillment at the service of art?

The most smoothly run careers of course feed an artistic
fame, no other kind, and here Joan Sutherland is emblematic.
There was never much to say about her as a public figure beyond the facts that she wasn't high-hat and had married her
coach. She didn't sweep into and out of the stage door, didn't
make like a diva when she spoke, didn't theorize about opera
as a system of moral entitlements. No, Sutherland was a series of encounters in the opera house, a fame made entirely of
performances. After that first parlous Violetta she chose her
roles carefully; this was especially true at La Scala and the
Met, key houses in making oneself internationally manifest.
Her Met Lucias, in the same ruined zoo of a production that
had insulted Callas, had been preceded by daunting PR hoopla,
yet Sutherland actually bettered her reputation; and at La
Scala, in those glorious pageants the Milanese used to put on
regularly four or five times a season, she was a smash from
the first. They love Stimmdiva in Milan.

Sutherland never seemed to suffer *Traviata* jitters at these
houses, never was miscast or in dubious voice. La Scala set
her off well; it was that house's particular delight to evolve
productions around singers' individual strengths, osmotically,
almost unnoticeably. Whether through director's imagination,
conductor's sympathy, designer's foresight, or—one sus-
pects—all in cahoots, this was a company made for triumphs
(provided one was willing to *demand* star's rights). Nor did
Sutherland err in her choice of debut. After spot appearances
about the boot, to encourage rumor and wonder, she walked
into La Scala, gave them her Lucia in a standby revival, and
blew the house away. Not since Tebaldi had the hall so rung
with cheers; not since early Callas had there been such fever
over a foreigner's singing of Italian.

Sutherland la Stupenda consolidated her first impression
in succeeding Scala productions, now brand new ones and each
a study in how to adore a star while respecting a work—the
storybook *Les Huguenots* or the ponderously classical *Semi-*

ramide. It has not been said enough, and not entirely understood by the general public, that Covent Garden has for some
time been a house most comfortable with self-starting talents,
with the more intense singers, the more theatrical personalities. Given an intelligent, even half-decent production, they will
thrive. Thus one thinks of the house as the place of Schwarzkopf, Christoff, Pears, Richard Lewis, Gobbi, Callas, Veasey,
Vickers, Marie Collier, and Amy Shuard, artists not hopelessly dependent on directors' connivance. Not that the company has not taken advantage of strong directors (especially
lately). But the house has been strong in both company members and habitual guests with an opera-as-theatre initiative.
Neither La Scala nor the Met has this advantage. Without it,
a house must create a pervasive set of production styles (as
La Scala did) or suffer an era of costumed concert (as the Met
did under Bing).

This is a factor in calculating one's career: which does a
diva need more, independence or showcasing confinement?
Choosing David Webster's Covent Garden for a debut meant
one thing to an expanding career, Ghiringhelli's La Scala another, Bing's Met a third. Renata Tebaldi was happy at the
Met, protected. Newcomers were warned not to touch her while
she was singing and directors who pressed her were subdued
(no matter who: Tyrone Guthrie was nearly asked off a *Traviata* for harrying Tebaldi with theatre thinking). Maria Callas was not happy at the Met, unsupported. There was nothing for her to bite on, nothing *doing.*

Sutherland fit into the old Met rather well. Like Tebaldi,
she would be encouraged, placed, advised with discretion: centered. The rest of the evening would lack the comely grandeur
of the Scala spectacle and the intelligibility of Covent Garden,
but New Yorkers had grown accustomed to stand-and-deliver
Stimmopera, and Sutherland's first Met special, *La Sonnambula,* was an ideal encore debut. Here's a piece that can be
beautifully and incisively realized—again, think of Callas and
Visconti—but also works nicely as pure song. It is without
question the soprano's opera. She has the anticipatory entrance, nearly all the tunes that anyone cares about, and the
final twenty minutes virtually to herself, from Sleepwalking

Scene on Perilous Bridge through a sumptuous elegy on to an embellished rouser, the curtain falling on her glorious high B flat. There was another virtue in the work's qualified novelty, for it was well known as a Bellini title but unfamiliar to New Yorkers as an experience. True, some complained that the piece is too slight to support so much in the way of honor and expense, but this was nonetheless New York's first taste of the bel-canto *riesumazione,* and this too fanned Sutherland's glow. In the end, the production was silly, the critics more than usually obtuse, the conducting slack, and the Met audience unused to Bellini: *La Sonnambula* was not appreciated. But Sutherland was, as the new Stimmdiva who can sell out in anything.

Of all debuts, the most critical is not necessarily the first, the encore, the house, or that in the great role, but a certain gala moment that is perfectly timed to carry one from note to true celebrity. Lotte Heinotz' emphasis on timing is very apropos here, for this debut comes after the reputation is won but before it has expanded beyond the elite and buff publics. It is a very exposed debut, a go-for-broke at one of the world's greatest houses in an imposing production with every ear in opera listening in. Jessye Norman's Met debut at the opening of the 1983–84 season, as Cassandre in *Les Troyens,* is a splendid example of this very fraught debut: an American who has sung opera at Paris, Milan, Vienna, Hamburg, Aix-en-Provence, and London (Cassandre, in fact) at last comes to glory in her homeland, not only at the top of the *cartellone* but in the house's proudest (anyway, biggest) staging, in one of opera's great stints, the Cassandre-Didon tradeoff.* This is a very vulnerable debut, sure to be either cum laude or flunk—with so much feeling in the air, so much waiting and watching, no middle grades will be awarded. Granted, a diva of Norman's quality is not likely to suffer disaster; the better you are, the bigger the success in such prominent exhibition. But mediocrity, so thoroughly exposed, can suffer career calamity, even devastation.

---

*Berlioz' two woman leads switch parts from night to night, supposedly to avoid exhaustion but actually to mix casting chemistry.

Careers do not take care of themselves even after they have been launched with consideration and luck. Win fame and you must maintain it: not only by staying in voice but by exploring your specialties, arranging for PR, and taking part in headline-cast recordings: making, in short, personal identification as a star. Some of this may be ordered, but some of it runs wild. The uncontrollable side, largely, is the journalism, as critics' reviews, magazine profiles, and the television tie-in. The controllable meshes with this in that a good PR agent can influence magazine decisions on whom to profile, can even, rarely, put one on the air. Then there are the special events, such as arranging the publishing of one's memoirs or biography.

Going back to Lotte Heinotz' day, we find little of the above, and what of PR that did exist then has evolved beyond practical comparison. The day-to-day "news" of musicians' personal lives was unheard of then; even a controversial liaison, like that of the young Geraldine Farrar and the German Crown Prince, was reported so circumspectly (if with patriotic outrage) that no one outside the royal circle could make out whether they were chaperoned picnic partners or *amants fous*. (At that, the merest hint of innuendo sent Farrar's father off to kick a newspaper publisher about the floor of his bedroom till he promised a retraction.)

Farrar had come to Europe to make her beginning and scored a fine success *als Gast* in Berlin. As an American she was a novelty, as a beautiful woman and a self-plundering actress she was a novelty worth talking about. Naturally the royal family came to hear her, and the Prince conceived a passion. This is the Cinderella story that Americans love; but Germans don't. To some it was already objectionable that the American Farrar was ensconced in major roles at the Royal Opera (today's Staatsoper)—and singing Marguerite in *Faust*, no less! All right, it's not a German opera, but it should have been.

Eventually Farrar left Europe to establish herself at the Met. She did not forget her Prince (they met again after World War I), but neither did she speak of him. Imagine how their relationship might have been treated today. One needn't imagine: just recall how the press covered the Callas-Onassis affair, tirelessly printing those telling photographs of the decisive yacht trip, with Winston Churchill on hand for historical glister, Callas in bathing suits for divas-are-like-you-and-me mobocratic putdown, and Meneghini sour as old yogurt for that whisper of adulterous intrigue.

Another difference between Heinotz' day and ours is the passing of the claque. This formidable instrument of PR flotation has its origins in certain disturbances that rocked theatres in the 1800s because of personal vendetta. A spurned lover, a discharged singer, or a jealous competitor would hire a troupe of bravos, issue them tickets, and lead them in demonstration on the night of a prima in hopes of wrecking the performance. *Norma*'s premiere was hurt in this way, by arrangement of the Countess Samoylof, the very good friend of Bellini's rival Pacini. "Fiasco!!! Fiasco!!!" Bellini wrote to a friend. "Solemn fiasco!!!" *Norma* survived this first night to dominate the rest of the Scala season and immediately entered the world repertory. But the *ad hominem* booing committee remained an effective weapon for decades. No theatre seems to have maintained it on a regular basis—what impresario wants a disturbance-in-residence? But at some point someone thought of engaging the noisemakers to boost rather than persecute, and so the claque was born.

The claque comprised practiced fans, usually standees and patrons of the top balcony, who made a calculus of applause, from sparse *bravi* to ovations, for a fee. Strongest in Italy, where minor corruptions are a routine of the social contract, powerful in South America and Vienna, weak in the North, and officially despised in England, the claque could be very helpful in scoring a *Sternstunde*. After all, a lot of applause can create a success out of an ordinary evening (it's difficult to reshape a disaster) and a little applause can sap the zing from a special one.

Through prudent leadership of the other spectators—a savvy cheer, a swelling, a carillon of cries, a moment seized, worried, and blessed—the claque leaders could create the climate of demented that opera strives for. The singers or some flunkey paid the leaders; the leaders paid the troops. It was a tolerable and perhaps necessary swindle, for audiences of the early 1900s accepted great performances more serenely than we do today. Without the claque, opera that wasn't dull might have felt dull. And claques were generally fair-minded, essentially taking tips for applauding singers they would have applauded anyway. Few claqueurs tried to hype third-raters or dismay the gifted; the chiefs approached the singers they admired and ignored the others. It was, in that more graceful time, the sole personal link between artist and buff.

Today fans are stage-door persons, in America especially, carting mountains of ephemera to dressing rooms for the stars to autograph, and complimenting, and asking, and hoping. The claque itself, as a salaried entity, has vanished. It's all amateurs now, though they hold the golden-age hysteria at the tips of their fingers and lips. When Rudolf Bing began to emphasize all-star performances at the Met—even his off nights had terrific people—the fans were startled into fanatic ovations, bowled over. James McCracken recalls being blackmailed by the claque, but generally the professional supporter was replaced by the *espontaneo,* for Bing brought demented back to the house on an almost nightly basis.

Bing himself was suspicious of the ruckus. As a Viennese, he felt sure there were claques at work somewhere; indiscreet inquiries revealed a very few miserable individuals angling for a tip (probably the same people who approached McCracken). The Met has continued to be a house of receptions on the grand scale, rivaled only by Vienna and way ahead of Covent Garden, La Scala, and Berlin in cheer quotient. And the claque? A tale is told every so often. Early in her career Leontyne Price supposedly offered an Italian claque money *not* to cheer her; there has been a scam here and there. But generally today's divas can count on their talent and fans' loyalty, not on accomplices, in the making of a hit.

The memoir scene, too, has altered beyond its due. This was once the province of genuine autobiographers: Farrar, Alda, and others sat down and wrote their books. Of course, this was back in the days when everyone could read and write. Today, ghosting or heavy editorial improvement is unavoidable. Moreover, the general success of the many books on Callas, a

publishing sub-industry in biography, recollection, and appreciation (including one in Russian), points to the opera-person-
ality book as a money-spinner—a product, like Garfield T-shirts
and *Star Wars* lunchboxes. Publishers like them because they
are at least safe and sometimes lucrative; singers like them
because they are very respectable PR. With the American expansion of opera's potential for big-league exploitation, biographies became *ne plus ultra* in the demonstration of fame
and the styling of image. No longer was a singer, upon retirement, to look back over a career played out to its extent, with
the completeness of perspective that affords. Now mid-career
bios have begun to proliferate, to the point at which any diva
who has not had her say or been spoken for appears, in default, second-rate.

The results are greatly variable. Rosa Ponselle's autobiography was published posthumously, and of course this was of
the old approach, with the career long finished, all lessons
learned and processed as advice to younger singers, and the
major part of the personal history considered and revealed:
what did I offer, how did I arrive, and why did I leave? Somewhat comparably, Dorothy Kirsten looked back from the leisure of the days after the final bow. Janet Baker produced a
kind of journal of her last year in the theatre before limiting
her activity to the concert platform, so this, too, has the shape
of a farewell and is, indeed, meditatively climactic. But singers still at work and (one hopes) growing lack perspective. Nor
can they speak freely of their experiences. An offended conductor, director, or impresario might cut them out of jobs.
Anyway, the bio as PR is not a bio; it's a four-hundred-page
greeting card. *Kiri,* David Fingleton's book on Te Kanawa, is
exemplary here: the eventless adventures of an artist who is
prominent but of minor consequence, and in any case yet in
her prime. What have we to learn from such a book?

What, while we're at it, have we to learn from critics, whose
reviews amount, to the impressionable reader, to a day-to-day
report on the opera world? Criticism is the most treacherous
variable in operatic PR, for it is as vain and vindictive as opera itself; yet, unlike the musicians who man opera, critics
never need defend their credentials. An intemperately loud

tenor is demonstrably a boor. A characterless soprano *is* characterless to eye and ear. Dull direction looks dull, and lank conducting sounds like a mess. But criticism calls for specialized knowledge that is mostly hidden from direct view, and few readers of newspaper or magazine music columns attend all the performances the writer attends, and therefore cannot match his experience with theirs. The reader must take their word for it, lacking that specialized knowledge and not having seen most of the performances in question.

Worse yet, readers assume that people in those positions of authority must deserve them. In fact, most critics lack expertise and taste; many cannot even write a sensible paragraph. As for their authority, they got their positions because there was an opening, the managing editor didn't know whom to hire, and an opportunist pushed in. This is the rule in the provinces, less so in the cultural capitals; but it is the bane of opera in America in particular, where an ancient Print Street superstition fears hiring specialists for mass-market positions. It's a disaster that careers are hostage to the opinions of such creatures. Rave notices can assist, even make careers; bad ones can harm or destroy others. The foolish read critics as if they were Solomons, even prophets—but in a reasonable world praise does not reward talent: talent demands praise. Divas who have been treated kindly think of critics as their benefactors. Wrong. If singers deserve approbation, approvers are only doing their job. If singers don't deserve it, approvers are misleading the public.

The best critics can take creative part in the evolution of opera, serving as archons of tradition and wistfully advising the future. Those who cannot ought at least to become funnels of sensitive report, making that day-to-day column a chronicle of contemporary operagoing, from the latest developments at Bayreuth and the premiere of an important new work like *Die Soldaten* or *Lear* to the analysis of seasons at the Met or San Francisco. Even this is beyond the reach of most writers. And consider the ruin they can make of history. Rosa Ponselle's literally overnight rise owed much to the New York critics' correct if cautious report on her amazing instrument. That night was climacteric. The entire Met, from Gatti to the janitors, knew that house reputation rode on the debut of a soprano who had never sung a note of opera before. "If she is a success," Gatti reasoned, "the doors of the Metropolitan will be opened to other American singers because she will have made it possible."

Caruso had brought Ponselle to Gatti, and Caruso now asked, "And if she fails?"

"Then Signor Gatti," Gatti assured him, "will be on the first ship back to Italy."

History. And it stood upon not only Ponselle's performance, but *what was said of it.* One might imagine that, with a voice like Ponselle's, the critics could not fail to praise. But it was the critics' assault on Ponselle's Carmen, when she was still in prime, that shattered her security and (combined with other factors) drove her from the stage. Again, it was the New York critics who utterly failed to hear what Maria Callas was doing until it became clear that to belittle Callas was to belittle oneself. Remember, writers become famous for disdaining, not for enjoying; and naturally critics are crazed to become famous, because they spend their lives writing about what other people do. No one ever wanted to know about a critic.

Why don't opera's people speak out against them? They fear reprisals. In private, among America's musicians, the New York critics are a laughingstock, but in public, critics are not only invulnerable but can strike back, as Ponselle revealed in a postmortem on Olin Downes' *Times* review of her Carmen. Granted, only the less influential reviewers touted Ponselle's gypsy; the major critics registered disappointment with the characterization, some with the singing as well. But Downes described the performance in terms one seldom hears applied to a major name, and it seems disquietingly coincidental that, two years before this, Downes had earnestly sought Ponselle for his Brooklyn concert series, wouldn't meet her fee, and was turned down. One diva pointed out, not for attribution, that composers and librettists do the creating, musicians the re-creating, and reviewers only gossip. "You can have opera without critics," she points out. "You can't have opera without musicians. *We* are opera." Grace Moore used to say that she made her career on bad notices. Another diva (who couldn't care less who knows that she said it, but whom I will nonetheless shield) phrased it most succinctly. "Critics," she says, "are scum."

All of the above—the journalism, the fans, the books, and the reviews—has long been a part of opera history, changeable but present. Some parts of PR are entirely new, produced by the postwar age of technomedia communications—and this new matter has substantially changed the shape of the diva's rise and fall. A burst of appearances in print and on television, correctly timed—"timing is the first need!"—can turn an artist into a world-famous personality. What recordings did for Caruso and Galli-Curci, an American Express commercial did for Luciano Pavarotti. A telecast from the Met can reach more people in one airing than some singers reach in their careers, and such familiar television guests as Joan Sutherland, Marilyn Horne, and Beverly Sills—whether in proscenium-bound performances, galas, or cable documentaries—have won a mandate for fame that even the epochally iconographic Geraldine Farrar never knew.

Opera as input for video has its ludicrous side—Carol Neblett singing "Vissi d'arte" in Italian on the Johnny Carson show, for example, causing millions of unmusical Americans to wonder why the broad with the fancy chest is making strange music in a foreign tongue. Television opera has its delightful surprises, too, as when Horne and Eileen Farrell joined Carol Burnett for an operatic version of *The Three Little Pigs* that showed the two divas as wickedly apt in shtick as Burnett. Television opera has its innocent, terrible power as well, felt in the decisions about who deserves to appear and who not. At one Met gala an eleventh-hour indisposition thrust substitute Catherine Malfitano into importance in the Final Trio from *Faust,* for, in an evening dominated by the same old headliners purveying tired Gems From the Opera, Malfitano came off as fresh and vital, inadvertently representing the younger generation that would replace these same headliners as the stars of the 1980s.

Who deserves to appear and who not? Opera has been televised for thirty-five years, but only lately has it made champions of the participants. Who, after all, had television when the Met broadcast Edward Johnson's last opening night? NBC's

"Opera of the Air," produced in the studio in the 1950s, made no stars. Leontyne Price was "well received," as they used to put it, in *Dialogues des Carmelites* and *Tosca,* but it was her Met debut that put her over. Typically, then, not till the Met got back into television in the 1970s, this time pandemically, did opera take its place in electromagnetic culture, assume power. To be a star of the top class and sing at the Met and *not* get a Met telecast is to be a star of the second class.

How much simpler opera PR was three decades ago, before television mattered, before Elsa Maxwell took up the Callas-Tebaldi debate, before recordings threw off their status as a quaint supplement to the real thing and became a competitive thing-in-itself. In the early 1950s, PR fell into two categories: one, the reviews-records-memoirs cycle, for the general public; and, two, the interviews-news-and-notes approach of the opera magazines, for the musical community and committed buff. Only in the English-speaking world did magazines wield crucial influence. England's *Opera,* launched in 1950 by the Earl of Harewood and Harold Rosenthal, built slowly on a characteristically British sensibility, tending to the polite and the academic, with emphasis on the London opera scene and a patriotic platform, most strongly expressed in the editorial militance on opera in English, the occasional twee fanfare for some British singer guesting in foreign parts,* and a certain ethnocentric eccentricity, as when some newcomer would be likened to "the young Jill Gomez" or some other less than internationally renowned artist. Where *Opera* most affected the diva was in the pervasive consistency of its reviews; singers seldom had the feeling that they had impressed one writer only to disappoint some other for comparable work. *Opera*'s reviewers seemed to comprehend a point of view in the general. There were also *Opera*'s profiles, little biographies that gave a singer the sense of having arrived. The magazine was published by experts for everybody and most impressive for the

---

*This courtesy was extended even to non-British singers who somehow touched British opera history. Thus one sensed an amusing loyalty toward Brigitte Fassbaender in her first appearances because her father, Willi Domgraf-Fassbaender, had been an installing member of the Glyndebourne Mozart style.

passion of its reason—it was, and is, in the best sense, a record of What Happened.

Opera News, on the other hand, was founded as the Metropolitan Opera Guild's house organ. There would be none of
Opera's adversary editorializing about the state of the national opera house, little editorializing at all. *Opera News* was
even squeamish about reviewing performances. As it obviously couldn't analyze Met performances, why should it discuss any? The Guild was organized in the Depression by
Eleanor Robson Belmont as a fund-raiser for the Met, to forge
an American opera-loving community so the middle classes
could participate in Met charities along with the Knickerbocker grandees. Where Opera's burning issue was Covent
Garden's house style, where *Opera*'s deity was a superintendent genius who might pull such a style together, where *Opera*'s favorite place was where great music theatre was heard,
Opera News had no issue, its deity was Mrs. Belmont, and its
favorite place the Met, even when it was empty and silent: and
let's all tune in, now, folks, for the Saturday-afternoon Texaco
broadcast.

Opera's format has remained changeless for thirty-five
years, but *Opera News* underwent modification. Sometime after
the war it developed a chummy quality, reveling in informal
photographs of the stars posed about a Christmas tree or exercising on the beach, haphazardly snapped by spouses and
well-wishers. To balance *Opera*'s profiles, *Opera News* en-
dorsed the interview, polite rather than candid but at least a
glance deeper into backstage than one had in *Opera*'s formal-
ized third-person narratives. The Met and its broadcasts remained *Opera News*' focus over the years, but its scope was
broadened to take in the international scene. Unlike *Opera,*
which had long viewed the world as a mosaic of artwork, theory, and re-creative talent, all to foment healthy controversies, *Opera News* began to follow the postwar jet lag, tracing
stars' hither-and-yon while prudently outlawing controversies
of any kind. Thus it became in part a medium for singers' PR,
a chance for them to implant their schedules, silly opinions,
dreams, and likenesses upon the American readership.

In 1974, when Robert Jacobson replaced the old guard at *Opera News,* Belmontism was dismantled. In sure steps the magazine became tighter, more adult, and idealistic. The "opera stars at play" Brownie candids were banished, the clubhouse-sheet layouts reordered, the "reports" of performances turned into reviews. Still published by the Guild, still given to Saturday-broadcast data, *Opera News* otherwise retired the philosophy of Met self-congratulation and became the Met's toughest and fairest critic. (Jacobson's reviews of Met and other performances, along with Andrew Porter's in *The New Yorker,* amount to the most accurate information on what goes on in American opera performances.) Circulation rose notably, the magazine's fund-raising power along with it. *Opera News* became more than ever essential in the extrapolation of a national opera culture—but vitally self-willing at the same time. Veteran singers, used to dropping into the offices (in the old Met) on their way to or from a rehearsal with a sheaf of glossies and forceful chat, found it difficult to crash into the new offices, removed to the Lincoln Center neighborhood (but two blocks from the Met, as if emphasizing its independence). Making the cover of *Opera News* became almost as difficult as getting a "Live From the Met" telecast, getting the interview treatment more prestigious—and worthwhile—than winning a profile in *The New York Times.* The magazine has reflected the growth of the art in postwar America, moving out of Mrs. Belmont's ladyfingers sorority into high tech.

Opera is a money-spinner now, big business, for if the performing companies themselves incur deficits, a business corporation that makes public love to opera in charitable alliance reaps a fortune in moral oneupmanship, and the subsidiary opera of the home recording has been lucrative for over eighty years. Not all recordings make a fortune; some lose one. But the distinctly upmarket audience means the high tariff is not prohibitive—on the contrary, it was partly the expense of the Victrola and the Caruso records that established the opera disc as an upper-midcult status symbol. Appealing largely to people with a sizable discretionary income and covering a market roughly the size of the free world, from San Francisco to Vienna, records now serve as the very outline of the opera world, the stars' letters patent and the newcomers' credentials of arrival. Note the Catch-22: one needs recordings to become prominent, yet one cannot make recordings unless one is prominent already.

This was not always the case. Till 1925 recording and reproducing equipment were very primitive. The sound they made was surprisingly alive, and still impresses for its forward presence when played on appropriate machinery. But it was only vaguely representative of the sounds fed into its acoustical horn; nor could the horn accommodate much orchestral accompaniment. Many singers regarded it with misgivings, and those who threw themselves into recording were never quite sure what manner of art it called for. It couldn't handle opera-house dynamics—in the early days singers had to back away from the horn when they hit a big note. Caruso and the gramophone fit together as naturally as Mary Pickford and the camera, but many singers made few or no recordings, and the small sales of the complete sets marked home listening as a sometime thing.

However, the application in 1925 of the electrical pickup— a microphone adeptly replacing the horn—reinstituted opera records, and by the late 1930s they could provide a fierce PR for a singer striving for greater fame than even Met appearances could achieve. Columbia had snapped up Ponselle within days of her Met debut in 1918, and this adventurism became standard procedure: great voices would make great records. Consider, then, how Helen Traubel felt when Victor snapped her up on contract but, strangely, did not seem to want to record her. Possibly the firm was protecting its prior investment in Kirsten Flagstad, who sang exactly the same repertory. Why partition the territory? Traubel, who had dreamed of joining Caruso, Farrar, and Galli-Curci on those ubiquitous and illustrious "red seal" labels since childhood, was decimated. Victor allowed her a piddling series of Lieder-with-piano, but kept stalling on her Wagner, though this was just the time when a packaged supplement for the listening room would most enhance her reputation. A sympathetic A-and-R man stepped in with a dazzling proposition: the Immolation Scene conducted by Toscanini—this in the face of Victor's standing version with Flagstad and the underpowered Edwin McArthur. The session went off without incident, and Traubel readied herself for glory. But the records did not appear: Toscanini suddenly decided that, as Flagstad's Immolation came out on four 78s and his (made on less adaptable equipment) came out on six, Victor was undermining his sales appeal, and he effectively banned Traubel's discs from the stores. This is that other Toscanini that the legend-bearers never mention, the marplot who used his authority as much for wicked sport as for artistic perfection. Traubel was so unhappy that she left Victor for Columbia. Her Immolation Scene finally came out in 1956—after Traubel had departed the opera stage.

When the LP came in in 1949, complete sets superseded 78 selections. But the situation did not open for the singer—not at first. The market sat tight, with two or three versions of the popular operas and few of anything unusual, so only the most famous or luckiest of divas could make a place on the lists. Take *Madama Butterfly*. Stretching up to the dawn of stereo in 1957, there were versions by Renata Tebaldi, Victoria de los Angeles, Eleanor Steber, Maria Callas, and Clara Petrella (plus some importations known to few). Steber is a bit of a surprise here, for Americans were not considered glamorous. Exceptions were made for such as Risë Stevens' Carmen; and Anna Moffo proved to be American *and* glamorous. (She made the first stereo *Butterfly*.) But Dorothy Kirsten, though a Met mainstay and a regular participant on the Saturday broadcasts, never got to leave anything on disc but arias and a few operettas—not even Butterfly, supposedly her best part. One feels the lack, for her contemporaries are very much with us in their records. There are some who hold that—barring Leontyne Price—authentic Verdi has not been heard in America since Zinka Milanov . . . since Zinka Milanov last sang Aida into their Sony headphones.

Besides reifying a diva's reputation, records can acclimatize the ear to an unusual art. Callas made records her deputies. If Walter Legge's promotion of her in the early-middle 1950s characterized her as rival to Decca-London's Tebaldi and the Victor Met-based group, the records themselves revealed how singular an artist she was, one (as she constantly reminded the press) without rival. Moreover, the more thoughtful precinct of the music room gave the ear a chance to savor Callas' peculiar timbre, follow her reading of the libretto. In the theatre her beguiling personality might undermine one's study of her singing; or, on a bad night, one might hear too little of what she could do at her best. The records gave one thinking time, and came out so frequently that people with little or no access to her stage work could experience her versatility at first hand—the *Puritani* Elvira so different from the Norma, the Tosca from the Aida. It is entirely possible that Callas' career would have been much less successful without her extensive body of recording, for it was Legge's program to set standards in his recordings. His releases would not merely delight in their season but amaze the generations. Callas' recordings made her omnipresent in glorious company, protecting her when the voice failed and, later, when she gave up without actually retiring. Some divas are less interesting on records than in the theatre, accepting studio taping as PR proclamation rather than as demiurgic opportunity; not Callas. She was erratic in the house but at her finest on records, and so the legend lives, as it doesn't on Patti's discs and does but dimly on Farrar's.

Schwarzkopf, too, enlarged her presence through recordings, playing a repertory vaster than that she trusted in the theatre. As Legge's wife she became EMI's house diva, prepared for anything—and, unlike Callas, she was a tireless dispenser of the Lied, chanson, and carol that disc so intimately transcribes. In 78 days records were a flier singers took, fearful that the mechanical reproduction of their art might cheapen them. By the 1950s the whole thing had turned over: reproduction was loyal and packaging a formal showcase. Participation had become estimable.

It was but a hop from estimable to essential, but now that Legge's ideal of superb performances has given way to a shabby headliner sweepstakes, there is no concern for style and Fach, no responsibility, no air of entitlement. There is Ricciarelli, Domingo, Raimondi or Freni, Pavarotti, Milnes, great Stimm' but largely uncommitted singing. Worse yet, cursory perfor-

mances can make such a powerful impression by their sheer
weight of stardom that house performances try to emulate re-
cord-studio lab conditions, everything clean and pretty and
everyone a notch or two above Fach. Montserrat Caballé passes
a store window, spots her recording of *Turandot,* says, "Gee, I
guess I *can* sing it," orders the foot-long fingernails, and onstage she goes. It's a glittery malarkey; but it makes too much
money to be questioned.

Stardom, once an element of opera, is becoming opera's
ruination. We can admire the architecture of a sound career
in many of the divas who rose in the postwar years—Leontyne Price, for example. Price had luck in her first breaks, the
acute specialization in Verdi, a good head for choosing appropriate debuts, the quick claim upon such great roles as Aida,
Donna Anna, and Tosca, and an attractive pursuit of somewhat unusual roles later on, such as Manon Lescaut and
Strauss' Ariadne, tasty reviews (even the mixed ones read as
raves), an abundance of PR from her unique contribution to
the racial integration of bigtime opera, and a voice that adapted
wonderfully to recording technique. Some of this happened to
Price, some she took upon herself in free choice. Still, one way
or another, this is admirable career-building. Could a young
Price of the 1980s so naturally make her way, given opera's
collapsed ideals? Would she mark out her specialties in the face
of the miscellaneous offers every singer gets? Would she master the great roles at opera's treadmill tempo? Would she record what she does well or what Caballé and Te Kanawa turn
down? Would she defend her values, even bother to frame any?

Catherine Malfitano's career serves as a model here, for
planning, proceeding at sensible tempo, coping with bad luck,
and keeping those first plans in trim as fame starts to grin
and the tempo picks up. Malfitano cites "guidance" as the first
priority, along with a "support structure"—the guidance by an
expert who knows the Business, the support from one's family
and friends. And the structure one erects for oneself.

Support helped Malfitano weather her first setbacks at
Juilliard, where a teacher tried to limit her to soubrette parts
and where her first audition for the advisory panel yielded the
intelligence that Malfitano ought to give up opera altogether.

Perhaps the attempt to imprison her in Soubrette City was more offensive than the attempt to run her out of music, for it hurt her "sense of self-belief," a key factor in the development of one's artistic image. True, as a lyric-leggiero, Malfitano knew she was in for a certain amount of little-sister parts at first, and she paid her dues in Gretels and Marzellines. But she was projecting her graduation to the summit of her Fach, in Violetta, Manon, Lulu, Mimì, and the dangerous but irresistible Butterfly.

Malfitano looked for a logic in opera, would not simply fold into its devices. One must seek stimulation, not repetition; acute art, not salaries. When she got the chance to create heroines in operas by Carlisle Floyd and Thomas Pasatieri, she liked the honor and loved the work, glad to share in a little history instead of racking up another dozen Rosinas. When agent Matthew Epstein expressed interest with the agent's characteristic "Call me," she didn't—if he's interested, she thought, let him call her. (Pasatieri brought them together.) When the City Opera offered her Donna Anna and all about her urged her forward, she accepted and then, realizing that local taste favors dramatics in the part, pulled out. When a vocal siege threatened, she set to work and broke it rather than attempt to sing around it (which, in other cases, has led to atonal Puccini and early retirement). When the Met invited her for a look-in on a little-sister part, she found a graceful way of asking to wait till they thought her capable of finer things; and they did. Support is integral and guidance crucial, but in the end, Malfitano observes, "A singer has to become horribly independent."

This appears to be the elemental word, virtually the secret of greatness in diva from Schröder-Devrient on: know thyself, hold true to self, and say no to everything else. Felsenstein, remember, saw opera's downfall in the passing of the independent singer, the self-inventor, and every special diva has had to conquer impresarios, critics, and even audiences in order to succeed—think of Mary Garden saying no as early as her first lesson with the celebrated Marchesi. One must gamble on one's self-belief.

Conservative in general, Malfitano takes very specific dares, as in attempting the four *Hoffmann* heroines in Salzburg with James Levine and Jean-Pierre Ponnelle. Malfitano, a superb Antonia, had been considering Offenbach's impossible quartet for years, and when Teresa Stratas, queen of no, bowed out of the production, Malfitano was called in. This was a controlled gamble, for with dependable colleagues Placido Domingo and José van Dam on hand and the sympathetic Levine in the pit, Malfitano could limit the experiment to what she felt she could handle. A poor gamble trusts a messy staging or intolerant co-workers; in Salzburg, Malfitano had everything going for her, including her talent.

The smart diva splits the difference between luck and independence, giving the latter the edge. In Malfitano's early years with Epstein, singer and agent devised "three-to-five-year plans" as if to direct the luck, render it incisive. Distrusting PR apparatus, Malfitano reluctantly tried it and gave it up; can one afford to? Has she missed out on anything for lack of push? In the twelve years since her debut, as Nannetta in Central City in 1972, she has forged an international career, paid her visit to television in *Street Scene* and *The Saint of Bleecker Street,* gained the Met in a new production and her role of choice,* glided onto the big-league recording schedules as Juliette, Poppea, and Susanna. Hers is an exemplary career, oriented to rather than limited by Fach and capable of expansion. The Donna Anna would probably have been a mistake; she thrust it aside. The *Hoffmann* was hazardous but possible; she bit. She is a contender, intoxicated by opera.

If Malfitano lacks anything, it is an image, that immediately personalized essence that makes divas into what the Germans call *Weltstars;* and this will come as she perfects her Violetta, her Manon, her Marguerite, perhaps Amina and

---

*The new role was Poulenc's Thérèse in *Les Mamelles de Tirésias* and the great role Violetta, in which she is superior to the Met's present alternates. Malfitano reminds us, however, that no diva ever completes her study of *La Traviata:* "There is no freezing of that part." It was, by the way, the television *Saint* that led to the Met offer; thus one right choice and/or good break leads to another.

Louise, roles she was born to try. She will have to make her mistake somewhere along the line, and there will be the dummy directors to contend with. (Her personal *bête noire,* she says, is the reckless costume designer who builds dresses as the Aztecs constructed their temples. It's like singing while dressed in a lead safe.) By holding to her ideals and drawing on the guidance and support, she has retained independence. Only thus can one stay hale and involved, sensible of the adventure of making it and sturdy enough to hold it when one gets there.

You newcomers, ask yourself: what is your program? What nationality, style, company, role? Will you, through three-to-five-year plans, reach a given summit in time, or plummet before you reach a height? Some of opera's favorite stories tell of defeat and despair, for if fables of the rise inspire, those of the fall astound. Everyone loves a juicy disaster.

CHAPTER

11

FALL

The cruelty and speed with which the New York public forgets is extraordinary.
Rudolf Bing

Let us hope this singer will be allowed to cherish her special gift and not just end up . . . as another tired to death . . . Mimì.
Philip Hope-Wallace
on Renata Scotto
1958

She has been too happy— that is her misfortune.
Maria Malibran on
Henriette Sontag

It is said that there are a thousand tales of a diva's rise and only one of her fall: the voice dies. This is romance. Eventually the instrument does give out, but the saga includes a great many non-vocal reasons for yielding the stage, and many different ways of yielding. In Germany one sings till one drops, stepping down to small or Sprechstimme parts, and more than one Isolde extended her career as *Lulu*'s Countess Geschwitz or the Garderobiere, a tiny part in the last scene of Act One, scarcely heard amid the tumult of Lulu's dressing-room fainting fit. Martha Mödl passed the whole second half of her career in what amounted to a second career in colorful parts like *Mahagonny*'s Widow Begbick and Britten's Mrs. Herring (in German, which gives, for "Bloody little fool!," "So ein dummer Kerl!"). In Italy, where divas resist demotion, they turn instructor, following the ancient Neapolitan adage that any musician is, by the impartive nature of the art, a teacher. In America a media directive dating to the 1920s holds that anyone famous remains exploitable forever after, so even a voiceless singer is good for broadcast appearances, a wave from the audience, or just showing up, as Maria Jeritza did, front and center in her white hair and dark glasses, dreaming of her Maytime of feuds and furor.

Even divas who firmly and permanently go still face a host of options. They might make an end in a Gala Farewell in Their Very Own House, as Nellie Melba did at Covent Garden, singing an act each of *Roméo et Juliette, Otello,* and *La Bohème* and, at the close, delivering a valedictory, bursting into tears, and sweeping off to close an era. They might seek out a *Sternstunde* finale in some amazing part—but to bring this off one must retire in one's prime, and what diva wants to? By the day that nature hands them their ticket-of-leave, even their most trusty roles are behind them. Another possibility is to slip into less demanding forms, as Callas tried film and Ponselle the home musicale, holding formal concert about the piano with old friends and youngsters. Ponselle eventually became impresario, as head of the Baltimore Civic Opera, and others have turned their experience into savvy to run their own companies—Janina Korolewicz-Wayda in Warsaw, Emma Carelli in Rome, Kirsten Flagstad in Oslo, Beverly Sills in New York. Mary Garden had a bash at it in Chicago while she was still active as a singer,* but didn't enjoy administrative control and never tried it again, though the temptation to reprove one's former master by leading a company through seasons of beauty, glory, and fun must be a strong one.

On the other hand, maybe Garden's way of leaving is the healthy one. Her instrument in ruin, she was going out the hard way, having disasters in unimpressive places, when she suddenly remembered herself and proudly walked off into a quiet retirement. Unquestionably, running a house would have been more amusing; but then she wouldn't have died, as she did, a few weeks short of her ninety-third birthday.

Garden did at least make an official farewell of sorts. Others fade wanly from the scene without ado, as Bidú Sayão did at the Met, there one night and gone the next, having found

---

*A favorite cliché recalls Garden's billing herself as "directa." However, she refers to her managerial episode several times in her memoirs without using the neologism, so perhaps it's time to forget it. We might also stop flogging her for dropping a fortune in her sole season: her backer had offered her carte blanche, and I can't think of a better way for a wealthy businessman to spend his money.

no admirer in Rudolf Bing. Others momentously Return, though this of course has its dangers. The faithful will attend in force to cover every gaffe with a bravo, true, but younger buffs will just sit and listen, and how can a blasted voice live up to the lore it inspired in its prime?

Opera's most famous such instance is the return of Pasta, in London in 1850, thirteen years after retirement to her Italian villa. "Nothing more inadvised could have been dreamed of," Chorley wrote of this evening of scenes from *Anna Bolena*. Pasta, remember, was not just a diva but one of the divas of the age, so demented that Bellini wrote Norma for her (also Amina—and Anna Bolena, too, was Pasta's first). Her voice was never secure, and "its state of utter ruin on the night in question passes description." Old-timers cringed in their seats and the rude young, such as the actress Rachel, openly jeered.

One newcomer watched in sorrowful awe: Pauline Viardot, herself a reigning diva after her creation of Fidès the year before and now hearing Pasta for the first time, if we can call this concert a hearing and this soprano Pasta. Chorley tells us how Viardot witnessed Pasta's last terrible attempt upon Anna's mad scene:

> When, on Ann Boleyn's hearing the coronation music for her rival, the heroine searches for her own crown on her brow, Madame Pasta wildly turned in the direction of the festive sounds, the old irresistible charm broke out; nay, even in the final song, with its roulades, and its scales of shakes ascending by a semitone, the consummate vocalist and tragedian, able to combine form with meaning—the moment of the situation with such personal and musical display as form an integral part of operatic art—was indicated: at least to the apprehension of a younger artist. "You are right!" was Madame Viardot's quick and heartfelt response (her eyes full of tears) to a friend beside her; "You are right! It is like the *Cenacolo* of da Vinci at Milan—a wreck of a picture, but the picture is the greatest picture in the world!"

Some singers are smart enough to anticipate their last nights by programming them relatively early, thus to spark interest in a Farewell Performance, rekindle interest in a Second Farewell by Popular Demand, enflame interest in an Absolutely Guaranteed Last Farewell Performance!, flicker into the provinces for a lengthy tour, and flare up in town, freshly combustive. Giulia Grisi sang farewells for seventeen years.

Perhaps the most energizing stunt in this cycle of approach and avoidance is the premature retirement and successful return, more satisfying than Pasta's rash encore and more spontaneous than Grisi's protracted finale. When Pasta's contemporary Henriette Sontag married an Italian diplomat, his superiors insisted she abandon the stage or risk social upheaval, not to mention the crushing of her husband's career. Sontag dutifully retired, and, as the Countess Rossi, vanished from the public arena after a highly famous nine years that had taken in the top line of score in the world premieres of Beethoven's Ninth Symphony and Weber's *Euryanthe*. The Countess kept her voice in trim at soirées of salon, however, and when the Count abandoned *his* arena, Sontag was free to make her comeback. She had been away for eighteen years.

Opera doesn't change much in two decades, but a voice can. Chorley, attending Sontag's London return, noted the peril of an orchestra larger than Sontag had known in her youth. But the house was not overlarge, and anyway Sontag's prime concern (aside from the money she and Count Rossi desperately needed) was the challenge of rising above the fanatic popularity of Jenny Lind, who had ruled London since Sontag's retirement and had only just yielded the opera house herself.

Sontag triumphed. Lind's partisans would not give way, but Sontag gave them no clear line of attack, no opening for a scandal. Not only did Sontag go on to revive her old successes; she tried new roles, even created a few. The very return itself was unprecedented in opera; that Sontag brought it off so well proved a deliciously nervy act, a very center of demented dared and won. Was it Sontag's success that inspired Pasta's disastrous comeback two years later?

Sunday critics might point out that Pasta's return was as doomed as Sontag's was blessed, that neither the one's failure

nor the other's victory should surprise. Pasta's was an un-
manageable voice, the kind that fails quickly; Sontag was a
nightingale, singing not on the interest but on a kind of
Christmas Club, saving for future need. By this logic, verismo
experts should fail most quickly and never dare a comeback.
Yet one who retired in 1941 returned ten years later to re-
launch a career that lasted over three further decades, and in
some of the most rapt singing in postwar opera: Magda Olivero.

Olivero's comeback itself does not shock if one considers
the lyrical flavor of her first years. She was no canary. Her
Liù was intense, her Violetta desperate, her Adriana epic. Yet
she somehow worked out portrayals that were *deftly* lurid, her
technique defending her even as she strode out upon the field
unarmed. Marriage took her from the stage, till composer
Francesco Cilea, nearing death, begged to see Olivero as his
Adriana for one last time. Although he died just before she
made her return in the part, as postwar Italy was running short
of verismo idols, impresarios clamored for this miraculous
Adriana—and, while she was at it, why not Fedora, Francesca, Minnie?

Bowing to *force majeure,* Olivero settled back into The Life,
her lyric strain building into verismo thrust. She prowled
through the repertory in full cry, yet the voice never failed.
Perhaps it was a case of indomitable physique—Olivero's iron
stomach muscles were the talk of the business. So, also, was
her bizarrely antique style, artificial but supremely committed. Olivero belonged to an age that liked its Toscas to stalk
into Act One carrying a beribboned Bo-Peep crook in the grand
old manner, and as the years passed and the conventions
changed around her, Olivero observed the old ways, crook and
all.

Her timbre darkened and her glottal attack became pervasive, yielding a somewhat unattractive sound, especially in
the very fully composed middle voice. Still, like it or not, it was
an ur-basic verismo instrument, if not born to thunder and
weep, then certainly developed to those ends. Just as Callas
could turn any role into bel canto through her classical *espressivo,* Olivero could make anything into verismo, even Cheru-

bini and Janáček. She became a legend, not only for her age and style but because she flunked some of the tests of solid career-making, yet flourished. She seldom sang outside of Italy, had not recorded an opera since 1938, and knew nothing of PR. Still, her fame spread: Olivero taking over La Scala's *Francesca da Rimini,* intended for Callas; Olivero presenting her Adriana at the Edinburgh Festival; Olivero's Iris photographed *in media res,* a fifty-year-old adolescent with the overbite of a small dragon; Olivero taping her first complete opera in thirty years; Olivero making her American debut in Dallas, then circling New York as the fans drove out to welcome her, to Hartford, to Newark . . . and Olivero, at last, at the Met for two Toscas at the age of sixty-one, possibly the only time she went on without the crook. Who else in the last sixty years celebrated an entrance into a major theatre by slowly casing the house from floor to topmost balcony and taking what may have been the very last of the golden-age debut bows?

Comebacks are intriguing, but rare. What we must know, above all, is why a career ends in the first place. Obviously, there are some ground rules:

Singing on the principal shortens a career; singing on the interest lengthens it.

Tackling roles beyond your Fach will ruin you for *all* roles.

Nervousness, feuds, geschrei, and other backstage capers waste energy.

The only person who knows how great a diva is is the diva herself.

Consistent greatness is not enough; you must become ever greater.

Specialization may strangle versatility.

Demented devours.

Ljuba Welitsch might be cited as the diva who merrily ignored some or all of the above and made the most of it in a brief heyday. Welitsch was a delightfully total diva; with her plaintive timbre and all-out projection, her wild red hair, and abundant oomph that she could pour as easily into Donna Anna as into Tosca, Welitsch was torrid candy, easily the most successful Salome of the postwar years. She was as well a formidable Verdian, a moving Aida, and a fixture in British opera history for her participation in the famous Glyndebourne *Un Ballo in Maschera* with Mirto Picchi, Paolo Silveri, Alda Noni, and Jean Watson under Vittorio Gui at Edinburgh in 1949. Moreover, Welitsch practiced a tempestuous Musetta— so tempestuous that Rudolf Bing recalls using her to punish Patrice Munsel when the latter forced him to give her a try at Mimì: with Welitsch announced at the last minute, Munsel didn't even show up.*

This is the stuff of great stardom—talent, glamour, eccentricity, beauty wild. Yet by the mid-1950s, less then ten years after she became famous, Welitsch had run out of voice, out of any claim on lead roles. She turned up in the quite minor part of the duenna in von Karajan's *Rosenkavalier* recording—an unprecedented demotion at the time, not unlike Sutherland's singing Clotilde (today) in someone else's *Norma*—swung into film, materialized in a ridiculous walk-on bit in the Sutherland *Fille du Régiment,* and ended up in Vienna singing the *alte Weib* parts in operetta. Only those who have seen authentic Viennese musical comedy know how abysmal these roles are, short, virtually written for defunct voices, and usually assigned to the oldest pensionary in town not literally dead.

Why must opera exact such a price of those who give most eagerly to it? Why does independence become so expensive just when, one would have thought, the world star has won her liberty? On the contrary, it is the early years in which singers experiment freely, even the middle years. The late years, usually those of greatest reputation, are hemmed in by certain expectations, both from colleagues and from public. This is not simply a matter of age limiting a diva, for age does not dwin-

*Bing tells the story in the first volume of his memoirs, but the Met annals correct his memory. Welitsch sang her sole Met Musetta with Dorothy Kirsten, not at the last minute; and Munsel sang her sole Met Mimì with Brenda Lewis, not a particularly tempestuous Musetta. Good story, though.

dle in Isolde, Tosca, or Lucia the way it does a movie actress. Like those fifty-year-old Beatrices of the Ellen Terry era, divas actually age into young parts. But divas do become prisoners of their celebrity, unable or unwilling to move into other kinds of roles, different music. It is as if one spends one's youth learning great roles and one's seniority becoming their victim. Look at Welitsch—some Vienna, some Covent Garden, some Met, and out into the void of the campy comprimaria.

Welitsch did in fact make her debut (in Sofia) in 1934, and sang throughout the following years: she was not a flash, here then gone. Yet two decades of opera work does not seem like a fair lifetime's allotment, especially given that only the second decade "counts": plays to sophisticated audiences and international fame. (Sofia may be lovely in spring, but it is somewhat less than the world's capital of Divakunst.) It is becoming a fact of opera life that Wagnerian voices die young, but that is because today's Wagnerians bite in too early. Welitsch was not a Wagnerian; anyway, it was a naturally big voice. Why withdraw? Lisa della Casa retired to help nurse an ailing daughter back to health, Denise Duval because the opera establishment was not as committed as she was, Anita Cerquetti and Rosanna Carteri for family reasons. All this has nothing to do with the state of the voice. Other divas retire because the instrument has run out after long use—Melba, Flagstad, Milanov. Understandable, sensible, inevitable. Welitsch doubtless ran out of voice early, sang on the principal, and lost the toss. But what of the endowed diva who wants to sing and *can* sing . . . and retires? What of Rosa Ponselle?

The question of independence bears heavily on Ponselle's case, for who would have more artistic latititude than the proudest voice in opera's most honorable Fach, the lyric-dramatic? Who was better berthed than Ponselle, the Met's most permanent and enthusiastic resident? Who had a nicer relationship with her impresario? Who chose major roles with keener tact, each a great one? Yet Ponselle retired when still in voice, in 1937, nineteen years after her debut. There was no illness, no stupendous feud, no crushing failure like Melba's Brünnhilde, no climax. She quit, *futsch,* gone! To understand this in context, imagine Joan Sutherland having stayed

almost exclusively at Covent Garden after her world-shaking
Lucia, running through her Elvira, Amina, and Norma, perhaps some Meyerbeer or Elsa or Strauss' Ariadne, then, quite
suddenly, in 1978, crossing her name off the roster without
public explanation and slinking off to her Swiss home, silent
forever after.

For decades Ponselle's retirement remained a favorite opera mystery, though insiders knew something of it. She deals
frankly with it in her memoirs. Yes, she was in her prime, but
her Carmen, poorly reviewed though a popular success, seemed
a bitter reversal of her fortunes—it was the first role she had
undertaken in which just about every opinion-maker didn't see
her as ideal. The role meant a lot to her, moreover. Not only
did she enjoy the gypsy as a character, she found the music
lay rather lightly on her instrument—at last, a part that didn't
keep her up nights worrying how to get through it! Worse yet,
her Gatti was gone, replaced by Edward Johnson; and Johnson coolly refused to give Ponselle her requested production of
Adriana Lecouvreur, bane of impresarios and delight of divas.
Ponselle felt entitled to the piece, however questionable as art
and box-office, after all she had done for the Met in bread-and-
butter titles, not to mention Joseph Breil's odious contribution
to Gatti's Americana mania, *The Legend,* which Ponselle so
detested that she burned the score. Then, too, there was her
stage fright, always calamitous. She had just married, and the
temptation to get out from under the pressure of being re-
peatedly stupendous was fetching. So all this happened at once,
meshed into a sort of logic called Retirement. But why didn't
Ponselle change her mind after a year or two of nothing? Why
didn't Johnson try to talk her out of *Adriana* into something
more agreeable and comparably flattering? How could the
irreplaceable Ponselle simply be let go?

One reason lies in the character of the impresario's vanity, which demands that his takeover of a house, no matter
how noble it was, see nights of yet more formidable nobility.
A change in leadership means a change in look, staff, repertory, production style, and PR, with lots of new voices. An incoming intendant is known by the quality of artists he *brings
into the house.* Johnson could not thrive on Gatti's fixtures any

more than Gatti could on those of his predecessors. A leader leads, into a new golden age; or so he intends. So if Ponselle was not *per se* replaceable, she was all the same an excrescence, even a reproach—and a checklist of Johnson's incoming divas shows how strong the Johnson Met was going to be. In 1934, one year before he took over,* Lotte Lehmann made her debut. In 1935, the year of Ponselle's Carmen and the Johnson installation, Kirsten Flagstad and Marjorie Lawrence joined the company. Gina Cigna arrived in 1936, Bidú Sayão and Zinka Milanov in 1937 (and Grace Moore returned on her first substantial contract), Risë Stevens in 1938, a reasserted Helen Traubel in 1939, Eleanor Steber and Jarmila Novotna in 1940, Astrid Varnay in 1941. Only Cigna and Milanov shared Ponselle's Fach, neither as gracefully as Ponselle—Cigna was a Turandot and Milanov an Aida, but Ponselle was Norma. Still, this was irrelevant to Johnson. His need in diva was ingenuity and fame, not exact replacements for Gatti's artists.

So when Ponselle dug in her heels over *Adriana Lecouvreur,* Johnson made no effort to coax her out of it. He had no call to fire Ponselle, nor did he truly hope to lose her; he was, let us say, amused by the chance to live without her. Thus, while the backstage of the Johnson regime was decorated by anecdotes of Johnson's cajoling a singer, Johnson's promising extra desserts, Johnson's wheedling and doling, Johnson let Ponselle work out her own problem. This, though she does not say so straight out, must have been the last and worst humiliation, the one that definitively hurled her out of the business. Bad enough that the critics can treat her as if she were some neophyte from the provinces; worse that the Met did not think *Adriana* a valid draw with Ponselle (and she had offered to sing the first twelve performances without payment). Worst of all was Johnson's cavalier manner—his implication that Ponselle was not important enough to treat importantly. So marvelous was she, and so celebrated, that she could only see her-

---

*Technically, Johnson was to have served as assistant to Herbert Witherspoon, Gatti's appointed successor. But Witherspoon died shortly after taking office and Johnson, supposedly Gatti's own choice, replaced him.

self with the rights of a marvel and the tokens of celebrity. Everyone wants to be cherished; but some have earned the right to be, and the sad truth of the matter is that Rosa Ponselle had finally become taken for granted.

It couldn't happen today. With greatness in short supply, everyone in the opera community, from managers to reviewers, is more dependent upon and respectful of it. Ponselle's fall came about through conflict between her expectations and the prevailing cynicism of business-as-usual—the intransigence of impresarios, the recklessness of critics, the inertia of the public. All of these had heard Ponselle regularly without a break since 1918, and not till a few years had passed did some realize what they had lost. There were attempts to petition Johnson to recall her, and in a strange way Ponselle and he effected a reconciliation, not as diva and intendant, but as former colleagues, for nostalgia's sake. Ponselle had been hurt too badly to go back in without a great struggle, and it must have been chilling for her to learn, on her visit to Hollywood, how limited an operatic reputation can be. Out of the parish, most people don't even know who you are; told who, they don't care. It must have seemed to Ponselle that the entire world was ungrateful. She had a right to be the rage on a steady basis, and was tragically alienated when that right was not upheld. The only person who knows how great a diva is is the diva herself.

Another career-ending trap lies in the limited perception that the world takes of a singer, Fach as image. Achieving success in certain kinds of part sometimes forbids one's crossing over into other kinds. Try to picture Kirsten Flagstad working out a deal with time by going out as Mrs. Herring or Leocadia Begbick. On the contrary, other than her Met Alceste and Dido at Bernard Miles' first (not the present) Mermaid Theatre, Flagstad continued to sing the repertory that had made her famous, almost to the end, simply moving into the recording studio when she left the stage. Flagstad even added a part, learning the *Rheingold* Fricka for the Decca-London recording. There was no possibility of her branching out into supporting or operetta parts (though she had sung

operetta in her youth) in the Mödl or Welitsch manner. Flagstad sang Wagner and more Wagner, retired to help found the
Norwegian National Opera, and died.

The American Flagstad, Helen Traubel, not only didn't
sustain but prematurely lost her career by fighting her image.
She shared with Flagstad a resemblance of timbre, the wisdom to wait till age forty before singing Wagner, and a Val-
kyrie's physique. But Traubel didn't share Flagstad's renown.
Wagnerian trend in the 1940s ran against the American in favor of the Nordic European; anyway, New York is not sophisticated enough to celebrate two Isoldes. Reviewers conde-
scended to Traubel as they wouldn't have dared do to Flagstad,
grumbling about Traubel's Isolde costume or some other irrelevant nonsense, or fastening upon her evasive top notes as if
Wagnerian style consisted entirely of high Bs and Cs. Flagstad had the recording career that would have been Traubel's
had she made the summit five years earlier, Flagstad took the
anecdotes and the PR, and Flagstad returned to the Met after
the war to coopt Traubel's glory all over again. By the late 1940s
Traubel had to admit that opera had not done as much for her
as she had for opera. She decided to explore her bent for pop
culture.

Traubel had never been anything but American midcult
when off the stage, the very opposite of a Callas with her European *panache* and *tempesta*. Traubel was a baseball fan, a
big eater, a hearty laugher, a chum. So she took this into music—in a duet record with Jimmy Durante spoofing opera, in
nightclub dates, in the writing of mysteries. This did not suit
Rudolf Bing's idea of official Met behavior. Bing liked *panache*
and *tempesta*—the one he could market and the other he could
crush. The Met needed Traubel—Flagstad was about to retire,
Astrid Varnay could not control the Wagnerian heroines sin-
glehandedly, and the only other Brünnhilde on hand was the
less than inspired Margaret Harshaw. But a shortage of alter-
natives never fazed Bing. No doubt he had never liked Traubel; her directness and independence were qualities he admired in impresarios, not in singers. As it was, he used her
for only two performances in 1951–52 and two in 1952–53, and
asked her to abandon her nightclub work during her Met en-

gagements. Irate at his take-it-or-leave-it attitude—just as Ponselle had been at Johnson's—she went off to Hollywood to see about doing musicals. So the Met didn't need Traubel after all.

Sad to say, no other medium did, either. By the time she got to Broadway, playing a bordello madam in the Rodgers-and-Hammerstein musical *Pipe Dream,* based on John Steinbeck's tales of the raffish idlers of the Monterey canneries, Traubel's singing was labored, not safe above an A. The voice was still glorious as sound, but its structure was collapsing; besides, Traubel had felt miscast and bewildered by the whole thing, from rehearsals through tryout to opening night and some really rotten notices.* *Pipe Dream* was more or less the end of Traubel: no gala recording addenda, as with Flagstad, and no stage comeback. There was a bit more nightclub work, the usual memoirs, some ghastly film and television stints, and silent retirement in Santa Monica. Mary Garden has told us, "Once you make your name, you can do what you like"—but this isn't always the case. Having set herself up as the most important American Wagnerian of her time, Traubel could not take on any other character, any other job, even. Specialization may strangle versatility.

Clearly, writers who speak of opera's perils and despairs are not exaggerating—not if the woman who is now acknowledged as one of the greatest singers of the century was so blithely dismissed, not if an extremely resourceful talent could not follow up her Isolde with a change of style. There is exaggeration in PR, of course. Opera is flooded with hype, from the promotion of the latest conductor, tenor, or *Ring* recording to such articles as that profile of Franco Corelli, run in the *New York Times Magazine,* which pictured the tenor nearly fainting with exhaustion after singing the Siciliana from *Cavalleria Rusticana.* What, after *that* little piece?

Hype obscures the hard work, the tenacity, and, yes, the peril (for instance, of going onstage in poor voice because your cover is unavailable) and despair (of having everything opera

---

*She didn't even get the show's title right in her autobiography. It must have been rather heavily ghosted.

needs in musicianship, but none of what the public wants in vocal gold). Opera not only combines the exertion of athletics, the imagination of theatre, and the beauty of music—opera combines them at hurricane force: demented or else. Opera thrives on scandal, challenge, disaster. The public doesn't care for mediocrity, but a failure is interesting and a success hurtling into doom truly enchanting. Peril and despair.

Thus it was that Maria Malibran was as much remarked upon for her outstandingly vivacious style of life as for her singing, as loved for her increasingly daredevil vocalism as for her fragile plastique. Let Malibran equip her Venetian gondola and she (in her own words) "revolutionized the reflections in the canals." For four centuries the Serenissima's sumptuary laws forbade the citizenry any color but black in the outfitting of gondolas; decoration was for municipal or festival use only. Malibran's gondola was gray, with a scarlet interior, blue curtains, gold and silken ropings, and gondoliers to match. "Whenever I pass," she noted with glee, "everyone knows who it is." Or let a rival soprano pull off a rousing embellishment on Malibran's stage and Malibran would double-embellish the upstart a third higher—would sing her off the stage or die. Malibran in fact expected to die young, and did seem to be speeding to her destiny offstage and on. It was part of her attraction, perhaps elemental in her image. If Schröder-Devrient's independence was that of the singer who bends canto to realism of character, if Viardot's independence was that of the remarkable woman whose singing is but one aspect of her cultural influence, Malibran's was that of the woman whose life is fantastical, a kind of art.

How long can one live on the fantastical level? Mary Garden would have been shocked at how frivolously Malibran balanced a heavy concert schedule with an active social life. As the pride of a musical family, Malibran had no trouble getting into the business—her father was as much impresario as teacher and singer. Malibran could skip Garden's three years of absolute application—in her family one applied oneself to music from birth—and throw herself into The Life early on to sustain it at a furious rhythm till she died . . . at the age of twenty-eight.

It was a terrible death. While horseback riding in Manchester she fell and, her ankle locked in the stirrup, was dragged and badly hurt. Of course she had chosen the most dashing horse in the stable; she was Malibran! The accident did not kill her at once, and she heedlessly carried on her public and private lives as if nothing had happened. She said nothing; would let nothing be said. But her associates saw that she was suffering, her temperament wavering between the manic and the suddenly debilitated.

She was racked by headaches, but dared not complain. She feared that her dazzling program of life-art, the diva as Malibran, would be canceled on her behalf by well-wishers. She was known for certain acts; she must accomplish. When her doctors tried to dissuade her from fulfilling a concert engagement, she became hysterical, and they had to give in—but so did she: no sooner did she arrive at the hall than she collapsed in agony and was taken home. "Oh, how I wish I could have sung," she cried, "for I was never in finer voice!"

By then it was general knowledge that Malibran was about to pass from the scene, and the news was big. It was as if opera's great wish had come true, a proof that heroines really do die in beautiful delirium.

Yet because Malibran had delayed admission of her illness so long (and hidden it from the audience so well, singing at full force onstage only to faint in the wings), it was some while before realization took hold. Once it did, an informal theory arose that Malibran had died not of a riding accident but of the admirable arrogance of greatness. Opera does not kill. But it does take too much if you want to be the best. Malibran, the legend runs, gave too much and could not survive. She was pure diva, and must die of it—no flaps about her new productions or whether or not she might try alternative artistic venues, no living out a retirement in Baltimore or reminiscing of a lazy afternoon. Ponselle drifted off and Traubel was harassed, but Malibran was taken from us—by Malibran. Singing was her definition of self, to the point that one cannot imagine her surviving retirement. It is tempting to envision her dying in her prime by arrangement—as if she were too good to live.

Independence pays different prices in different eras, but always the most self-willed divas, given the talent to back up their claims, are the most famous. They are not always loved. Malibran was, but Schröder-Devrient was rather admired, Garden was misunderstood, Olivero was regarded as pleasant camp, and Scotto is disliked. Does opera want independence?

Impresarios don't. Most stage directors don't. Most critics don't; they want everyone as vapid as they are themselves. The maestro is the only member of the staff who needs a diva to make the wild magic, who is as much a part of the music as she is. Still, the diva had to yield some of her independence to him to initiate their collaboration. Malibran didn't—but in her day maestros were virtually the stars' employees. Opera, then, was reinless, an emporium of the unique. Anything could happen, the most wonderful, the most shocking. That was opera's charm. One minute, a lovely *jeune fille* tries over a sonnet at the spinet; next minute, Dr. Miracle is taking her pulse.

Few rises today are as quick and neat as Malibran's, few falls as drastic. Different times know different rules. One rule, however, has held from then to now: independence is marvelous and dangerous. We have our wise Freni and Horne, imperturbably superb; but we also have Stratas, who dares. Stratas seems as wary of independence as determined upon it—she sees its traps. Perhaps she knows the story of Malibran, who sang herself to death.

Demented devours.

CHAPTER
12
IMMORTALITY

*I hope I never have need
of friends.*
                    Maria Callas

Opera is so big that at times even the mediocre seems legendary, but the biggest legends belong to the biggest talents. Shortage of such talent intensifies the standing legends, especially the younger ones, which call to us from the experiential intimacy of the performances we attended, broadcasts we heard, records we play. To think of Malibran!: but we *heard* Tebaldi, Milanov, Nilsson, hear them yet.

Opera needs immortality as no other theatre art does. The spoken stage has a mere catalogue of greats, names attached to anecdotes. Bygone dancers are very dead. And the lighter musical stage is devoted to novelty. Opera alone lives on its lore, eternally promotes its past. We do not cherish the latest Leonore as we do Flagstad's; or the next Aida as we do Rethberg's; or the current Marschallin as we do Lotte Lehmann's. Perhaps this is because it takes most of a career to implant a notion of one's range and precisions—a photograph, so to say, of one's gifts. And by that time one is in decline, the range imploding and the precision losing grip, the photo fading. When a singer has reached greatness, he or she is already turning into history.

Greatness in opera is not self-effacing, for all its dialogues, ensembles, and concept productions. Opera cannot use the team player any more than an Olympic decathlon can. Greatness against heavy odds calls for self-belief, self-belief in turn develops independence, and independence creates the unique image. And it is the image that serves, condones, and actuates immortality, in transformation out of historical existence into symbolic existence.

The image varies directly with the great roles—or, rather, with the characterizations. A motherly Isolde, Alceste, and Leonore with a serenely lovely timbre yields one image; a furious Isolde with a timbre of white fire yields another, especially if she also delivers a Salome. Aida reflects differently upon a black American than upon a native Italian. Thaïs in the nude, a Norma with a stormy personal life, Mélisande in finishing-school finesse, a Carmen who sweats—all such may define a diva's personality as well as her art, for hearing is believing. Their PR may bear on it, or their ease on the concert platform, or their occasional stints in film. But if divas are their roles, was Callas Médée or Violetta, vindictive or fragile? Was Flagstad more the Nordic heroine or less when the charges of Nazi sympathy harassed her postwar return? Why, of all her roles, was Renata Scotto most like—no, not Norma, not Hélène, not Musetta, but Gioconda?: a singer, better yet a resourceful and ubiquitous singer, best of all a singer whose great love (Enzo: opera) is ungrateful.

This imagistic complexity sets opera stardom apart from all other stardoms. In spoken theatre, an actor's image is based on a certain focus of talent, whether for Shakespeare, Method naturalism, low farce, mime, and so on. In film the biggest names generally carry a fixed identity from movie to movie, like whores celebrated for a particular technique. Pop music, from ragtime to rock, is most limited of all, even if (especially when) Ethel Merman sang to disco arrangements of her old standards. But consider the changes an opera diva undergoes—from sweet Sophie von Faninal on to the impetuous Octavian, thence to the wise Marschallin as the voice shifts its center of power over the years; or from Mimì to Tosca, Marguerite to Esclarmonde, Cherubino to the Countess. In a single season a diva plays *femmes fatales* and trouser parts, princesses of *morbidezza* and tense verismo queens. She commands

Handel, Donizetti, Berlioz, Britten. True, an enthusiasm for bel canto or Wagner will identify one. Yet once fame is won a singer moves beyond specialty, and the image expands. Geraldine Farrar expanded logically, out of contemporary opera into contemporary technology: the movies. Janet Baker, on the other hand, compressed, also logically, emphasizing her renowned textual intensity by leaving opera for the concert platform. These moves make sense not only artistically but dramatically. Baker was never mistaken for her characters, however truly she interpreted them. She is neither Didon nor Maria Stuarda, but rather the woman we have encountered in recital, the compleat musician. But Farrar was popularly assumed to be some facsimile of Butterfly, Zazà, Madame Sans-Gêne. It seems fair that Baker abandon theatre portrayal without regret and that Farrar try the realism of the movie camera, where one virtually becomes what one appears to be.

It is not surprising, then, that so many favorite images of diva conduce to doom, for doom is what most operas are about: Norma, Marguerite, Anna Bolena, Brünnhilde, Salome, Fidès, Luisa Miller, Katya Kabanova, Tosca, Manon, Cassandre, Kundry, Desdemona, Lulu, Carmen. If such great roles inform image, and if the most persuasive artists bring commitment and temperament to bear on the musicianship of a superb voice, we inevitably think of them in terms of decline, despair, and death.

Yes, many of opera's proudest biographies sing of voices fully exploited in long careers—Pauline Viardot, who helps found the mezzo principal and tells Berlioz how to compose and Turgyenyef how to write; Kirsten Flagstad, who becomes the first soprano in Wagnerian history to be thought of as the supreme heroine of her time and quietly resists bad postwar PR; Joan Sutherland, who takes her early neglect like a sport and breaks out of bel-canto typology into Massenet, Puccini, Adriana Lecouvreur, and just about anything that attracts her. We like these stories: who wouldn't? But they don't fascinate the way doom fascinates—or why aren't there more books on them?

Why is Callas, opera's most tragic figure because most noble and most destroyed, the most documented of opera's heroines? Of all sad tales, hers is the most accessible, because contemporary, because recorded and photographed and filmed, because we were there. Even those who missed her stage performances attended her doom; and it's not over yet. We hear her asserting her self-belief in interviews; hear her establishing independence as the Stimmdiva of born-again bel canto; witness her shipboard wake, styled as the collapse of *ancien régime*, in Fellini's film *And The Ship Sails On;* and collect her art and life into the image of the greatest diva who was inevitably the most wretched. She could teach those stinkers out there, could will herself beautiful, could win one of the world's most powerful men, and could never be happy.

Callas is the personification of demented, as singer, actress, and citizen. Without her, opera's demented would have been less textured, would have been all musicianship and temperament—the professional parts—and have lacked the paradoxical personal elements of will battered by insecurity and success terrified of failure. Nor is all this biographical hindsight, for even as Callas rose to her international fame in about 1955–56, she was already generating suspense out of the difference between Callas flawless and Callas in trouble, already making defiant statements that measured Callas tyrant against Callas victim—and was presently to begin the series of walkouts and wars that would cut her off from the stage while she was yet capable of taking on new great roles. (What a Didon she would have made in *Les Troyens,* what a Sélika, Luisa Miller, Mélisande, Anne Trulove!) Attending a Callas night, one could expect anything from disaster to the greatest performance of music theatre ever heard: from filth to demented. This was one reason why Callas was never taken for granted as Ponselle was, as Sutherland is. For a single night, demented is flawless as a rule; over the course of a career, demented is unpredictable.

This in itself might have made Callas insecure, for she was so reluctant to cancel a commitment that she would go out in sluggish voice determined to grind it into order by Act Two, bend technique to her command. But she had worse problems, mainly a psychology of unworthiness that made her wary of beauty, worshipful of power, fearful of intimacy. Think of the happy legends: Viardot at Pasta's unseemly comeback, tears in her eyes as she acknowledges the greatness in the ruin; Flagstad standing by the Met in its dark time, missing her husband, and getting a lot of knitting done; Sutherland getting along with just about everybody she meets, asking only that she be allowed to bring her own costumes.* Then think of Callas: despising colleagues leading and supplementary, feuding not only with impresarios but with whole companies, losing her husband and her extra weight to become cocktail Callas of the chic cafés, and making all sorts of demands on everyone. The woman was out of control, caught, it appears, between conflicting needs: one, to prove her worthiness publicly through her art, and, two, to prove her worthiness privately in her relationships.

She could spend a day working onstage with Visconti and Bernstein, concentrated on the aesthetics of bel canto, then, after dinner, chase through Milan after the two men, jealously tearing them apart because she was afraid they loved each other more than they loved her. She could go out hating the audience for not realizing that she alone of her day was reviving opera's first principle of librettistic *espressivo*, come back loving the audience because she had made them realize it and they had cheered, then go out the next night hating them again. She could make such bizarrely self-contradicting statements as "I'm not interested in money, but [my fee] must be more than anyone else gets." It was not unlike trying to become who she were even as she affirmed who she was. In Callas, demented is a paradox, for her private life spilled into her public life, not only as tabloid headlines but as antagonistic tics in her artistic dealings.

Nor could Callas have worked it any other way, for to do what was good for Callas and for opera she had to enforce her independence: but to enforce it she had to come up against the machine. Callas was too self-willing for impresarios. They loved to humiliate her. Rudolf Bing hasn't got over it yet; when her name comes up and others trot out their testimonials to her artistry, Bing rehearses his reasons for firing her.

* And conductor.

The truth of it is that Callas came in during the rise of the multi-national opera corporation, which destroys independence. Callas ran a counter-revolution, back to the golden age, when originality was cherished. Typically, Callas alone is regularly compared to opera's most venerable legends—to Schröder-Devrient for acting, to Pasta for the unruly instrument made to play through work and will, to Malibran for the somewhat feverish quality of her offstage life.

Thus opera links its immortalities as no other art can, for no other art consists, largely, of succeeding generations constantly playing the same parts the preceding generations played. Dance has a comparatively smaller core repertory and, besides, even its most formidable classics may be choreographed anew, wholly changing their form and yielding new roles of old character names. Various dancers have played *Le Sacre du Printemps'* Chosen One in contrasting stagings totally unlike each other; but imagine singers trying *Carmen* recomposed with new melodies. The spoken stage does have its Portia, Millamant, Mother Courage, Mrs. Tyrone, great roles of unchanging text; but thespians are more concerned with premieres than with revivals, while opera is currently very weak in new work. Who but an opera diva, then, can so minutely and broadly express her historical antecedents? Callas personally instigated her immortality, aligning her image along Classical and bel-canto lines. She might have echoed Malibran's "I will live or die as Norma!" Yet the cry itself is Romantic—not Classically even and symmetrical, but emotional and haphazard.

And arrogant. Who is Callas to compare herself to Pasta and Malibran? She didn't use the names, it is true, but the sense of outraged mission with which she carried herself was unmistakable, even offensive. So when the series of scandals came, many people both in and out of opera were pleased. Hubris must be checked. There was the *Sonnambula* "walkout" at La Scala's Edinburgh visit—no walkout at all, we know, but Callas turned her back on the press, went to a party, and let Ghiringhelli make the statement, knowing that he had never been her supporter in any important way. Ghiringhelli said nothing. There was the *Norma* walkout in Rome, halfway through a performance she should never have attempted—but there was no understudy to field for her and Italian honor was at stake. There was the Scala *Pirata,* in which she pointedly addressed a line directly at Ghiringhelli's box so that she seemed to be telling the audience, *"There* you see the executioner's place!" ensuring her departure from La Scala. There was the goading of Bing, ensuring her departure from the Met. There was this chain of uproars and terrors, followed by a departure from opera altogether. In the mid-1950s she seemed to be everywhere, in much-heralded stagings and a stream of recordings. In 1961 there was one recording and five performances of one role in two places. In 1962 there was one recording and two performances. In 1963 there were two recordings and no performances. Because by then she was in the grip of Aristotle Onassis.

One element that divides immortals from more workmanlike divas is concentration, an apotheosis of commitment. One might also call it "living for art"; less sentimentally, it is the power to throw all one's resources into one's work: the musicianship that learns a role in a week at the piano, the temperament that cannot call a rehearsal over till it is finished, the imagination that grips a great role in its breadth and detail. Without concentration one's immortality is compromised, no matter how attractive one's image. Consider the difference between, say, Mary Garden and Lina Cavalieri, both quite famous in their day. Garden did it the hard way, in mostly out-of-the-way repertory and a quiet private life, while Cavalieri sang potboilers, married often and infamously, and picked up three million dollars' worth of jewelry with as much fanfare as possible. Yet Garden's memory has utterly overwhelmed Cavalieri's. The latter's scandal-sheet career is recalled only by specialists: Garden retains a chapter in the popular annals, for what she did *onstage.* This is opera's immortality, centered on singing.

Concentration was Callas' assault and defense, inaugurating her art as it shielded her from anxiety. It was by weakening her concentration that Onassis destroyed Callas. He would have no other gods before him, and opera had been her god—in her prime there was literally nothing else in her life.

Onassis filled her life to the exclusion of her music, so that by the time he dropped Callas to collect the one woman who was more fabulous—Jackie Kennedy—Callas had nothing. Opera had been her sublimation of the love she couldn't find in her family or anyone else. While she showed those stinkers out there, she also showed the stinker inside, proved herself worthy. She forged an image that allowed her to like herself. When Onassis offered her the love she sought, tangibly, in true romance, she let the image wither, didn't need it. Onassis gone, she turned to retrieve her music. But it, too, was gone, the neglected voice in shreds, the concentration shattered, the hazards of celebrity too bitter to dare again. She did show up here and there, contemplated offers, even sang. Yet only one thing could revive her: reconciliation with Onassis. Eventually Callas retrieved her tycoon, but nothing more; and when he died, she died, too.

Callas' immortality comprises all the parts of diva, from the debuts and installation of the great roles through the alliances and feuds with her cohorts on to the fall and even the comeback, a mortifying aria concert with Giuseppe di Stefano. Callas *contains* diva, and still has the strongest hold on what immortality means in opera, what it comprehends of peril and despair. It is most devastating when the greatness is flawed, most telling when the supreme talent cannot live with itself, when deathless art is made most human because demented devours. "Ah, that miserable woman!" Visconti said. "She will pay for this!"

She did.

BIBLIOGRAPHY

Henry Pleasants' *The Great Singers* (Simon and Schuster, 1966; updated 1981) is favored for its highly readable illustrated history of opera stardom from the castrati to Sills and Pavarotti. The venerable Henry F. Chorley is more limited, but his survey of London seasons, *Thirty Years' Musical Recollections* (Knopf, 1926; reissued by Vienna House, 1977), has the advantage of ear-witness reports on such as Jenny Lind, Maria Malibran, Pauline Viardot, and Henriette Sontag. While Chorley's writing is dense in the manner of the day, he speaks with a historian's perspective, comparing and summing up even as he "reviews." Everyone quotes him. Colonel Mapleson, similarly heavy with his pen, recounts many a bizarre adventure in his autobiography, shortened and edited by Harold Rosenthal as *The Mapleson Memoirs* (Appleton-Century, 1966). If Chorley is the instructor in singing style, Mapleson is the storyteller, just as quotable.

Moving back to contemporary writers, we visit with the world's leading musicians in Robert Jacobson's collection *Reverberations* (Morrow, 1974). Jacobson interviews Arroyo, Rysanek, Price, Nilsson, and others such (divos, pianists, and conductors as well) with expertise and charm. Unlike many practitioners of the musician interview, Jacobson knows the artist *as* artist, and frames his probe to invite them into significant utterance. Here's a fine place to learn how Price regards Fach, how Eileen Farrell left the Met (it wasn't pleasant), what Ljuba Welitsch has been up to lately, and the secret of Rysanek's high notes of death.

Michael Scott's two volumes on *The Record of Singing* (Scribner's 1977; Duckworth, 1979) precisely accompany his twelve-disc albums of 78 transcriptions of great and near-great names of the acoustic era in aria and song. Aiming at a representative collection rather than a "best of," Scott included too many humdrum performances for some tastes, but the first volume, limited to 2,500 copies, sold out so quickly that it fetched exorbitant collectors' prices in short order. The books may be bought separately, and stand nicely on their own, the blend of anecdotes and analysis within the biographical framework yielding a lively read. One thing Scott should know is why Rosina Storchio didn't go to the Met when her Scala colleagues Gatti and Toscanini moved there—Scott calls it "a mystery." Storchio and Toscanini's romantic involvement had become public gossip in Milan, to Carla Toscanini's humiliation. Storchio even bore Toscanini's child. A thus troubled marriage nearly collapsed when four-year-old Giorgio Toscanini, the legitimate heir, died of diphtheria. Stricken and repentant, a confirmed if straying family man, Toscanini relegated Storchio to the status of an episode when he and Carla left for New York.

Buffs have a field day comparing Scott's description of the recordings with the playbacks, and, barring some odd opinions, his mordant commentary is a fine guide to late golden-age vocalism. Newcomers be warned: Scott prefers Stimm' to Kunst, and underrates what he calls "cosmetic talents" who got by on theatricality. If opera is theatre, is theatricality a makeweight or a necessary? Discussing Carmen Melis' "N'est-ce plus ma main?," Scott applies Beckmesser chalk to her "devices of verismo: the dolent and fluttering tone, sudden lurches in the line, exaggerated and pinched sounding subito pianos, and a quantity of aspirates and sobs," admitting only Melis' "genuine charm" and "the warm and expansive tone." Then you play the aria, and hear possibly its most enchanting interpreter. EMI has reissued the first volume's discs corrected to pitch, along with addenda deleted from the original issue.

Similar in conception to Scott's books but complete to the present and emphasizing what is great rather than what is typical is J. B. Steane's *The Grand Tradition: Seventy Years of Song on Record* (Scribner's, 1974). This is a gem, a desert-island volume one can never tire of. Steane is generous with praise and eloquent in description—as in Sembrich's "bold-ness of stride and speed of strike" or Galli-Curci's "running her tongue in playful determination round 'Mi lascia reggere.'" I choose at random.

One defect of books on recorded opera is their tendency to ignore the crucial difference between opera in the studio and opera in the house. To compare Flagstad's lab recordings to relays of her stage performances is to jump from a reading to a portrayal. Her famous EMI Isolde under Furtwängler is glorious but staid; her Scala Brünnhilde, from the same era with the same conductor, has bite. (She nearly blows Set Svanholm off the mountaintop with her "Heil euch, Götter!") Studio taping remains the favored medium in opera's record market (except among the underground labels, which have dealt in live performances for decades). However, now that transcriptions of in-house opera have proliferated in good sound on foreign labels, buffs have become spoiled and are losing interest in sanitized studio renditions. With Mödl and Varnay in Bay-reuth Wagner; Schwarzkopf in the world premiere of *The Rake's Progress* and the famous Piccola Scala *Cosi* under Guido Cantelli; Callas, Sutherland, and Scotto at La Scala; and Leyla Gencer in a host of roles, not a note of which she got to leave on commercial discs (through politics and vendetta, she darkly notes), why take the less intent studio tapings? Thus Scott's sampling is representative of opera *recordings,* not of opera; and Steane's eloquence at times outweighs that of his subjects by the neutralizing of the medium.

Now for biography. One bel-canto heroine comes alive for us in Howard Bushnell's *Maria Malibran* (Penn State University Press, 1979); can we hope now for a comparable work on sister Pauline? Melba has inspired nearly as many books as

Callas, but only John Hetherington's *Melba* (Farrar, Straus, 1968) gives full measure in research and readability. Melba may not have been one of the great demented divas, but she *was* one of the great divas, and Hetherington really catches her. She helps him with her sharp wit and fearless temper. Malibran was more influential, Melba more fun.

Geraldine Farrar, Frances Alda, and Mary Garden, of the following generation, left their own documents, very much in their own voices (Garden's told to Louis Biancolli, but expansively *in propria persona*). Farrar's volume has two voices. She wrote *Such Sweet Compulsion* (Greystone, 1938) in alternating chapters by The Mother and The Daughter (i.e., the then-late Mrs. Farrar and Geraldine), thus, I suppose, to lend objectivity to the vulgarly subjective art of talking about oneself for hundreds of pages. It's a prim book, a little constipated, as its lavender title suggests. Alda's *Men, Women, and Tenors* (Houghton Mifflin, 1937) is, as *her* title suggests, more direct. *Mary Garden's Story* (Simon and Schuster, 1951) is most telling. I love the way the righthand running heads (the identifying rubrics at the tops of the pages) change with Garden's action like silent-film title cards. Thus we get "Maeterlinck's Defeat" and "Maeterlinck's Revenge," "I Meet Melba," and "Persistent Turk."

Ponselle: A Singer's Life (Doubleday, 1982), adorned with the Columbia Records PR photo of Madonna Ponselle, is lively reading, just raw enough to be the writing of a singer who could write. James A. Drake edited in some way—he admits to a prelude, footnotes, and conclusion; I imagine he contributed somewhat more. The book is honest, discreet, and telling, although Ponselle herself cannot explain how she learned to sing without instruction. Her coaches (Romani and Serafin) must have been something. Elisabeth Söderström's *In My Own Key* (translated, Hamish Hamilton, 1978) is disappointingly light-weight, but speckled with arresting observations. Janet Baker's *Full Circle* (Watts, 1982) carries the author through the backstage of her last year of stage work, in a Covent Garden *Alceste,* an ENO *Maria Stuarda,* and a Glyndebourne *Orfeo ed Euridice.* It's an introverted work, dealing with self-belief rather than with image—but note the characterological perception of Zoë Dominic's photographs.

With Callas we have come to a veritable library. Her mother and husband have had their say, Evangelia in *My Daughter Maria Callas* (Fleet, 1960) and Meneghini, with the help of Renzo Allegri, in *My Wife Maria Callas* (translated, Farrar, Straus, 1982). The mother's volume is foolish and unattractive, however much it contributed to Callas lore—some favorite tales of the hardheaded Callas originated here, for instance the one in which, charged with sister Jackie's poor professional prospects, the Maria suggests Jackie throw herself out the window. Meneghini recalls a more vulnerable woman, though he also reveals her defiantly putting impedient impresarios in their place, one of them quite violently. Coauthor Allegri and translator Henry Wisneski between them made a fascinating document of Meneghini's attempts to regulate Callas' reputation, as intriguing for Meneghini's delusions about himself as for his backstage anecdotage. Yet another relative joined the group, cousin Steven Linakis, in *Diva: The Life and Death of Maria Callas* (Prentice-Hall, 1980), a very poorly written book, useful for some report on the soprano's youth in New York—the only time when Linakis had access to her. How, then, can he write of her life or death? Worse yet are the errors involving opera, unforgivable in an opera bio. Linakis several times refers to Verdi's first Shakespearean adaptation as *Lady Macbeth* and tells of Callas singing "a selection from *Tosca*" and goes on, "No doubt this was when Tosca, tall candles in hand, walks over the body of Scarpia." Tosca doesn't walk over the body, but around it—and this "selection" is mimed, not sung.

Arianna Stassinopoulos' *Maria Callas: The Woman Behind the Legend* (Simon and Schuster, 1981) delivers on its subtitle's promise and has become the standard biography, though buffs prefer John Ardoin and Gerald Fitzgerald's *Callas* (Holt, 1974) for Ardoin's analysis and the witness of Fitzgerald's interviews with Callas' associates. This is obviously to be the source for future Callasiana—indeed, already is: Stassinopoulos used so much of it that her publisher had to settle out of court with Fitzgerald for a diva's ransom. Ardoin went on to discuss Callas' studio and in-house recordings in *The Callas Legacy* (Scribner's, revised, 1982), absorbing in its delineation of Callas' tour through the great roles and useful in isolating which of various performances holds the gold.

I can't say much for the bulk of present-day diva bios, so let's skip on to the house staff. Helena Matheopoulos' *Maestro* (Harper and Row, 1983) presents interviews with nearly all the leading conductors of the day, some of them—Claudio Abbado, Colin Davis, Riccardo Muti, and James Levine—of interest for their notes on opera. Von Karajan, I'm sorry to say, utterly snowed her. The two most influential conductors before him, Mahler and Toscanini, claim a number of books each, often mere "reminiscence." The standard bios are Henry-Louis de la Grange's huge *Mahler,* Vol. I (Doubleday, 1973) and Harvey Sachs' *Toscanini* (Lippincott, 1978), fair and expert at reducing one of music's most apotheosized figures to human size.

Impresarios of the twentieth century haven't left books as commonly as those of the nineteenth did, but Rudolf Bing, ever exceptional, published two volumes. First, *5000 Nights at the Opera* (Doubleday, 1972), written with Martin Mayer, captures Bing's voice, wit, and elegance; but the sequel, *A Knight at the Opera* (Putnam, 1981), badly needed editing: disorganized, dull, often ungrammatical, and printed in insultingly large type to use up paper and thus meet a stiff price. What did Bing have to say that wasn't in the first volume? Nothing. The memoir as product.

There have been diva novels plangent and lubricious, but the only one that comprehends demented in its extravagance and exaltation is James McCourt's *Mawrdew Czgowchwz* (Farrar, Straus, 1975), the saga of a soprano who can sing everything better than anyone. (Her Fach is great roles—all of them.) Set at the old Met, among the standees, the gentry, the musicians, and the journalists, the novel has the eerie rightness of a fantasy that doesn't invent. Revealing the audience's corollary to demented—*divadienst*—McCourt lays out a reverent satire (sample character names: dish columnist Halcyon Q. Paranoy and composer Merovig Creplaczx) that has become the essential opera novel, forcing Willa Cather and Marcia Davenport, yea, even Robert Merrill to the side. Mystery buffs might, however, investigate Helen Traubel's *The Metropolitan Opera Murders* (Simon and Schuster, 1951), which ends "Never trust a tenor." Incidentally, it's pronounced "Mardew Gorgeous."

I most strongly recommend *The Last Prima Donnas* (Knopf, 1983), Lanfranco Rasponi's interviews with and recollections of fifty-six divas of the inter- and postwar years, from Gilda dalla Rizza and Lotte Lehmann to Sena Jurinac and the Maria. Somehow Rasponi got them all to speak openly of work and life, bitter disappointments along with glories. Some of the subjects are utterly forgotten—Gemma Bosini Stabile, for instance. Others—Iva Pacetti, Sara Scuderi—are little more than names. But all contribute to the picture of committed and musicianly artists whose successors are opportunists with neither dedication nor poetry. Rasponi began publishing his pieces at *Opera News* when I was on its staff; in the office we had a black jest to the effect that Rasponi was killing off two generations of divas, for no sooner would he speak to one than she would die. Sadly, the joke bit back when Rasponi himself died just after his book came out. He was a gentleman. Don't miss it.

INDEX